MOON

WASHINGTON HIKING

CRAIG HILL

CONTENTS

WASHINGTON HIKING REGIONS

1. **Seattle and Vicinity**
2. **Mount Rainier**
3. **North Cascades**
4. **Central Cascades**

© MOON.COM

WASHINGTON HIKING
TOP EXPERIENCES

1 Explore the Columbia River Gorge (page 245).

2 Take in Pacific Ocean views and spot marinelife (pages 194 and 197).

3 Hike around Mount Rainier, Washington's tallest peak (page 59).

4 Wander through fields of wildflowers (page 18).

5 Chase waterfalls (page 20).

6 Walk beneath curtains of moss and towering trees in Olympic National Park's Quinault (page 232) and Hoh Rain Forest (page 223).

7 Swim in mountain lakes (pages 101 and 147).

8 Follow trails through the urban forests of Seattle (page 35).

9 Kick back with a post-hike beer (page 17).

10 Take in sweeping views. Climb to the top of one of the 93 fire lookouts across the state to see all the way to the horizon. (page 85, 119, and 316).

HIT THE TRAIL

The Evergreen State could take even the most dedicated hiker a lifetime to explore. There are 3 national parks, 9 national forests, 24 wildlife refuges, more than 100 state parks, and 4.5 million acres of protected wilderness.

But beyond the numbers are the experiences. There are the Olympic Peninsula's temperate rainforests, made lush by more than 10 feet of rain per year, and the wave-chiseled sculptures at Point of Arches, as well as the maritime playgrounds of Puget Sound and the San Juan Islands. Further east are the skyscraping volcanoes of the Cascades and the channeled scablands. Washington is also home to the quieter side of the Columbia River Gorge and the rewarding finishing stretch of the Pacific Crest Trail.

Our trails give generously to those who love to wander. Pause to skip rocks on Rialto Beach. Feel your pulse quicken as you stand on Burroughs Mountain or listen to avalanches rumble down Mount Rainier. Hear the haunting bugle calls of elk during the early fall.

Discover the fulfillment of challenges conquered and the rejuvenation that comes with solitude. Each step takes you a little farther from the stress of everyday life and a little closer to the peace nature delivers.

This book shows you the paths to take. Nature will take care of the rest.

▼ TABLE MOUNTAIN

HIKING GETAWAY

Camping the Coast

With a mix of sea stacks, lighthouses, towering capes, tide pools, and beaches, Washington's coast offers classic adventure. Pick a hike and then pitch a tent nearby for the night, or string these suggestions together—they're listed north to south—to hop your way down the coast on a hiking-camping trip. Driving time between successive campgrounds is typically between 1 and 3.5 hours.

Makah Indian Reservation, Neah Bay

Start your day with an easy walk to **Cape Flattery,** the northwesternmost point in the contiguous United States. Then make the longer hike to **Point of Arches via Shi Shi Beach** to catch sunset. Spend the night at **Hobuck Beach Resort,** an oceanside campground on Makah tribal land, conveniently situated between the trailheads.

Olympic National Park, Ozette

Two legs of the **Ozette Triangle** are boardwalks cutting through the forest to and from the middle leg, a walk on Washington's wild coast. Nearby you can spend the night camping on the shore of Ozette Lake at **Ozette Campground,** and learn about the homesteads that once occupied this area.

▼ SHI SHI BEACH

▲ KALALOCH CAMPGROUND

Olympic National Park, Rialto Beach
Time your visit for low tide and examine tide pools as you stroll along **Rialto Beach** to the sea arch known as **Hole-in-the-Wall.** Spend a night sleeping in the forest less than 1.5 miles from the Pacific Ocean at nearby **Mora Campground.**

Olympic National Park, Kalaloch
Head about 30 miles inland from the coast to hike through rain forest on the **Quinault Loop.** Then head back to the coast for a night at **Kalaloch Campground,** one of the most popular campgrounds on the Olympic Peninsula; sites are close enough to hear the ocean surf.

Ilwaco
Spend a night near where the Lewis and Clark expedition camped at **Cape Disappointment State Park** and take a walk on the **North Head Trail.** After a short side trip to an old military battery, the trail leads through the forest to a lighthouse with sweeping views of the Pacific.

BEST BY SEASON

Spring

- **Hall of Mosses and Hoh River Trail:** This is the best season to see wildlife at this popular Olympic National Park destination (page 223).
- **Dog Mountain:** In spring this peak is capped with vivid wildflower fields (page 267).
- **Kamiak Butte:** The rolling hills of the Palouse are most green in spring (page 313).

Summer

- **Second Burroughs Loop:** Alpine tundra, wildflowers, glacier views, and the rumble of rock and ice careening down Mount Rainier make this an epic summer hike (page 68).
- **Chain Lakes Loop:** Visit lakes on a North Cascades trail with views of Mount Baker and Mount Shuksan (page 101).
- **Steamboat Rock:** Start the day with a hike up a basalt butte in the Grand Coulee, and then spend the warmest hours playing on Banks Lake (page 284).

▼ CHAIN LAKES LOOP

▲ FALL COLOR ON MAPLE PASS LOOP

Fall

- **Maple Pass Loop:** For fall colors, it's hard to beat this North Cascades loop (page 110).
- **Granite Mountain:** This scenic climb is awash in reds, oranges, and yellows in autumn (page 150).
- **Lake Ingalls:** October is the time to see mountain goats wandering among golden larches (page 159).

Winter

- **Oyster Dome:** This popular trail is open year-round and sees fewer visitors in winter (page 26).
- **Nisqually Estuary Boardwalk Trail:** In winter, bald eagles fish for chum salmon at the refuge. In late January, hunting season ends and the final 700 feet of the estuary boardwalk reopens to hikers (page 54).
- **Point of Arches via Shi Shi Beach:** A worthy trip any time of year, you won't have to share the beach with as many visitors in colder months (page 197).

BEST WATERFALL HIKES

- **Twin Falls:** View this dynamic cascade in the forest from several vantage points (page 47).

- **Cedar Falls:** Make this easy hike early in the spring when the falls are at their most powerful (page 113).

- **Wallace Falls:** The trail to these falls is one of Washington's most popular hikes (page 132).

- **Lake Serene and Bridal Veil Falls:** This stack of waterfalls is so tall you can't fit it all into one view (page 135).

- **Quinault Loop:** Pass multiple waterfalls on this loop through lush rain forest greenery (page 232).

▾ UPPER TWIN FALLS

BEST BREW HIKES

In Washington, you're never too far from a brewery. One of the joys of hiking is kicking back with a beer afterward. Here are some of the best trail-brewery pairings.

- **Discover Park Loop, Seattle and Vicinity:** This gentle trail offers a taste of Seattle history, forested trails, and sweeping views of Puget Sound, Mount Rainier, and the Olympics. It's also just minutes from several Seattle breweries, including **Fremont Brewing Company,** one of the state's fastest-growing breweries thanks to its broad selection of award-winning beers (page 37). To try: Dark Star (imperial oatmeal stout) and Session Pale Ale.

- **Rattlesnake Ledges, Seattle and Vicinity:** Ham it up for a few family photos against a spectacular backdrop from a rock outcropping high above Rattlesnake Lake. Then head to the **Snoqualmie Brewery and Taproom,** where kids can enjoy freshly brewed root beer floats while parents savor an adult version, or some of the brewery's award-winning offerings (page 43). To try: Black Frog Nitro Stout Float, Haystack Hefeweizen, and Copperhead Nitro Pale Ale.

- **Colchuck Lake, Central Cascades:** Work up a thirst on this hike to a stunning lake and then head into the Bavarian-themed village of Leavenworth. The Icicle River, which you'll drive alongside on the way to town, is used to produce the beer at **Icicle Brewing Company** (page 146). To try: Bootjack IPA and Enchantments Hazy IPA.

- **Coyote Wall (Labyrinth Loop), Columbia River Gorge:** Every step of this trail offers picturesque views, and you can keep the views coming just five miles down the road in White Salmon, where you can sample the selection of session beers at **Everybody's Brewing** in view of Mount Hood (page 272). To try: Local Logger (lager) and The Cryo-Chronic (IPA).

- **Yakima Skyline Trail, Central Washington:** Admire views of the city of Yakima and the Yakima River canyon, then head to **Bale Breaker Brewing Company,** located on one of the area's commercial hop farms (page 292). To try: Field 41 (pale ale) and Topcutter (IPA).

ICICLE BREWING COMPANY

LOGGER LAGER

BEST WILDFLOWER HIKES

- **Skyline Trail Loop:** Conservationist John Muir's words are carved into the steps at the beginning of this hike and let visitors know what lies ahead: "the most luxuriant and the most extravagantly beautiful of all the alpine gardens" (page 78).

- **Skyline Divide:** Heather, aster, daisies, and lupine add a kaleidoscope of color to a ridge with up-close views of Mount Baker and Mount Shuksan (page 95).

- **Grand Valley:** Look for scarlet paintbrush, bluebells-of-Scotland, and more on this hike (page 226).

- **Dog Mountain:** Colorful lupine, columbine, balsamroot, and other wildflowers attract so many visitors that you need a permit to visit in spring (page 267).

- **Cowiche Canyon:** Golden balsamroot and pink bitterroot add spring color to the arid terrain near Yakima (page 293).

▾ LUPINE ALONG THE SKYLINE DIVIDE TRAIL

BEST DOG-FRIENDLY HIKES

- **High Rock Lookout:** Dogs aren't allowed on trails at Mount Rainier, but this hike just outside the park is the next best thing (page 85).

- **Lake Twenty-Two:** This climb past waterfalls, giant cedars, and a serene lake is a lovely treat for both you and your pet (page 122).

- **Mount Ellinor:** Young, fit dogs will love this short but steep hike, and you'll love the views (page 238).

- **Coyote Wall (Labyrinth Loop):** This is the rare hiking trail with an off-leash season (page 270).

- **Badger Mountain:** Leashes are available to borrow at the trailhead (page 296).

▼ HIKING AT HIGH ROCK LOOKOUT

EASY WATERFALL WALKS

The Pacific Northwest's renowned precipitation makes it quintessential waterfall country, and many don't demand a thigh-burning workout to appreciate. Visit in the spring to see them flowing at full force.

MARYMERE FALLS
Distance/Duration: 1.9 miles round-trip, 1 hour
Trailhead: Storm King Ranger Station, Olympic National Park
Depart from the ranger station and pass beach access to Crescent Lake before using a narrow tunnel to travel under U.S. 101. From here, the wide, smooth Marymere Falls Nature Trail passes two trails over a 0.5-mile stretch leading to the intersection with the Barnes Creek Trail. Turn right, cross bridges spanning Barnes and Falls Creeks, and climb 39 steps to a loop with two viewing areas (separated by 51 steps) of the 90-foot cascade splashing down a mossy cliff. After finishing the loop, return the way you came or explore other trails in the area.

SOL DUC FALLS
Distance/Duration: 1.8 miles round-trip, 45 minutes
Trailhead: end of Sol Duc Hot Springs Road, Olympic National Park
Sol Duc Creek splits into three falls, plummeting nearly 50 feet into a narrow canyon. A bridge and viewing platform overlook the falls, located next to the Canyon Creek Shelter. Built in 1939, the shelter is a year younger than Olympic National Park.

▾ FRANKLIN FALLS

SNOQUALMIE FALLS

Distance/Duration: 1.4 miles round-trip, 45 minutes
Trailhead: Salish Lodge, Snoqualmie

You can see Snoqualmie Falls' dramatic 270-foot plunge just a few steps beyond the Salish Lodge, but the 0.7-mile walk from this upper viewing area to the Snoqualmie River greatly enhances your visit. The trail is wide, steep, and lined with salmonberries, elderberries, sword ferns, vine maple, and other flora. At the bottom of the trail hikers pass a massive turbine and sections of pipe from hydroelectric plants that have harnessed the river's energy since 1898. The falls' significance to the Snoqualmie Indian Tribe predates the power plants; the tribe considered the falls to be the birthplace of their people. Follow a boardwalk along the river to the lower viewing area. If the trail seems too steep, you can drive to the lower parking lot.

FRANKLIN FALLS

Distance/Duration: 2 miles round-trip, 1 hour
Trailhead: Forest Road 5830 north of Denny Creek Campground, Mount Baker-Snoqualmie National Forest

Wander a family-friendly trail along the South Fork Snoqualmie River and stand at the foot of a 70-foot cascade. Just beyond the intersection with the Wagon Road Trail (an option for the return trip), descend to the base of the falls. Be careful: The rocks can be slippery and debris sometimes washes over the falls or drops from surrounding cliffs. In wintertime when the falls freeze (and closed roads might make this trip longer), there is the risk of avalanche from the steep slopes of Denny Mountain. With an elevated stretch of I-90 passing above, the area is a striking intersection of nature and civilization.

PALOUSE FALLS

Distance/Duration: 1.4 miles round-trip, 45 minutes
Trailhead: Palouse Falls State Park parking lot

Visible just a few steps beyond the parking lot, this stunning, nearly 200-foot plunge in the Palouse River takes almost no effort to view. However, a path at the north end of the parking lot takes hikers to the less-visited upper falls. You'll follow a path right along the edge of the canyon and gaze down at the massive falls, then make a steep descent through a hillside slit to active railroad tracks. Follow the trail along the tracks before descending the talus slope to the canyon floor and the upper falls.

SEATTLE AND VICINITY

Water or mountains? Vibrant city or the solitude of nature? The Seattle and Puget Sound area is an ideal hub for adventurers who don't want to make these tough choices. Twenty-five miles is all that separates the sound-view paths at Discovery Park from the short trail climbing to Poo Poo Point on Tiger Mountain. Whether you want to watch birds on the Nisqually Delta, explore history on Whidbey Island, or take in the majestic view from atop Oyster Dome, Puget Sound offers abundant opportunities within two hours of Seattle. And if you want to test your legs in the mountains, it's less than 40 minutes to North Bend, home of scenic local favorites such as Mailbox Peak, Mount Si, and the Rattlesnake Ledges.

▲ DECEPTION PASS BRIDGE

▲ PARAGLIDER AT POO POO POINT

◄ VIEW FROM THE TOP OF MOUNT SI

1 **Oyster Dome**
DISTANCE: 3.9 miles round-trip
DURATION: 2 hours
EFFORT: Easy/moderate

2 **Deception Pass: Rosario Head and Lighthouse Point**
DISTANCE: 3.3 miles round-trip
DURATION: 1.5 hours
EFFORT: Easy

3 **Ebey's Landing**
DISTANCE: 5.5 miles round-trip
DURATION: 2.5 hours
EFFORT: Easy/moderate

4 **Discovery Park Loop**
DISTANCE: 2.9 miles round-trip
DURATION: 1.5 hours
EFFORT: Easy

5 **Poo Poo Point via Chirico Trail**
DISTANCE: 3.8 miles round-trip
DURATION: 2 hours
EFFORT: Moderate

6 **Rattlesnake Ledges**
DISTANCE: 4.9 miles round-trip
DURATION: 2.5 hours
EFFORT: Moderate

7 **Mount Si**
DISTANCE: 7.6 miles round-trip
DURATION: 4 hours
EFFORT: Moderate/strenuous

8 **Twin Falls**
DISTANCE: 2.6 miles round-trip
DURATION: 1.5 hours
EFFORT: Easy/moderate

9 **Mailbox Peak: Old-New Loop**
DISTANCE: 8.2 miles round-trip
DURATION: 6 hours
EFFORT: Strenuous

10 **Nisqually Estuary Boardwalk Trail**
DISTANCE: 4.1 miles round-trip
DURATION: 2 hours
EFFORT: Easy

▾ BOARDWALK AT NISQUALLY ESTUARY

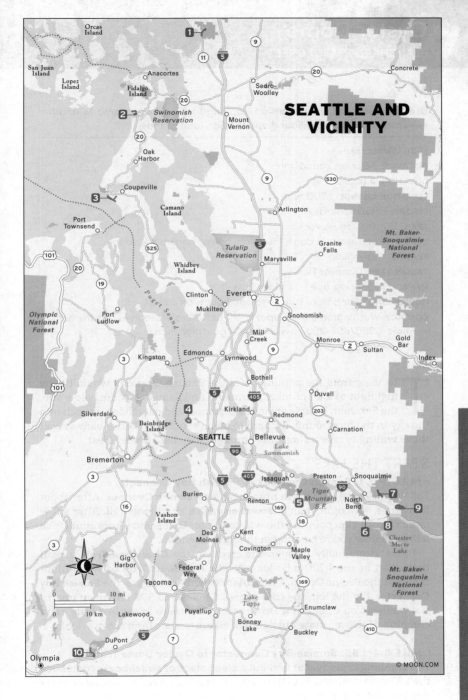

SEATTLE AND VICINITY

Oyster Dome

BLANCHARD STATE FOREST

Use forest trails to climb from an inspiring trailhead panorama to another sweeping view of Puget Sound and the San Juan Islands.

BEST: Winter Hikes
DISTANCE: 3.9 miles round-trip
DURATION: 2 hours
ELEVATION CHANGE: 1,200 feet
EFFORT: Easy/moderate
TRAIL: Dirt trail, roots, rocks
USERS: Hikers, leashed dogs, mountain bikers, horseback riders
SEASON: Year-round
PASSES/FEES: Discover Pass
MAPS: USGS topographic map for Bow
HOURS: One hour before sunrise to one hour after sunset
CONTACT: Washington State Department of Natural Resources, Northwest Region, 360/856-3500, www.dnr.wa.gov/blanchard

The view from the parking lot at the Samish Overlook would be the highlight of a lot of hikes. Farmland and Samish Bay are below you, the San Juan Islands are in the distance, and paragliders launch into the sky in the foreground. It's hard to believe, but even better views await those willing to take a short hike through Blanchard State Forest.

START THE HIKE

▶ MILE 0-0.4: Samish Overlook to Samish Bay Connector

Follow the gravel path north from the grassy **Samish Overlook**. After about four steps, stay right at an **intersection** with a short loop trail. After a few more steps, a **sign** pointing the way to Oyster Dome and Chuckanut Drive lets you know you're heading in the right direction.

Descend gradually through the trees on the **Chuckanut Trail**, a path that's part of the 1,200-mile-long **Pacific Northwest Trail** between Montana and the Pacific Ocean. After 0.4 mile turn right to join the **Samish Bay Connector**. (To the left, the trail drops 1.4 miles and 900 feet to an unofficial trailhead on Chuckanut Drive; some start there to get in a little extra climbing. However, state officials ask hikers to start from the overlook.)

▶ MILE 0.4-1.65: Samish Bay Connector to Oyster Dome Trail

The climbing is gradual at first but a steep stack of **switchbacks** completes the 1.25-mile connection to the Oyster Dome Trail. While crossing streams and passing under cedars and Douglas firs it's easy to see why the 4,500-acre forest has a long logging history. Today timber and biomass (residual limbs and small pieces of wood) are sold by the state to help fund schools,

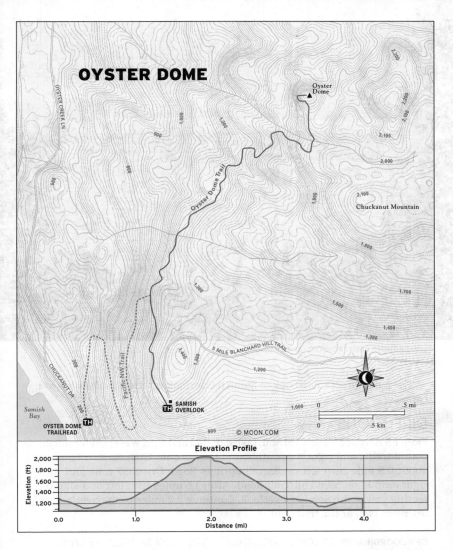

OYSTER DOME

Oyster Dome ▲

Chuckanut Mountain

Oyster Dome Trail

Oyster Creek Ln

5 MILE BLANCHARD HILL TRAIL

Pacific NW Trail

CHUCKANUT DR

Samish Bay

SAMISH OVERLOOK TH

OYSTER DOME TRAILHEAD TH

© MOON.COM

0   .5 mi
0   .5 km

Elevation Profile

Elevation (ft): 2,000 / 1,800 / 1,600 / 1,400 / 1,200

Distance (mi): 0.0   1.0   2.0   3.0   4.0

roadwork, hospitals, and other services. Before the junction with the **Oyster Dome Trail**, pass a mangled interpretive sign explaining that a mile-high glacier creeped through this area 18,000 years ago.

▶ **MILE 1.65-1.95: Oyster Dome Trail to Oyster Dome**

Continue straight as you join the **Oyster Dome Trail**. The path is a bit vague as it approaches a creek, but it becomes clearer after you step over the stream. Finish this 0.3-mile stretch by scampering over rocks and roots and then popping out of the trees onto a **rock outcropping** with views of Puget Sound, the San Juan Islands, and the Olympics. Look for bald eagles and other birds circling overhead. Watch your step as you snap photos and stake out a place to relax; the rock is slippery when it's wet.

▲ PARAGLIDER SEEN FROM OYSTER DOME

The most direct route back to Samish Overlook is to return the way you came.

DIRECTIONS

From I-5 north of Mount Vernon, take exit 240 and turn west (left for northbound traffic and right for southbound traffic) onto Lake Samish Road. In about 0.5 mile turn left on Barrell Springs Road. Drive 0.7 mile and turn right onto Blanchard Hill Trail Road. After 1.6 miles turn left at a sign directing you to the Samish Overlook. Continue 2.2 miles to the overlook. A restroom is near the trailhead.

GPS COORDINATES: 48.609757, –122.426313 / N48° 36.5854' W122° 25.5788'

BEST NEARBY BITES

A star of the Bellingham burger scene since it opened in 1989, **Boomer's Drive-In** (310 N. Samish Way, 360/647-2666, www.boomersdrivein.com, 11am-10pm Sun.-Thurs., 11am-11pm Fri.-Sat.) is the perfect place for a post-hike cheeseburger and shake. Let a carhop bring a quarter-pound Boomer Burger to your window or grab a seat around the circular fireplace inside the 1950s-themed diner. From the trailhead, the 16.5-mile drive north takes less than 30 minutes via I-5.

Explore the perimeter of Bowman Bay to find views of Rosario Strait, the Olympics, islands, and an iconic bridge.

DISTANCE: 3.3 miles round-trip
DURATION: 1.5 hours
ELEVATION CHANGE: 500 feet
EFFORT: Easy
TRAIL: Dirt, gravel
USERS: Hikers, leashed dogs
SEASON: Year-round
PASSES/FEES: Discover Pass
MAPS: Green Trails Map 41S for Deception Pass
PARK HOURS: 6:30am–dusk daily summer, 8am–dusk daily winter
CONTACT: Deception Pass State Park, 360/675-3767, http://parks.state.wa.us

D eception Pass draws more visitors than any other Washington state park, and it's evident why as you stroll around Bowman Bay. The boat launch parking lot accesses several short out-and-back hikes, including this scenic duo that is easily fused into one sublime, longer hike.

START THE HIKE

▶ **MILE 0-1.8: Rosario Head Loop**
Heading northwest from the parking lot, walk through the **picnic area** and past the **Civilian Conservation Corps Interpretive Center.** The center pays tribute to Franklin Roosevelt's Great Depression-era program responsible for developing so many state and national parks. Past the **picnic shelter**, find a path entering the woods. The trail bends left after an awkward section that seems destined to lead you through a campsite.

For the next 0.4 mile, walk among Douglas firs and madrone while crossing a steep hillside above the bay. The trail quickly deposits you at another picnic area at **Sharpe Cove.** Stay left, arcing along the cove, and follow a short gravel path past an access point to Rosario Beach.

The Maiden of Deception Pass welcomes visitors to **Rosario Head.** Carved from cedar in the early 1980s, the story pole depicts Ko-Kwal-al-woot, legend of the Samish Indian Nation. From the maiden, make a 0.25-mile loop around Rosario Head. Standing atop cliffs dropping sharply to Rosario Strait, enjoy a view that includes Vancouver Island, the San Juans, and the Olympics. Return the way you came (1.8 miles round-trip). The parking lot is also the starting point for part two of this hike.

Deception Pass: Rosario Head and Lighthouse Point

SEATTLE AND VICINITY

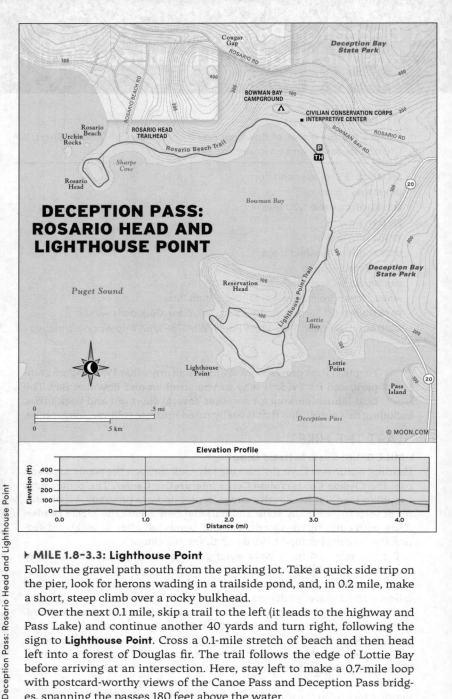

DECEPTION PASS: ROSARIO HEAD AND LIGHTHOUSE POINT

Elevation Profile

© MOON.COM

▶ **MILE 1.8–3.3: Lighthouse Point**

Follow the gravel path south from the parking lot. Take a quick side trip on the pier, look for herons wading in a trailside pond, and, in 0.2 mile, make a short, steep climb over a rocky bulkhead.

Over the next 0.1 mile, skip a trail to the left (it leads to the highway and Pass Lake) and continue another 40 yards and turn right, following the sign to **Lighthouse Point**. Cross a 0.1-mile stretch of beach and then head left into a forest of Douglas fir. The trail follows the edge of Lottie Bay before arriving at an intersection. Here, stay left to make a 0.7-mile loop with postcard-worthy views of the Canoe Pass and Deception Pass bridges, spanning the passes 180 feet above the water.

After completing the loop, return to the parking lot (a 1.5-mile round-trip) and pick your next adventure in the 3,854-acre park.

▲ THE MAIDEN OF DECEPTION PASS

DIRECTIONS

From the Clinton ferry dock on Whidbey Island, follow Highway 525 north for 22 miles and then continue straight on Highway 20 for 26 miles. Shortly after crossing the Deception Pass Bridge, turn left on Rosario Road.

From Mount Vernon, take Highway 536 west to Highway 20. (From Burlington, access Highway 20 at exit 230 on I-5). Continue straight on Highway 20 for 7 miles to a traffic circle. Take the second exit in the traffic circle and follow Highway 20 south for 4.4 miles; turn right on Rosario Road shortly after entering Deception Pass State Park.

After turning on Rosario Road, take an immediate left onto Bowman Bay Road and drive 0.4 mile to the parking area. A restroom, playground, beach access, and picnic tables are available at the trailhead. Camping is available nearby.

GPS COORDINATES: 48.416739, –122.650780 / N48° 25.0043' W122° 39.0468'

BEST NEARBY BITES

Make the 15-minute drive north to Anacortes to sample the pizza and beer menu at **Rockfish Grill** (314 Commercial Ave., Anacortes, 360/293-2544, www.anacortesrockfish.com, 11am-9pm Sun.-Thurs., 11am-10pm Fri.-Sat.). The pizza is made with local ingredients and prepared in a wood-fired oven. Anacortes Brewery crafts the beverages next door. From the trailhead, the 9-mile drive north takes about 15 minutes via Highway 20.

Get a history lesson while admiring Admiralty Inlet, the Olympics, and Whidbey Island's prairie.

DISTANCE: 5.5 miles round-trip

DURATION: 2.5 hours

ELEVATION CHANGE: 300 feet

EFFORT: Easy/moderate

TRAIL: Dirt, sand, gravel, beach

USERS: Hikers, leashed dogs

SEASON: Year-round

PASSES/FEES: None, but Discover Pass required if you park at Ebey's Landing State Park parking lot

MAPS: USGS topographic map for Coupeville, WA

CONTACT: Ebey's Landing National Historical Reserve, 360/678-6084, www.nps.gov/ebla

Saved by local citizens from the hands of developers, Ebey's Landing became the country's first national historical reserve in 1978. Today, Ebey's offers plenty of trails amid its 17,572 acres; the following route links the Ebey's Prairie Ridge and Bluff Trails to sample the best of this Puget Sound gem.

START THE HIKE

▶ **MILE 0-0.5: Ebey's Prairie Ridge Trail Trailhead to Pratt Loop Trail Intersection**

Starting from the trailhead for **Ebey's Prairie Ridge Trail** near the historic Sunnyside Cemetery, follow the wide gravel path as it makes its way 0.3 mile along an alfalfa field to **Ebey House,** open Memorial Day through Labor Day weekends (10am-4pm Thurs.-Sun.). From the house, the trail dips to the left of a barbwire fence and descends gradually as it makes its way toward **Admiralty Inlet.**

In 0.2 mile, pass the **intersection** with the Pratt Loop Trail, continuing straight and enjoying an unobstructed view over the prairie. Occasionally the silence is broken by the thunderous jet engines at nearby Whidbey Island Naval Air Station.

▶ **MILE 0.5-1.4: Pratt Loop Trail Intersection to Bluff Trail**

After another 0.4 mile, you'll reach the **Bluff Trail** above the glistening water. Turn left and descend 0.4 mile to a bench with a view of the ferry route between Whidbey Island and Port Townsend. Drop 0.1 mile to the **parking lot** and a restroom. (Note that this parking lot off Ebey Road, the Ebey's Landing State Park parking lot, requires a Discover Pass.)

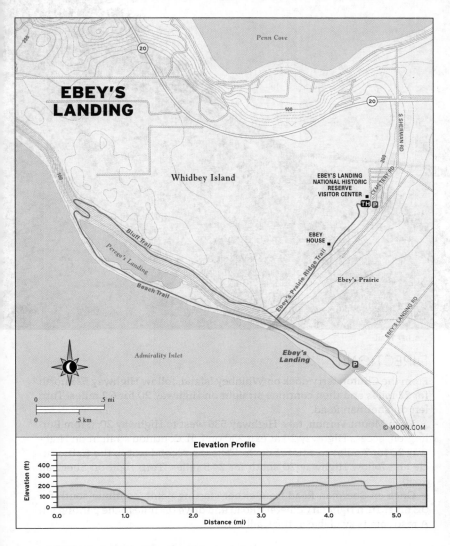

EBEY'S
LANDING

Penn Cove

Whidbey Island

Ebey's Prairie

Admiralty Inlet

Ebey's
Landing

0   .5 mi
0   .5 km

© MOON.COM

Elevation Profile

▶ **MILE 1.4-3.5: Bluff Trail to Perego's Lake**

Facing the water, turn right and stroll 1.7 miles on the rocky, driftwood-lined **beach**. Gulls and the occasional bald eagle soar overhead. Seals poke their brown heads out of the water. At the far end of **Perego's Lake,** regain the **Bluff Trail** and climb 200 feet over the next 0.3 mile to the top of the bank. (For a gentler climb, hike this loop in the opposite direction.) The view from the grassy slope looking over the lake and Puget Sound might be the best in the reserve.

▶ **MILE 3.5-5.5: Perego's Lake to Ebey's Prairie Ridge Trail**

For the next 1.1 miles, walk the edge of the bluff along the **Robert Y. Pratt Preserve** to complete the Bluff Trail Loop. Turn left on the **Ebey's Prairie Ridge Trail** and follow the familiar path 0.9 mile back to your car.

▲ BLUFF TRAIL

DIRECTIONS

From the Clinton ferry dock on Whidbey Island, follow Highway 525 north for 22 miles and then continue straight on Highway 20 for 6.2 miles. Turn left on Sherman Road.

From Mount Vernon, take Highway 536 west to Highway 20. (From Burlington, access Highway 20 at exit 230 on I-5). Continue straight on Highway 20 for 7 miles to a traffic circle. Take the second exit in the traffic circle and follow Highway 20 south for 24.5 miles. Turn right on Sherman Road.

Once on Sherman Road from either starting point, continue south for 0.3 mile. Turn right on Cemetery Road and drive 0.3 mile to the parking lot. A restroom is available at the trailhead.

GPS COORDINATES: 48.204608, –122.707119 / N48° 12.2765' W122° 42.4271'

BEST NEARBY BREWS

Less than 1.4 miles and five minutes northeast of the trailhead, **Penn Cove Taproom** (103 S. Main St., Coupeville, 360/682–5747, www.penncovebrewing.com, hours vary) has 14 taps serving local brews, including its own Madrona Way IPA. It's all about the beer here; the menu's modest food options include nachos, hot dogs, and popcorn.

Loop through Seattle's largest park while enjoying views of Puget Sound, Mount Rainier, and the Olympics.

BEST: Brew Hikes

DISTANCE: 2.9 miles round-trip

DURATION: 1.5 hours

ELEVATION CHANGE: 300 feet

EFFORT: Easy

TRAIL: Dirt, gravel, sandy and paved paths

USERS: Hikers, leashed dogs (not allowed on beaches), bikes (paved surfaces only)

SEASON: Year-round

PASSES/FEES: None

MAPS: Free maps at visitors center or online at www.friendsofdiscoverypark.org/maps

PARK HOURS: 4am–11:30pm daily

CONTACT: Discovery Park, 206/684-4075, www.seattle.gov

START THE HIKE

The 534-acre park is Seattle's largest, and its forest, well-maintained trails, and views of Puget Sound make for an easily accessible oasis.

▶ **MILE 0-1.3: Visitors Center Parking Lot to Discovery Park Boulevard Intersection**

Starting at the northeast corner of the **visitors center parking lot**, walk down a few steps and into the woods. In less than 0.1 mile arrive at the **intersection** where the **Loop Trail** begins and ends. Go right and take a **tunnel** under Discovery Park Boulevard.

The trail has some modest inclines but is mostly flat and wide. Pass under Douglas firs, maples, and alders, wind in and out of lush green drainages, and cross four roads in the first 1.1 miles. Upon crossing the fourth, follow signs left to stay on the loop.

In another 0.1 mile, cross **Discovery Park Boulevard**, a road that can be busy at times, and stay right at the **intersection** just past the restroom.

▶ **MILE 1.3-2: Discovery Park Boulevard Intersection to Magnolia Bluff**

The park's famous view from atop **Magnolia Bluff** unfolds before you in another 0.4 mile. As you spend the next 0.3 mile walking the **sandy trail**, watch ferries cut across Puget Sound and seaplanes soar overhead; Rainier is visible to the south. You'll be tempted to stay long enough to watch the sun set behind the Olympics. To the west, in the middle of the park, what looks like a giant golf ball is an FAA radar dome that was relocated to Fort Lawton from McChord Air Force Base in 1960.

SEATTLE AND VICINITY

Discovery Park Loop

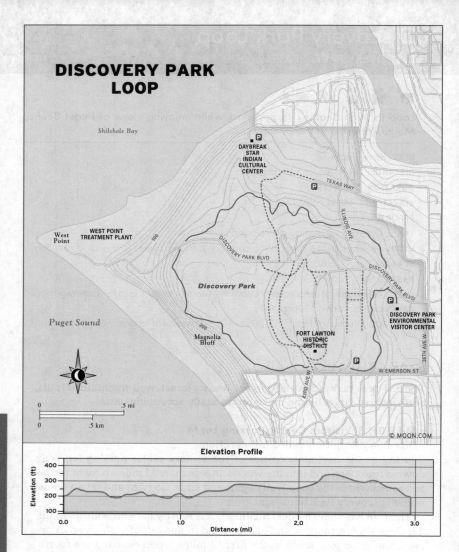

DISCOVERY PARK LOOP

Shilshole Bay

DAYBREAK STAR INDIAN CULTURAL CENTER

TEXAS WAY

ILLINOIS AVE

WEST POINT TREATMENT PLANT

West Point

DISCOVERY PARK BLVD

Discovery Park

DISCOVERY PARK BLVD

DISCOVERY PARK ENVIRONMENTAL VISITOR CENTER

Puget Sound

36TH AVE W

Magnolia Bluff

FORT LAWTON HISTORIC DISTRICT

43RD AVE W

W EMERSON ST

0   .5 mi
0   .5 km

© MOON.COM

Elevation Profile

Elevation (ft)

400
300
200
100

0.0   1.0   2.0   3.0

Distance (mi)

▶ **MILE 2-2.9: Magnolia Bluff to Visitors Center Parking Lot**

From the bluff, the trail turns inland for a 0.4-mile jaunt to the **south parking lot** (an alternative starting point). Continue on the **Loop Trail** for 0.5 mile (passing shortcuts to the visitors center) before closing the loop. Turn right at the familiar **intersection** and make the short walk back to the parking lot.

DIRECTIONS

From I-5, take exit 167 and follow Mercer Street toward Seattle Center. After 1.6 miles veer right on Elliott Avenue. Travel 1.9 miles as Elliott Avenue becomes 15th Avenue, and then take the Emerson/Nickerson exit. Stay right and follow Nickerson Street 0.2 mile to a stop sign; turn left on Emerson Street. In 0.5 mile turn right on Gilman Avenue. Continue 1.1 miles as

▲ PUGET SOUND

Gilman becomes Government Way and then Discovery Park Boulevard. In the park, take the first left to the visitors center and the east parking lot. Restrooms are available in the building (8:30am-5pm Tues.-Sun.), behind the building, and along the trail.

Additional parking is available in the south parking lot. Get there by returning to the intersection of Government Way and 36th Avenue and turning right on 36th. Turn right on Emerson Street after 0.3 mile, then drive west 0.4 mile and turn right to enter the park. Drive 0.2 mile to the south parking lot.

King County Metro's Route 33 ends at the park. Exit at Government Way and 36th Avenue and make the 0.1-mile walk to the visitors center trailhead. Route 24 stops at Emerson Street and Magnolia Boulevard, 0.1 mile from where the loop trail passes the south parking lot.

GPS COORDINATES: 47.658218, –122.406216 / N47° 39.4931′ W122° 24.373′

BEST NEARBY BREWS

Post-hike brews are easy to find in Seattle. Local favorites like the **Pike Brewing Company** (1415 1st Ave., 206/622-6044, www.pikebrewing. com, 11am-midnight Sun.-Thurs., 11am-1am Fri.-Sat.) and **Old Stove Brewing** (1901 Western Ave., Pike Place Market, 206/602-6120, www. oldstove.com, hours vary) are less than 8 miles southeast and about 20 minutes away via 15th and Elliott Avenues. Even closer is the **Fremont Brewing Company** (1050 N. 34th St., 206/420-2407, www.fre-montbrewing.com, 11am-9pm daily), just 3.8 miles and 13 minutes east via Nickerson Street.

Make the climb from a paraglider landing strip to the launching pad while enjoying views of Mount Rainier, Mount Baker, and Lake Sammamish.

DISTANCE: 3.8 miles round-trip
DURATION: 2 hours
ELEVATION CHANGE: 1,700 feet
EFFORT: Moderate
TRAIL: Dirt trail, rocks
USERS: Hikers, leashed dogs, paragliders
SEASON: Year-round
PASSES/FEES: None
MAPS: Green Trails Map 204S for Tiger Mountain
CONTACT: Washington State Department of Natural Resources, 360/825-1631, www.dnr.wa.gov

START THE HIKE

▶ MILE 0-0.9: Parking Lot to Chirico Trail

The trail starts at the north end of the **gravel parking lot**. In the first few steps, you'll encounter a **wooden sculpture** of a winged lion. The popular hike to Poo Poo Point starts at a paragliding landing strip (at the parking lot) and climbs all the way up to the launching pad. The trail was built by Marc Chirico, owner of Seattle Paragliding (11206 Issaquah-Hobart Rd. SE, Issaquah, 206/387-3477, www.seattleparagliding.com), which will fly you down for $225-250.

From the winged lion, pass under the **Chirico Trail** sign and follow the trail for 0.1 mile before it turns into the woods, passes through a gate, and starts climbing. After 0.7 mile of climbing along **Yah-er Wall,** Poo Poo Point's steep, fern-lined face, you'll arrive at a log bench that tempts hikers to pause to catch their breath. If you skip this one, don't worry—there's another one in 0.1 mile. Stay left at each bench to continue climbing the Chirico Trail.

▶ MILE 0.9-1.9: Chirico Trail to Poo Poo Point Launch Site

The ascent continues over the next 0.6 mile past Douglas fir, western hemlock, and purple foxglove before hitting an **intersection;** turn left here to stay on Chirico. In 40 yards you'll hit another **intersection;** keep left yet again. After another 0.2 mile you'll arrive at a **clearing,** used as the south paragliding launch site. The views of Puget Sound and Mount Rainier to the south are this trail's first big reward. You might glimpse an eagle soaring overhead. Stay left here and catch the trail at the edge of the clearing for the final 0.2-mile uphill push to the main **Poo Poo Point launch site.**

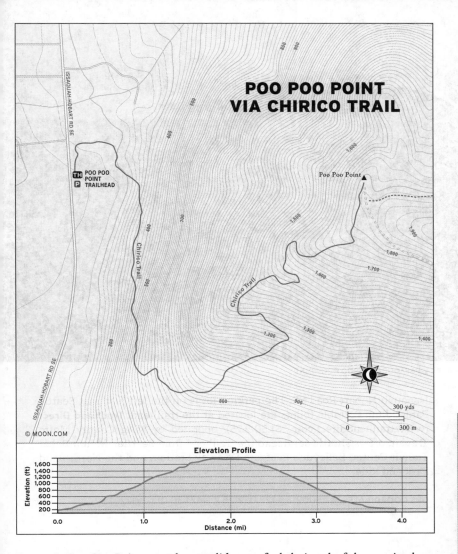

**POO POO POINT
VIA CHIRICO TRAIL**

Poo Poo Point ▲

Elevation Profile

At Poo Poo Point, watch paragliders unfurl their colorful canopies before they soar off to become part of the scenery, which includes neighboring Squak and Cougar Mountains, Issaquah, Lake Sammamish, and, on particularly clear days, Mount Baker. Note that the point's amusing name has nothing to do with what jumping off the side of the mountain might scare out of you, or the scat from bear, deer, and other animals you might see along the way. Rather, the name refers to the sound made by old steam whistles when loggers worked the forest.

If you don't fly down, simply retrace your path to the trailhead.

DIRECTIONS

From Seattle, follow I-90 east to exit 17 in Issaquah. Turn right and merge onto Front Street North and then continue 2.8 miles as the road becomes

▲ PARAGLIDER AT POO POO POINT

Issaquah-Hobart Road SE. The parking lot is on the left just past Seattle Paragliding. Portable toilets are located at the trailhead. **Trailhead Direct** (www.trailheaddirect.com, $1.50-2.75), operated by King County Metro Transit, offers shuttle service to the trailhead from Seattle's Mount Baker Transit Center, Bellevue's Eastgate Freeway Station, and the North Bend Park and Ride.

GPS COORDINATES: 47.500216, –122.022128 / N47° 30.013' W122° 1.3277'

BEST NEARBY BITES

Signs on the windows at Issaquah's **XXX Root Beer Drive-in** (98 NE Gilman Blvd., Issaquah, 425/392-1266, www.triplexrootbeer.com, 11am-9pm daily, cash or check only) read "Warning: Nothing that you eat or drink here is good for you!" But after a day of hiking, it's easy to justify a burger and a huge root beer served in a frosted mug. And the 1950s-diner vibes—think classic-car memorabilia and a jukebox playing Elvis tunes—transport you to a time when the world was blissfully unaware of trans fat. From the trailhead, the 3-mile drive north takes 9 minutes via Front Street.

Rattlesnake Ledges

RATTLESNAKE MOUNTAIN SCENIC AREA, NORTH BEND

Reach a trio of rock outcroppings high above Rattlesnake Lake and the Cedar River Watershed via a moderate climb up one of Washington's most popular trails.

BEST: Brew Hikes

DISTANCE: 4.9 miles round–trip

DURATION: 2.5 hours

ELEVATION CHANGE: 1,600 feet

EFFORT: Moderate

TRAIL: Dirt single track

USERS: Hikers, leashed dogs

SEASON: Year–round

PASSES/FEES: None

MAPS: Green Trails Map 205S for Rattlesnake Mountain/Upper Snoqualmie Valley, USGS topographic map for North Bend

CONTACT: Washington State Department of Natural Resources, 360/825–1631, www.dnr.wa.gov

START THE HIKE

▸ **MILE 0–1: Parking Lot to Rattlesnake Lake Viewpoint**

Slip past the gate at the northwest edge of the parking lot to start your hike on the **Rattlesnake Ledge Trail.** Listen to the greetings of chirping birds and croaking frogs while following a wide gravel path along the perimeter of Rattlesnake Lake.

After 0.25 mile, you'll have access to portable toilets. A large **kiosk** displays a map of the trail. Notice a sign warning of steep cliffs; this isn't to be taken lightly, as people have fallen to their deaths here. The trail is often accessible in winter, but hikers should check conditions before attempting during cold months. From the kiosk, the trail climbs through a forest of western hemlock, cedar, and Douglas fir, passing a bench in 0.75 mile that offers a view through the trees of **Rattlesnake Lake.**

▸ **MILE 1–2: Rattlesnake Lake Viewpoint to Lower Ledge**

After admiring the view, continue on the trail, which skirts the **Cedar River Watershed** (the source of Seattle's water). The gurgle of this stream not visible from the trail lures some hikers off the path, but don't follow their lead; signs warn that hikers can be prosecuted for wandering off-trail.

After 1 mile, you'll reach a **sign** that directs you along the Rattlesnake Mountain Trail to East Peak. The sign signals your arrival at the first ledge. Turn right and continue about 50 yards to the **lower ledge** (Rattlesnake Ledge), which offers views of the Cedar River Watershed, Rattlesnake

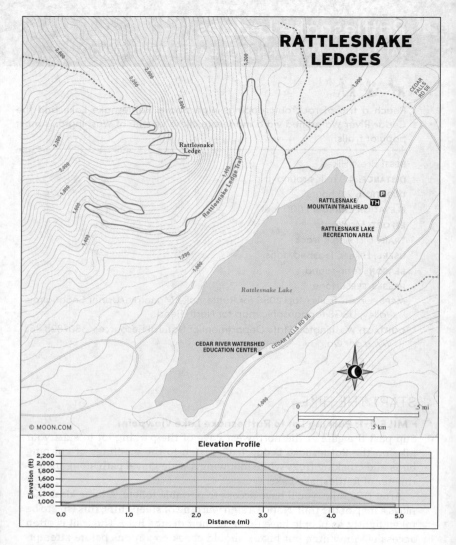

RATTLESNAKE LEDGES

Rattlesnake Ledge

Rattlesnake Ledge Trail

RATTLESNAKE MOUNTAIN TRAILHEAD

RATTLESNAKE LAKE RECREATION AREA

Rattlesnake Lake

CEDAR RIVER WATERSHED EDUCATION CENTER

CEDAR FALLS RD SE

© MOON.COM

0   .5 mi
0   .5 km

Elevation Profile

Elevation (ft): 2,200 / 2,000 / 1,800 / 1,600 / 1,400 / 1,200 / 1,000

Distance (mi): 0.0   1.0   2.0   3.0   4.0   5.0

Lake, the Cascades, and North Bend. This is as far as most people go, making this rocky outcrop crowded on most sunny days.

▶ MILE 2-2.45: East Peak to Middle and Upper Ledges

The upper ledges offer more solitude—and arguably even better views—for just a bit more work. Turn left at the sign for the lower ledge and continue another 0.2 mile through the forest until you reach an unsigned spur trail at a switchback. This short trail leads to the **middle ledge.** Continue up another 0.25 mile to find the unsigned spur to the **upper ledge.** The spur is easy to find on the right at a switchback. The views seem a little more exclusive the higher you go, even though they're separated by only about five minutes of hiking. From the upper ledge, you can see the throng of hikers 300 feet below on the lower ledge. And here's a fun trick to make

▲ MIDDLE LEDGE OF RATTLESNAKE MOUNTAIN

the view even more special: Get up early and hike by headlamp to the upper ledge to watch the sun rise over the foothills—and then scoot down to the middle ledge to watch it rise again.

When you're finished enjoying the scenery, return the way you came.

DIRECTIONS

From Seattle, follow I-90 east to North Bend and take exit 32. Turn right on 436th Avenue SE. Drive 2.8 miles, continuing straight as the road becomes Cedar Falls Road SE. The parking lot will be on the right. Portable toilets are available at the parking lot and about 0.25 mile into the hike.

GPS COORDINATES: 47.434701, –121.768716 / N47° 26.0821' W121° 46.123'

BEST NEARBY BREWS

A short drive from the trailhead, the **Snoqualmie Brewery and Taproom** (8032 Falls Ave. SE, Snoqualmie, www.fallsbrew.com, 425/831-2357, summer 11am-9pm Sun.-Tues., 11am-10pm Wed.-Sat., winter noon-9pm Mon.-Thurs., 11am-10pm Fri.-Sat.) has a menu that ranges from creative (Black Frog Nitro Stout ice cream float) to Canadian (poutine with beer-battered fries). However, it's best known for its brewers' greatest hits: Copperhead Pale Ale, Haystack Hefeweizen, Steam Train Porter, and many more. From the trailhead, the 8.5-mile drive northwest takes about 20 minutes via 436th Avenue and Highway 202.

7 Mount Si

MOUNT SI NATURAL RESOURCES CONSERVATION AREA, NORTH BEND

Seattle's StairMaster, Mount Si is a popular workout destination for hikers looking for a challenge that rewards with views of the Cascades, Olympics, and Snoqualmie Valley.

DISTANCE: 7.6 miles round–trip

DURATION: 4 hours

ELEVATION CHANGE: 3,200 feet

EFFORT: Moderate/strenuous

TRAIL: Dirt single track, large boulders

USERS: Hikers, leashed dogs

SEASON: April–November, but conditions often suitable for winter hiking

PASSES/FEES: Discover Pass

MAPS: Green Trails Map 206S for Mount Si

CONTACT: Washington State Department of Natural Resources, www.dnr.wa.gov/mountsi

START THE HIKE

▶ MILE 0-1.8: Mount Si Trail Trailhead to Snag Flats

At the north end of the parking lot, the Mount Si Trail starts with a flat, 0.1-mile gravel section that crosses a **bridge** before unleashing what makes this trail so famous: oodles of uphill. You'll ascend 600 feet in the next 0.7 mile before reaching the first of two **intersections** with the Talus Loop Trail. Keep left to stay on the Mount Si Trail, ascending another 750 feet in 0.9 mile before reaching the second intersection with the Talus Loop. Keep left again. (If the Mount Si Trail is proving too much, the Talus Loop is a convenient way to switch to an easier hike—3.7 miles round-trip with 1,400 feet of climbing.) Just past the second Talus Loop junction, Mount Si gives you a rare break with a level 0.1-mile section known as **Snag Flats.** Here you can see standing dead trees (snags), remnants of a 1910 fire. An interpretive sign on a short wooden boardwalk tells the story of a 350-year-old, 175-foot-tall Douglas fir damaged in the fire.

▶ MILE 1.8-3.8: Snag Flats to Mount Si Viewpoint

From Snag Flats, the trail dishes out its toughest section: 1,800 feet of elevation gain over 2 miles. There's not much in the way of views along the majority of this section—mostly ferns, hemlocks, cedars, and other flora. You might catch a glimpse of deer and there have been occasional bear and cougar sightings. At the end of this challenging stretch, step out of the trees and onto a **boulder field**. Take a few more steps and Si's famous view unfurls before you.

SEATTLE AND VICINITY

Mount Si

44

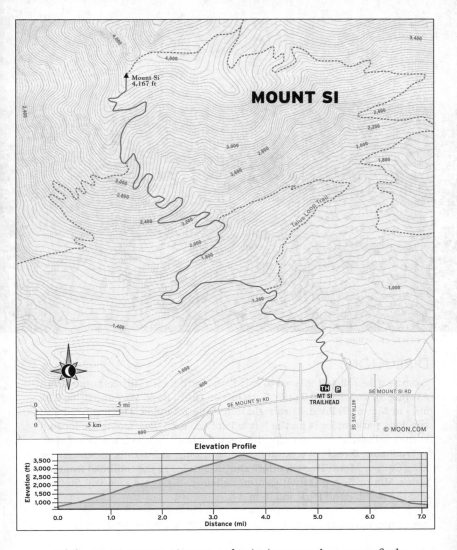

Elevation Profile

While snapping some pictures and enjoying a snack, you may find your-self intrigued by the rock feature above known as the Haystack. This is Si's summit but attempting it shouldn't be taken lightly; hikers have died fall-ing from this slope. Good footwear is essential. Reaching the top requires hiking around to the northeast side of the Haystack and then scrambling up a steep slope. Watch your step and stay alert for rocks knocked loose by people (or possibly even mountain goats) higher on the slope. Keep in mind that the view atop Haystack isn't much different from that at the main viewpoint.

After enjoying the view and resting your legs, return the way you came.

▲ VIEW FROM MOUNT SI

DIRECTIONS

From Seattle, follow I-90 east to exit 32 in North Bend. Turn left onto 436th Avenue SE and drive 0.5 mile. Turn left on North Bend Way and drive 0.25 mile to Mount Si Road. Turn right and drive 2.3 miles. The trailhead and spacious parking lot is on the left side of the road. Restrooms are located at the trailhead. Arriving early gives you the best chance at a parking spot.

Trailhead Direct (www.trailheaddirect.com, $1.50-2.75), operated by King County Metro Transit, offers shuttle service to the trailhead from Seattle's Mount Baker Transit Center, Bellevue's Eastgate Freeway Station, and the North Bend Park and Ride.

GPS COORDINATES: 47.488020, –121.723229/ N47° 29.2812' W121° 43.3937'

BEST NEARBY BITES

You might recognize Mount Si from the opening credits of the 1990s TV cult classic *Twin Peaks*, so it seems fitting to cap your hike with a visit to **Twede's Café** (137 W. North Bend Way, North Bend, 425/831-5511, www.twedescafe.com, 8am–8pm daily). Pick something from the extensive burger menu, or channel your inner Dale Cooper and order a slice of cherry pie and a "damn fine cup of coffee." From the trailhead, the 4-mile drive west takes about 10 minutes via Mount Si Road and North Bend Way.

8

Twin Falls

OLALLIE STATE PARK, NORTH BEND

🦌 🏞 🐾 🚶

Walk a gentle path along the South Fork of the Snoqualmie River to views of Twin Falls.

BEST: Waterfall Hikes
DISTANCE: 2.6 miles round trip
DURATION: 1.5 hours
ELEVATION CHANGE: 600 feet
EFFORT: Easy/moderate
TRAIL: Dirt single track, wooden bridges, stairways
USERS: Hikers, leashed dogs
SEASON: Year-round
PASSES/FEES: Discover Pass
MAPS: Green Trails Map 205S for Rattlesnake Mountain.
PARK HOURS: 6:30am–dusk daily summer, 8am–dusk daily winter
CONTACT: Olallie State Park, 425/455-7010, http://parks.state.wa.us

START THE HIKE

▶ **MILE 0-0.2: Parking Lot to South Fork Snoqualmie River**
At the southern end of the parking lot in Olallie State Park, find the well-marked **Twin Falls Trail** and start with a gentle 0.2-mile stretch along the **South Fork Snoqualmie River.** From the rumbling of the river and the sound of the water plunging over the falls to the occasional groan of a semitruck on nearby I-90, not a single step of this hike is quiet in spring and early summer.

▶ **MILE 0.2-0.4: South Fork Snoqualmie River to Switchbacks**
Ferns, vine maples, and salmonberry shrubs (*Olallie* is Chinook jargon for salmonberry) line parts of the trail. Various spots offer opportunities to get a little closer to the river and maybe catch a glimpse of a cutthroat trout. After 0.2 mile, the trail turns away from the river and climbs briefly using a few **switchbacks.** As you gain a little elevation an impressive carpet of sword ferns covers the forest floor.

▶ **MILE 0.4-1.1: Switchbacks to Lower Falls Spur**
Continue 0.3 mile to a series of benches that provide the first glimpse of the 135-foot **lower falls**. This spot alone is worth the trip, but keep going for more dynamic views. In 0.4 mile, reach a **staircase** that drops to a wooden platform with an up-close, top-to-bottom view of the lower falls. The falls' name comes from the Twin Falls Gorge it plunges through.

Twin Falls

▲ LOWER TWIN FALLS

▶ **MILE 1.1–1.3: Lower Falls Spur to Twin Falls Upper Falls**
To see more cascading water, continue 0.1 mile beyond the top of the stair-case, to a **bridge** that passes over the river and has views of the top of the lower falls and the bottom of the upper falls. The second **switchback** 0.1 mile beyond the bridge offers the best view of the **upper falls**.

This is an ideal place to turn around. Return the way you came.

DIRECTIONS

From Seattle, follow I-90 east to exit 34. Turn right on 468th Avenue SE and travel 0.5 mile to SE 159th Street. Turn left and follow SE 159th Street until it ends in the small trailhead parking lot. Signs mark the way to the trailhead. Toilets are located at the trailhead.

GPS COORDINATES: 47.453099, –121.705347 / N47° 27.1859 W121° 42.3208

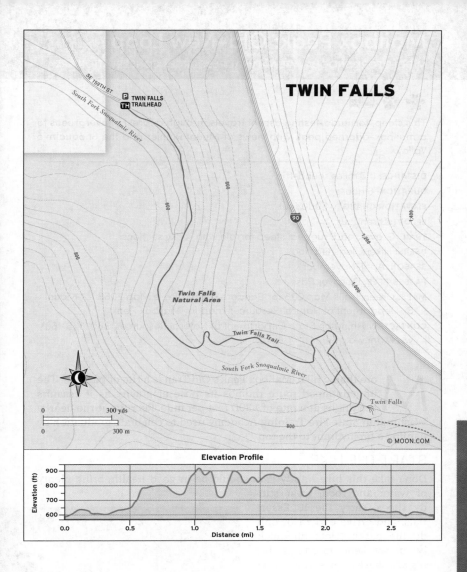

TWIN FALLS

Elevation Profile

BEST NEARBY BITES

Since it opened in 1998, the **North Bend Bar & Grill** (145 E. North Bend Way, North Bend, 425/888-1243, www.northbendbarandgrill.com, 8am-midnight daily) has established itself as a popular après-hike/ski/run/bike destination. It's easy to see why after you cap a hike with a draft beer and one-third-pound bacon Trail Burger served on a freshly baked bun. From the trailhead, the 5.5-mile drive northwest takes about 10 minutes via I-90 and Cedar Falls Way.

9

Mailbox Peak: Old-New Loop

MIDDLE FORK SNOQUALMIE NATURAL RESOURCES CONSERVATION AREA

✻ 🐾 🚌🚆

This steep, fortitude-testing ascent travels through a forest of evergreens to a mailbox-adorned peak with views of Mount Rainier and the Snoqualmie Valley.

DISTANCE: 8.2 miles round-trip

DURATION: 6 hours

ELEVATION CHANGE: 4,000 feet

EFFORT: Strenuous

TRAIL: Gravel road, rugged, steep terrain with rocky sections

USERS: Hikers, leashed dogs

SEASON: April-November

PASSES/FEES: Discover Pass

MAPS: Green Trails Map 206 for Bandera, Green Trails Map 206S for Mount Si, Department of Natural Resources map for Mailbox Peak

CONTACT: Washington State Department of Natural Resources, 360/825-1631, www.dnr.wa.gov

More than a hike, Mailbox Peak's Old Trail is a rite of passage. The unmaintained route thumbs its nose at gravity as it assaults the thighs at a rate of 1,300 feet per mile. Recruits at the nearby Washington State Fire Training Academy used to celebrate graduation by hauling a fire hydrant to the top.

START THE HIKE

Don't take this hike lightly: You should be in good health, bring plenty of water and food, wear sturdy shoes, carry the 10 Essentials, and arrive early. Not only do the parking lots fill quickly on weekend mornings, but it's also best to give yourself as much time as possible. Take the challenge seriously and Mailbox will deliver an immense sense of accomplishment.

▸ **MILE 0-0.3: Upper Parking Lot to New Trail**

Slip past the white gate at the end of the upper parking lot and follow a dirt road gently

THE MAILBOX ON MAILBOX PEAK ▸

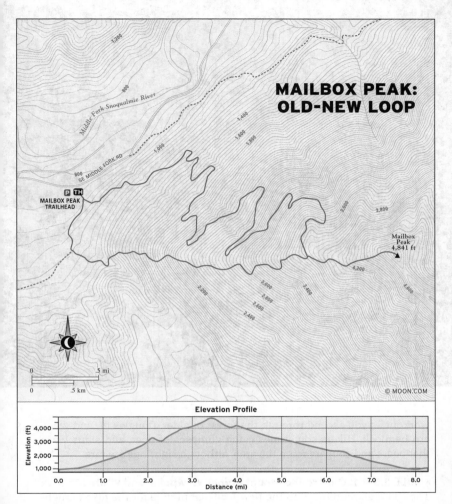

MAILBOX PEAK: OLD-NEW LOOP

Elevation Profile

upward. After 100 yards, take note of a trailhead on your left for the New Trail, which adds 2.5 miles to your hike (each way) but is significantly less steep than the Old Trail. To take on the famous **Old Trail** (which this hike follows), keep walking up the dirt road.

At 0.3 mile, you'll find one last warning. A sign bolted to a wooden **kiosk** cautions that what lies beyond is "steep, wet, unmaintained, difficult, challenging" and the site of frequent search and rescue missions. Still game? Then follow the path as it plunges into the woods and let the workout begin.

▶ MILE 0.3-2.3: New Trail to Old Trail

The next 0.2 mile of mellow ascent near a gurgling creek might lure you into thinking the route isn't as tough as you've heard. Those thoughts fall away quickly as the trail morphs into a ladder of roots and rocks. Let the **white diamond markers** posted on trees guide you as the trail refuses to relent for the next 1.8 miles. There are no views to distract you from the

▲ DESCENDING MAILBOX PEAK

workout as you ascend through the forest of alder, Douglas fir, and western hemlock. Hikers sometimes catch glimpses of deer, and signs warn that bears and cougars roam the area, although sightings are rare.

▶ **MILE 2.3–3.1: Old Trail to Mount Rainer Viewpoint and White Mailbox**
The Old Trail reunites with the **New Trail** just in time for the hike's toughest stretch: a 1,000-foot climb over 0.8 mile. A few **switchbacks** lead to a rocky **stairway** that cuts upward to an **open ridge,** where the destination finally comes into view. The final push up the ridge is the steepest yet. The challenge is rewarded with a sweeping view and one of the Northwest's most famous summit accoutrements, a large white **mailbox** that once stashed a summit register. It's now stuffed with surprises: letters, toys, and, if you're lucky, chocolate and whiskey.

▶ **MILE 3.1–8.2: Mount Rainer Viewpoint and
White Mailbox to Upper Parking Lot**
After refueling, taking in the views of Rainier and the Snoqualmie Valley, and snapping a selfie with the mailbox, return the way you came 0.8 mile to the **intersection** with the Old and New Trails, staying mindful of how your tired legs handle the steep descent. Stay on the longer yet gentler **New Trail** for the entire descent to give your knees and ankles a break. The path sweeps back and forth as its drops past evergreens, blossoming

trillium, and occasional salmonberry bushes on a 4.3-mile journey back to the parking lot. You'll cross two wooden bridges on the way down; after the second you're in the homestretch and it's safe to start celebrating your accomplishment.

DIRECTIONS

From Seattle, take exit 34 on I-90 and turn north onto 468th Avenue SE. After 0.6 mile, turn right on Southeast Middle Fork Road. Continue 2.6 miles, staying left at the junction with Dorothy Road, to a small parking area. Turn right and follow a short driveway to a larger parking lot if the gate is open. The gate closes at dusk and the upper parking lot is closed Monday-Thursday.

Trailhead Direct (www.trailheaddirect.com, $1.50-2.75), operated by King County Metro Transit, offers shuttle service to the trailhead from Seattle's Mount Baker Transit Center, Bellevue's Eastgate Freeway Station, and the North Bend Park and Ride.

GPS COORDINATES: 47.466669, –121.673748 / N47° 28.000' W121° 40.255'

BEST NEARBY BITES

Let North Bend's mayor cook you a cheeseburger at **Scott's Dairy Freeze** (234 E. North Bend Way, North Bend, 425/888-2301, 8am-9pm Mon.-Sat., 8am-8pm Sun.). Mayor Ken Hearing owns the nearly 70-year-old burger stand and often works the grill. Bagging Mailbox is also worthy of a milk shake, the second most popular menu item here. From the trailhead, the 6.2-mile drive northwest takes about 14 minutes via Middle Fork Road and North Bend Way.

This easy boardwalk trail on the Nisqually River Delta is a bird-watching wonderland and an ideal spot to introduce children to nature.

BEST: Winter Hikes

DISTANCE: 4.1 miles round-trip

DURATION: 2 hours

ELEVATION CHANGE: Negligible

EFFORT: Easy

TRAIL: Wooden boardwalks, dirt trail

USERS: Hikers, wheelchair users

SEASON: Year-round

PASSES/FEES: $3 adults, free children 16 and younger; America the Beautiful Passes accepted

MAPS: USGS topographic map for Nisqually, WA; free maps at visitors center and on the website

HOURS: Sunrise-sunset daily

CONTACT: Billy Frank Jr. Nisqually National Wildlife Refuge, 360/753-9467, www.fws.gov

Despite the sound of passing cars on nearby I-5, the Billy Frank Jr. Nisqually National Wildlife Refuge feels as if it's a world away from civilization. More than 275 species of birds visit the refuge each year, making it a popular destination for bird-watchers. Many believe the best time to visit is within two hours of high tide, when bird activity is at its peak.

START THE HIKE

▶ **MILE 0-1.1: Twin Barns Loop Trail to Nisqually Estuary Boardwalk Trail**
To delve into nature, head to the right of the visitors center (9am-4pm Wed.-Sun.) on the **Twin Barns Loop Trail.** You'll start by walking on a boardwalk (careful—it's slippery when wet) through a riparian forest for about 0.6 mile. Along the way, interpretive signs help visitors understand the habitat they're experiencing at the mouth of the Nisqually River. The trail passes a beaver dam and under a green, leafy canopy to an overlook of the Nisqually River. From here, turn left on a wide dirt path—the **Nisqually Estuary Trail**—and walk northwest about 0.6 mile to the **Nisqually Estuary Boardwalk Trail.**

▶ **MILE 1.2-2.2: Nisqually Estuary Boardwalk Trail to Estuary Observation Areas**
Continue on the elevated boardwalk for 1 mile, observing the estuary from several observation areas. Take a seat on one of the benches and watch

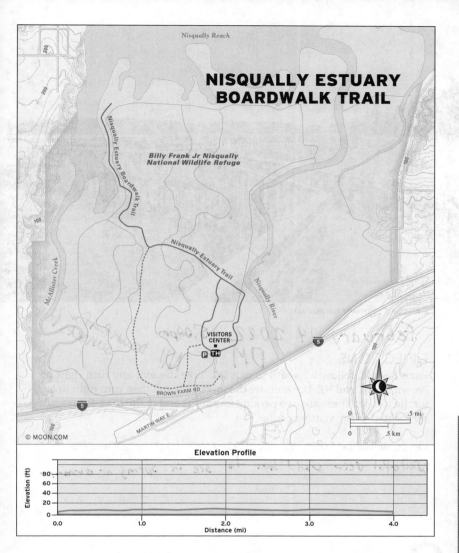

NISQUALLY ESTUARY BOARDWALK TRAIL

Nisqually Reach

Billy Frank Jr Nisqually
National Wildlife Refuge

Nisqually Estuary Boardwalk Trail

Nisqually Estuary Trail

Nisqually River

McAllister Creek

VISITORS
CENTER
P TH

BROWN FARM RD

MARTIN WAY E

© MOON.COM

0   .5 mi
0   .5 km

Elevation Profile

Elevation (ft): 80, 60, 40, 20, 0

Distance (mi): 0.0, 1.0, 2.0, 3.0, 4.0

Canada geese soar overhead while herons stalk fish. The boardwalk ends at a **covered area** with a telescope that can be used to observe wildlife or gaze up Puget Sound to Anderson and Ketron Islands, the Narrows bridges, and a sliver of Chambers Bay Golf Course. Note: The last 700 feet of the boardwalk closes October 15-January 25 for waterfowl hunting season.

▶ **MILE 2.2-4.1: Estuary Observation Area to Visitors Center**
Return the way you came. After 1.5 miles, you'll pass a gathering place with picnic tables and portable toilets in front of two large barns. Turn right off of the dirt path here, heading southeast on the **Twin Barns Loop** boardwalk to finish the hike. The final 0.4 mile of boardwalk cuts through the wetland. Listen for birds chirping in the willows as the trail returns you to the visitors center.

▲ NISQUALLY ESTUARY BOARDWALK

February 14 2022 5:00pm NY beautiful for sunsets ♡

DIRECTIONS

DM

From Seattle, follow I-5 south to exit 114. Take the exit and turn right on Brown Farm Road NE. Drive under the interstate and then turn right to enter the refuge. There are two parking lots at the end of the road. Restrooms are located at the visitors center.

GPS COORDINATES: 47.072453, –122.712959 / N47° 4.3472' W122° 42.7775'

Wonderful view would love to see in spring or summer

BEST NEARBY BREWS

In DuPont, just outside Joint Base Lewis-McChord, the **FOB Brewing Company** (2750 Williamson Pl. NW, Ste. 100, 253/507-4667, www.fob-brewingcompany.com, 3pm-11pm Tues.-Sun.) is decorated with military memorabilia and is staffed by workers in military gear. Even the beer pays tribute to the troops with names like SNAFU, 1000 Yard Stare, and Charlie Don't Surf (a reference to one of Robert Duvall's famous lines in the 1979 film *Apocalypse Now*). From the trailhead, the 7-mile drive northeast takes less than 15 minutes via I-5 and DuPont-Steilacoom Road.

Nisqually Estuary Boardwalk Trail

NEARBY CAMPGROUNDS

NAME	DESCRIPTION	FACILITIES	SEASON	FEE
Larrabee State Park	on the edge of Samish Bay beneath Chuckanut Mountain	77 RV and tent sites, restrooms	year-round	$12–50
245 Chuckanut Drive, Bellingham 888/226-7688, www.washington.goingtocamp.com				
Deception Pass State Park	three campgrounds in a popular state park	211 RV and tent sites, restrooms	year-round	$12–50
41229 State Route 20, Oak Harbor, Fidalgo and Whidbey Islands, 888/226-7688, www.washington.goingtocamp.com				
Fort Ebey State Park	the site of a World War II coastal defense fort on Whidbey Island	50 RV and tent sites, restrooms	March–October	$12–50
400 Hill Valley Drive, Coupeville, 888/226-7688, www.washington.goingtocamp.com				
Dash Point State Park	a popular destination on Puget Sound for everybody from beachcombers to skimboarders	141 RV and tent sites, restrooms	year-round	$12–50
5700 SW Dash Point Road, Federal Way, 888/226-7688, www.washington.goingtocamp.com				
Tinkham Campground	a forested campground on the South Fork Snoqualmie River	47 RV and tent sites, restrooms	early May–mid-September	$16.37–18.19
Tinkham Road, North Bend, Mount Baker-Snoqualmie National Forest, 877/444-6777, www.recreation.gov				

MOUNT RAINIER

In a land of mountains, Rainier is king. Locals refer to the stately peak simply as "the mountain." On clear days, the 14,411 feet of rock and ice rises above Puget Sound like a massive billboard beckoning people to get outside and explore. The most glaciated peak in the contiguous United States is the genesis of six major rivers and it brims with recreational opportunities. Here you can test your legs and lungs with a hike to Camp Muir (10,188 feet), stroll among the ancient trees in the Grove of the Patriarchs, wander through fields of colorful wildflowers, and visit fire lookouts. All the while admire the many faces of the famous mountain as you make your way around the park.

▲ SILVER FALLS

▲ CAMP MUIR

1 **Tolmie Peak**
DISTANCE: 6.2 miles round-trip
DURATION: 3 hours
EFFORT: Easy/moderate

2 **Spray Park**
DISTANCE: 5.8 miles round-trip
DURATION: 3.5 hours
EFFORT: Moderate

3 **Second Burroughs Loop**
DISTANCE: 6.4 miles round-trip
DURATION: 3.5 hours
EFFORT: Moderate

4 **Naches Peak Loop**
DISTANCE: 3.5 miles round-trip
DURATION: 2 hours
EFFORT: Easy/moderate

5 **Camp Muir**
DISTANCE: 8.2 miles round-trip
DURATION: 5 hours
EFFORT: Strenuous

6 **Skyline Trail Loop**
DISTANCE: 5.8 miles round-trip
DURATION: 3 hours
EFFORT: Moderate

7 **Grove of Patriarchs and Silver Falls**
DISTANCE: 2.6 miles round-trip
DURATION: 2 hours
EFFORT: Easy

8 **High Rock Lookout**
DISTANCE: 3.2 miles round-trip
DURATION: 2 hours
EFFORT: Moderate

▾ EUNICE LAKE

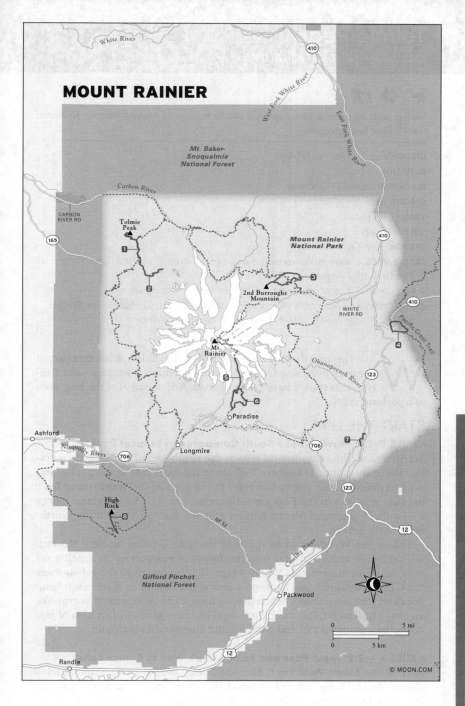

MOUNT RAINIER

White River

410

West Fork White River

East Fork White River

Mt. Baker-
Snoqualmie
National Forest

Carbon River

CARBON
RIVER RD

165

Tolmie
Peak

1

2

Mount Rainier
National Park

410

3

2nd Burroughs
Mountain

WHITE
RIVER RD

410

Pacific Crest Trail

Mt
Rainier

Ohanapecosh River

123

4

5

6

Paradise

706

7

Ashford

Nisqually River

706

Longmire

123

High
Rock

8

NF 52

12

Gifford Pinchot
National Forest

Cowlitz River

Packwood

0   5 mi
0   5 km

Randle

12

© MOON.COM

Tolmie Peak

MOUNT RAINIER NATIONAL PARK

Visit a pair of serene lakes as you climb to one of Mount Rainier National Park's four fire lookouts.

DISTANCE: 6.2 miles round-trip
DURATION: 3 hours
ELEVATION CHANGE: 1,100 feet
EFFORT: Easy/moderate
TRAIL: Dirt, rock
USERS: Hikers
SEASON: July–October
PASSES/FEES: 7-day national park pass, Mount Rainier Annual Pass, America the Beautiful Passes
MAPS: Green Trails Map 269SX for Mount Rainier-Wonderland
CONTACT: Mount Rainier National Park, 360/569-2211, Carbon River Ranger Station (May-Nov.), 360/829-9639, www.nps.gov/mora

While the long dirt road leading to Mowich Lake makes this part of the park less crowded than the tourist hubs at Paradise and Sunrise, this trail is busy on weekends. Arrive early for the best shot at a parking spot.

START THE HIKE

▶ **MILE 0-1.4: Mowich Lake South Campground to Ipsut Pass**

Starting from the campground area at the south end of Mowich Lake, follow the aptly named **Lakeshore Trail** along the west side of the park's largest and deepest lake. Signs also refer to the path as the **Wonderland Trail,** because it is part of the park's most famous trail. The Wonderland makes a 93-mile loop around Mount Rainier and is a dream trip for many Northwest backpackers.

Follow the Wonderland as it leaves the glacial basin holding Mowich after 0.7 mile and continues into the forest of evergreens. In another 0.7 mile, reach an intersection where a sign directs you left to the **Tolmie Peak Trail.** Before making this turn, go a few steps farther to stand atop **Ipsut Pass** and look across the Carbon River valley. If the Wonderland seems like an easy stroll so far, the steep drop from the pass gives you an idea of just how challenging it is to make the around-the-mountain circuit.

▶ **MILE 1.4-2.2: Ipsut Pass and Tolmie Peak Trail to Eunice Lake**

Back at the **Tolmie Peak Trail,** descend briefly before a short climb yields a nice reward. Here, 0.8 mile beyond the intersection, enjoy the view of the steep talus slopes of Tolmie Peak plunging to the azure waters of Eunice Lake. Meadows speckled with wildflowers and evergreens rim a lake that is often guarded by mosquitoes. Bears, deer, and smaller animals

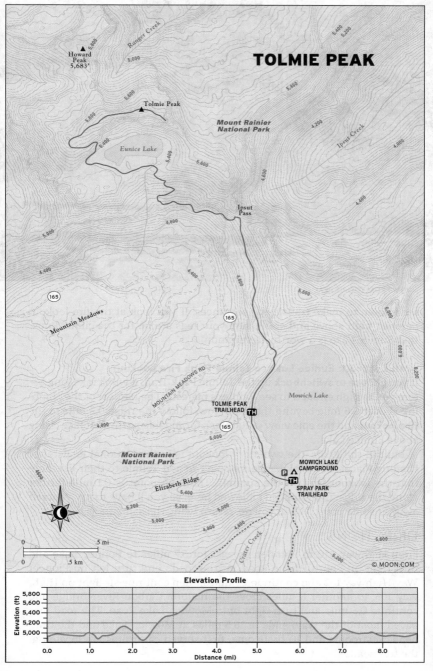

TOLMIE PEAK

Howard Peak
5,683'

Tolmie Peak

Mount Rainier
National Park

Eunice Lake

Ranger Creek

Ipsut Creek

Ipsut Pass

Mountain Meadows

165

165

MOUNTAIN MEADOWS RD

Mowich Lake

TOLMIE PEAK
TRAILHEAD **TH**

165

Mount Rainier
National Park

Elizabeth Ridge

MOWICH LAKE
CAMPGROUND

P ⛺ **TH**

SPRAY PARK
TRAILHEAD

Crater Creek

0   .5 mi
0   .5 km

© MOON.COM

Elevation Profile

Elevation (ft)		
5,800		
5,600		
5,400		
5,200		
5,000		

0.0   1.0   2.0   3.0   4.0   5.0   6.0   7.0   8.0
Distance (mi)

▲ VIEW FROM TOLMIE PEAK

are known to make trailside appearances. If you look at the fire lookout perched high above and aren't sure your legs are up for the climb, know that Eunice Lake is a worthy destination.

▶ MILE 2.2–3.1: Eunice Lake to Tolmie Peak Fire Lookout

If you choose to **switchback** up the Tolmie Peak Trail, it won't take long before you're high enough to see Rainier's majesty. The hardest of the climbing is over 0.6 mile beyond the lake. Now, follow the ridge 0.3 mile to the **fire lookout** and the epic view of Rainier's formidable northwest face rising above Eunice Lake.

Built in the 1930s, the two-story lookout is in the National Register of Historic Places. For peak baggers hoping to add Tolmie to their list, note that the lookout isn't on the summit. The high point is 0.1 mile farther along the ridge. Camping isn't allowed here, so you'll have to pry yourself away at some point. When you do, return using the same trails.

DIRECTIONS

From Highway 410 in Sumner, go east for 5.7 miles to Bonney Lake and turn right on South Prairie Road. At the road's end turn left on Pioneer Way/Highway 162 and continue 2.1 miles; then continue straight on Highway 165. In another 8 miles cross the historic Carbon River Bridge and continue 0.6 mile and turn right onto Mowich Lake Road. The road (unpaved most of the way) ends in 16.5 miles at Mowich Lake and the trailhead. Restrooms and 10 first-come, first-served campsites are located at the trailhead.

GPS COORDINATES: 46.933259, –121.864815 / N46° 55.9955′ W121° 51.8889′

Wander vast meadows of wildflowers under the icy slopes of Mount Rainier and make a quick side trip to a 300-foot waterfall.

DISTANCE: 5.8 miles round-trip

DURATION: 3.5 hours

ELEVATION CHANGE: 1,600 feet

EFFORT: Moderate

TRAIL: Dirt

USERS: Hikers

SEASON: June–October

PASSES/FEES: 7-day national park pass, Mount Rainier Annual Pass, America the Beautiful Passes

MAPS: Green Trails Map 269SX for Mount Rainier–Wonderland

CONTACT: Mount Rainier National Park, 360/569-2211, Carbon River Ranger Station (May-Nov.), 360/829-9639, www.nps.gov/mora

O ne of Washington's classic wildflower hikes, Spray Park can draw a crowd. Luckily the sprawling meadows offer plenty of places to find moments of solitude even on busy days.

START THE HIKE

▶ **MILE 0-0.25: Mowich Lake South Campground to Spray Park Trail**
Starting from the campground at the south end of Mowich Lake, follow the well-marked **Wonderland Trail** south into a forest of hemlocks. The trail makes a 93-mile loop around the mountain, but you'll spend just 0.25 mile on the century-old path. (Many Wonderland Trail backpackers use the Spray Park Trail as an alternative route because of the epic views.) At the intersection head left on the **Spray Park Trail.** Douglas firs and cedars mix with the hemlocks while huckleberries and rhododendrons line the trail.

▶ **MILE 0.25-1.9: Spray Park Trail to Spray Falls Spur Trail**
In another 1.25 miles, pass the **Eagle Cliff Viewpoint** on your right. This side trip is only a few steps and has a striking view of Rainier across the Spray Creek and Mowich River drainages. Keep an eye out for deer and listen for birds as you hike. In another 0.4 mile (after passing Eagle's Roost Camp), reach another worthy side trip: the **Spray Falls Spur,** a 0.2-mile round-trip to a 300-foot cascade.

▶ **MILE 1.9-2.9: Spray Falls Spur Trail to Spray Park**
The steepest stretch is up next. The trail **switchbacks** upward for 0.5 mile until it crosses **Grant Creek.** The next 0.5 mile ascends more gradually. You'll know you've arrived at **Spray Park** as pocket meadows awash with

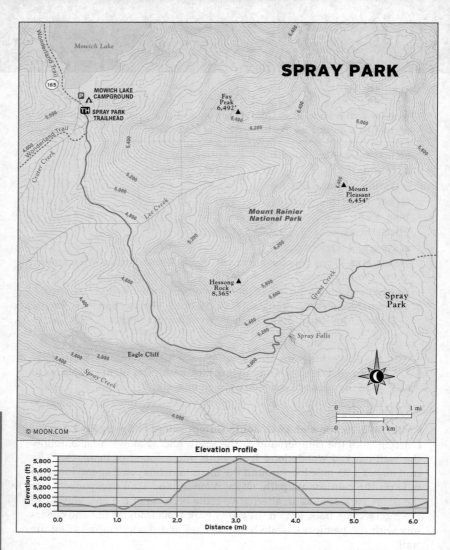

SPRAY PARK

Mowich Lake

Wonderland Trail

165

P · MOWICH LAKE CAMPGROUND

TH · SPRAY PARK TRAILHEAD

Wonderland Trail

Crater Creek

Lee Creek

Fay Peak 6,492'

Mount Rainier National Park

Mount Pleasant 6,454'

Hessong Rock 8,365'

Grant Creek

Spray Park

Spray Falls

Eagle Cliff

Spray Creek

© MOON.COM

0 ——— 1 mi

0 ——— 1 km

Elevation Profile

Elevation (ft) — Distance (mi)

summer wildflowers start allowing views of Rainier to the south and Hessong Rock and Mount Pleasant to the north. Gazing across fields of lilies, Rainier seems so close that you could casually stroll past Observation and Echo Rocks and up to the summit. Perhaps catch a glimpse of a marmot or a bear.

You can continue wandering or stay and enjoy the heavenly setting for a while. There's no landmark designating the turnaround point. That's up to you. When you're ready, return the way you came.

DIRECTIONS

From Highway 410 in Sumner, go east for 5.7 miles to Bonney Lake and turn right on South Prairie Road. At the road's end turn left on Pioneer Way/ Highway 162 and continue 2.1 miles; then continue straight on

▲ SPRAY PARK

Highway 165. In another 8 miles cross the historic Carbon River Bridge and continue 0.6 mile and turn right onto Mowich Lake Road. The road (unpaved most of the way) ends in 16.5 miles at Mowich Lake and the trailhead. Restrooms and 10 first-come, first-served campsites are located at the trailhead.

GPS COORDINATES: 46.933259, –121.864815 / N46° 55.9955′ W121° 51.8889′

BEST NEARBY BITES

Everybody enters through a door marked VIP at **Wally's White River Drive-In** (282 Route 410, Buckley, 360/829-0871, www.wallys restaurants.com, 8am-9pm Sun.-Thurs., 8am-10pm Fri.-Sat.). The most popular menu item is the Waltimate, a three-quarter-pound burger topped with grilled onions, sautéed ham, onion rings, Swiss and American cheese, lettuce, and tomato. You might need a knife and fork. From the trailhead, the 27-mile drive northwest takes 70 minutes via Mowich Road/Highway 165.

Second Burroughs Loop

MOUNT RAINIER NATIONAL PARK

Enjoy unobstructed views from tundra-topped mountains so close to Rainier you can hear the rumble of rockfall.

BEST: Summer Hikes
DISTANCE: 6.4 miles round-trip
DURATION: 3.5 hours
ELEVATION CHANGE: 1,400 feet
EFFORT: Moderate
TRAIL: Dirt, rock
USERS: Hikers
SEASON: July–mid-October
PASSES/FEES: 7-day national park pass, Mount Rainier Annual Pass, America the Beautiful Passes
MAPS: Green Trails Map 269SX for Mount Rainier–Wonderland
CONTACT: Mount Rainier National Park, 360/569-2211, www.nps.gov/mora

I f you're wondering how early you need to arrive to beat the crowds, well, it's in the name. Sunrise and Paradise (on the mountain's south side) are the national park's most popular destinations.

START THE HIKE

▶ **MILE 0–0.2: Sunrise Day Lodge Path to Ridge Trail**

At 6,400 feet, Sunrise is the highest you can drive on paved roads in Washington. Add in the up-close view of Mount Rainier, and it's understandable that you might need a minute to catch your breath before starting this hike. To make the classic hike to Second Burroughs, start on the paved path between the **Sunrise Day Lodge** and the comfort station. In 0.1 mile turn right at the **Sourdough Ridge Trailhead.** In another 0.1 head left at a **fork** and continue ascending to the ridge trail, where you'll turn left at another **intersection.** Look back down the steep meadow and watch cars hunting for parking spots.

▶ **MILE 0.2–1.5: Ridge Trail to Five-Way Intersection**

Pass the **Huckleberry Creek Trail** on the right in 0.4 mile before the trail descends slightly as you cross a **steep slope** and scree on your way toward **Frozen Lake.** In 0.6 mile, the trail switches back just below the small lake. Resist the urge to scamper up to the roped-off lake. The lake is the primary source of drinking water at Sunrise and access is prohibited. Stick to the trail and you'll get a good view soon enough. Stay right after the switchback and over the next 0.25 mile pass a **spur** to an overlook before passing Frozen Lake and arriving at a **five-way intersection.**

▲ SNOW ON MOUNT RAINIER

▶ **MILE 1.5–2.1: Five-Way Intersection to First Burroughs**

To ascend the Burroughs, take the **uphill trail** to the left. As you climb, look for bears, goats, marmots, and other animals below you. Be prepared for patches of snow in places where a fall could be treacherous. Snow can linger late into summer. It's often easily passable, but if you don't have an ice axe and traction, don't be shy about turning back if you don't feel safe. Check conditions before your hike by visiting or calling the White River Wilderness Information Center (located at the park's White River entrance, 360/569-6670).

In 0.6 mile, reach the top of **First Burroughs** where Rainier dominates the 360-degree view. Should you be tempted to do some *Sound of Music*-style hilltop twirling a la Julie Andrews, be careful to stay on the path. The tundra covering Burroughs is similar to that found in the Arctic and it's quite fragile.

▶ **MILE 2.1–2.9: First Burroughs to Second Burroughs and Peak**

Reach the **junction** with the Sunrise Rim Trail in 0.2 mile. You'll return on this trail but continue straight to visit **Second Burroughs**. In another 0.6 mile, arrive atop the **peak** where a rock bench awaits. Take a seat and enjoy the in-your-face view of Rainier as the sound of rockfall occasionally pierces the silence. Berkeley Park, Skyscraper Mountain, and Mount Fremont are visible to the north. The White River and Goat Island Mountain are to the southeast.

Second Burroughs Loop

MOUNT RAINIER

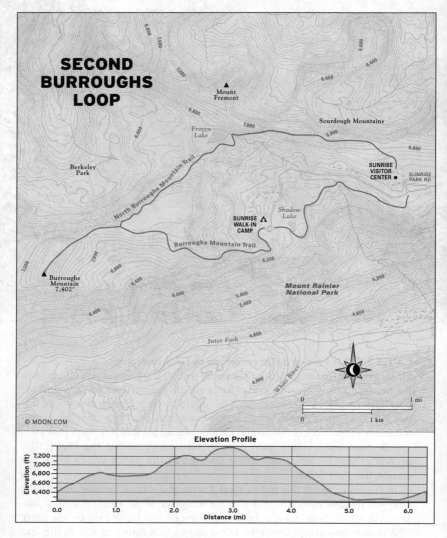

SECOND BURROUGHS LOOP

Mount Fremont

Frozen Lake

Sourdough Mountains

Berkeley Park

North Burroughs Mountain Trail

SUNRISE VISITOR CENTER

SUNRISE PARK RD

SUNRISE WALK-IN CAMP

Shadow Lake

Burroughs Mountain Trail

Burroughs Mountain 7,402'

Mount Rainier National Park

Inter Fork

White River

© MOON.COM

0   1 mi

0   1 km

Elevation Profile

Elevation (ft)

7,200
7,000
6,800
6,600
6,400

0.0   1.0   2.0   3.0   4.0   5.0   6.0

Distance (mi)

▶ **MILE 2.9-3.5: Burroughs Peak to Sunrise Rim Trail**

When ready, turn back and make a smaller loop by returning 0.6 mile to the **Sunrise Rim Trail** and turning right.

▶ **MILE 3.5-5.1: Sunrise Rim Trail to Shadow Lake**

Enjoy wildflowers and dramatic views of the White River Canyon as you descend. In 1.1 mile, pause at an **overlook** for a spectacular view of the Emmons Glacier giving life to the White River. In another 0.5 mile find a **restroom** at an intersection near Sunrise Camp and Shadow Lake. Go right here, passing short paths leading to the small lake. Summer wildflowers are especially brilliant beyond the lake.

▲ VIEW OF THE WHITE RIVER FROM BURROUGHS MOUNTAIN

▶ **MILE 5.1–6.4: Shadow Lake to Sunrise**
Over the final 1.3 miles pass the Wonderland's descent to the **White River Campground** and the scenic, kid-friendly **Silver Forest Trail** before returning to **Sunrise,** across the parking lot from where your hike began.

DIRECTIONS

From Enumclaw, follow Highway 410 east 37.2 miles to Sunrise Park Road and turn right. Four miles after the park entry station, turn right at the intersection with White River Campground Road and continue 10 miles to Sunrise. Restrooms, a cafeteria (which often serves ice cream), and a visitors center are located at the trailhead.

GPS COORDINATES: 46.914531, –121.640776 / N46° 54.8719′ W121° 38.4466′

BEST NEARBY BITES

Charlie's Café (1335 Roosevelt Ave. E., Enumclaw, 360/825-5191, 5am–2pm daily) in Enumclaw is a classic breakfast stop for those heading into the mountains and those with big appetites. In 2015, after setting the women's fastest known time by finishing the 93-mile Wonderland Trail in 22 hours, 4 minutes, and 7 seconds, Jenn Shelton of Colorado stopped at Charlie's and became the first female ever to finish the Bigfoot Challenge: an 8-ounce fried steak smothered in gravy, four eggs, hash browns, toast, and a pancake in 30 minutes or less. Feel free to order something a little lighter. From the trailhead, the 52-mile drive northwest takes 1.25 hours via Sunrise Park Road and Highway 410.

Starting from an alpine lake, enjoy sweeping views while using the Pacific Crest Trail to loop around Naches Peak.

DISTANCE: 3.5 miles round-trip
DURATION: 2 hours
ELEVATION CHANGE: 600 feet
EFFORT: Easy/moderate
TRAIL: Dirt trail
USERS: Hikers
SEASON: June–October
PASSES/FEES: 7-day national park pass, Mount Rainier Annual Pass, America the Beautiful Passes
MAPS: Green Trails Map 269SX for Mount Rainier–Wonderland
CONTACT: Mount Rainier National Park, 360/569-2211, www.nps.gov/mora

Using the Pacific Crest and Naches Peak trails, a quick loop around Naches Peak passes through colorful meadows with views of the surrounding valleys, Dewey Lake, and Rainier. Go clockwise for the most and best views of the Northwest's highest peak.

START THE HIKE

▶ **MILE 0-0.3: Parking Lot to Chinook Pass Bridge and Pacific Crest Tail**

From the parking lot, walk east toward Tipsoo Lake for about 100 yards and then turn left to follow the **Naches Loop Trail** as it climbs 0.25 mile through a stand of evergreens to the **Pacific Crest Trail.** Canada is to the left and Mexico is to the right. Turn right and reach a different kind of border in just a few steps. A **log bridge** over the highway doubles as the **Chinook Pass Entrance Arch** and sits on the boundary of Mount Rainier National Park and Wenatchee National Forest. Cross the bridge (built in 1936 and listed in the National Register of Historic Places in 1991) and follow the PCT along the north side of Naches Peak. The Rainier Fork of the American River and Highway 410 drop off to your left.

▶ **MILE 0.3-0.5: Pacific Crest Trail to William O. Douglas Wilderness**

In 0.2 mile enter the **William O. Douglas Wilderness,** named for the former U.S. Supreme Court justice who was a high school valedictorian in nearby Yakima. Scarlet paintbrush, columbine, purple aster, lupine, and other wildflowers color the slopes. An emerald pool sits trailside and snowmelt creates small seasonal cascades. Look for deer, marmots, and other creatures.

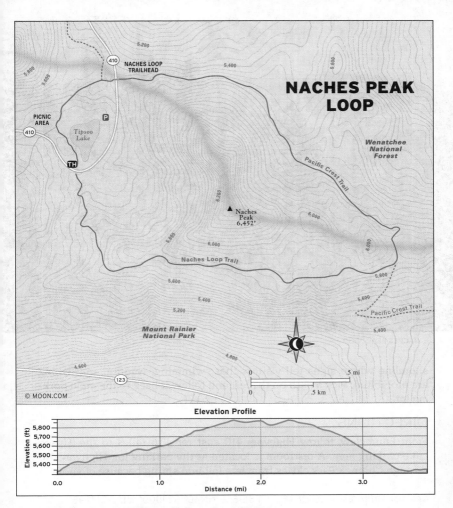

Elevation Profile

> ▶ **MILE 0.5-1.7: William O. Douglas Wilderness to Naches Peak Loop Trail**

An **overlook,** 1.2 miles after entering the wilderness area, offers views of Dewey Lake. A few steps farther, the PCT veers left and descends to the lake (a fun side trip if you have time), but go straight on the **Naches Peak Loop Trail.**

> ▶ **MILE 1.7-3.2: Naches Peak Loop Trail to Highway 410**

In 0.5 mile, find a trailside **rest spot** perfect for taking pictures of Rainier. The glaciated volcano highlights the scenery for much of the next 1 mile as you pass the Eastside Trail shortly before reaching **Highway 410.**

> ▶ **MILE 3.2-3.5: Highway 410 to Tipsoo Lake and Parking Lot**

Over the next 0.3 mile, cross the highway and pick up the trail again at the northwest end of a small **parking lot.** Descend to **Tipsoo Lake's** grassy

▲ NACHES PEAK LOOP

shoreline where signs tell visitors that swimming, wading, and fishing are prohibited. Pick a path on the left and follow it back to the **main parking lot.**

DIRECTIONS

From Enumclaw, follow Highway 410 east for 43.6 miles to the Tipsoo Lake parking area. A restroom is located at the parking lot. Highway 410 through Chinook Pass closes from late fall into spring because of snow.

GPS COORDINATES: 46.869848, –121.519659 / N46° 52.1909' W121° 31.1795'

BEST NEARBY BITE

About 26 miles (35 minutes) north of Chinook Pass via Highway 410, **Wapiti Woolies** (58414 Rte. 410 East, Greenwater, 360/663-2268, www.wapitiwoolies.com) is a popular stop for travelers craving ice cream. The huckleberry ice cream is popular, but Wapiti Woolies is best known for its creative winter caps.

Camp Muir

MOUNT RAINIER NATIONAL PARK

🦌 ❀ ♨

Trek above 10,000 feet to the most popular climber's high camp on Mount Rainier and take in the majestic, surreal views.

DISTANCE: 8.2 miles round-trip
DURATION: 5 hours
ELEVATION CHANGE: 4,700 feet
EFFORT: Strenuous
TRAIL: Pavement, dirt, rocks, steep snowfield
USERS: Hikers, mountaineers
SEASON: July–September
PASSES/FEES: 7-day national park pass, Mount Rainier Annual Pass, America the Beautiful Passes
MAPS: Green Trails Map 269SX for Mount Rainier–Wonderland
CONTACT: Mount Rainier National Park, 360/569-2211, www.nps.gov/mora, www.mountrainierclimbing.blogspot.com

There's a fine line between beauty and danger, and you're more likely to find that line when you're on the icy slopes of a volcano. This is a must-tick box on most Northwest hikers' bucket lists, but calling this trip a hike requires expanding your definition of the activity.

START THE HIKE

▶ **MILE 0-1.6: Jackson Visitor Center Steps to Skyline Trail**
Starting on the steps next to the **Jackson Visitor Center,** follow the paved **Skyline Trail** as you ascend through Paradise's colorful wildflower meadows. Skirt the west side of **Alta Vista,** a small hill that temporarily blocks your view of Rainier, and in 0.7 mile reach a wide paved area on the north side of the hill. Here, the pavement gives way to dirt trail as you continue walking toward Rainier. Over the next 0.9 mile, enjoy views of surrounding peaks, distant waterfalls, and the Nisqually Glacier. Keep your distance from wildlife such as bears, mountain goats, and marmots, which often make appearances around Paradise.

▶ **MILE 1.6-2.2: Skyline Trail to Muir Snowfield**
Turn left on the **Pebble Creek Trail** and, after another 0.3 mile, pass a trail leading right to the High Skyline Trail. Go straight for 0.3 mile, hop **Pebble Creek,** and prepare for the push up the **Muir Snowfield.**

▶ **MILE 2.2-4.1: Muir Snowfield to Camp Muir**
Over the next 1.9 miles from the creek to Camp Muir, you'll climb about 3,000 feet. Take a cue from the lines of climbers following their guides: They purposely travel slow and take breaks every hour as they acclimate to the thin air and conserve energy for their summit attempts.

There is no trail on the steep snowfield flanked by glaciers. On blue-sky days, the way is obvious, and you'll share the hill with hundreds of hikers. But the weather can change without warning. It is vital to check gear, weather forecasts, and the mirror before hiking to Camp Muir. You should be fit and skilled in route finding and snow travel to make this trip.

Above a rock outcrop known as **Moon Rocks** (9,200 feet), it's worth angling right toward **Anvil Rock** (9,584 feet) for a view across the gaping crevasses of the Cowlitz and Paradise Glaciers. Then angle upward back across the snowfield to Muir.

▶ MILE 4.1–8.2: Camp Muir to Jackson Visitor Center

Pat yourself on the back as you arrive at the **high camp** (10,188 feet) and plop down on a rock for a snack and a 100-mile view. Some days, you look out over cloud tops and it seems as if you could walk across a carpet of white fluff all the way to the upper slopes of Mounts Adams and Hood. It's no wonder this place was called Cloud Camp before it was renamed for naturalist John Muir, who climbed the 14,411-foot peak in 1888.

The ugly, battered **black box** is a shelter for climbers staying overnight with guide services. Meanwhile, rock shelters harmoniously blending into the landscape are more classic reasons Camp Muir is listed in the National Register of Historic Places.

Enjoy your time above the clouds but give yourself plenty of time for the return trip. The descent is usually riskier than the climb.

DIRECTIONS

From Highway 7 in Elbe, continue straight on Highway 706 for 13.6 miles to Mount Rainier National Park's Nisqually Entrance. Continue 17.5 miles inside the park to the large Paradise parking lot. Restroom facilities are located at the trailhead. The Jackson Visitor Center is open daily in summer and weekends and holidays in the winter. The Paradise Inn is typically open from May to mid-October.

GPS COORDINATES: 46.786070, –121.735881 / N46° 47.1642′ W121° 44.1529′

BEST NEARBY BITES

Lhakpa Gelu Sherpa, a 15-time Mount Everest summiteer, has helped many people climb the world's highest peak. As the owner of **The Wildberry Restaurant** (37718 Rte. 706 E, Ashford, 360/569-2277, www. rainierwildberry.com, hours vary) he brings a taste of Nepal to Rainier. In addition to burgers and traditional American fare, the Himalayan Special menu includes momo (steamed dumplings) and Sherpa stew. From the trailhead, the 19-mile drive southwest takes about 35 minutes via Paradise Road and Highway 706.

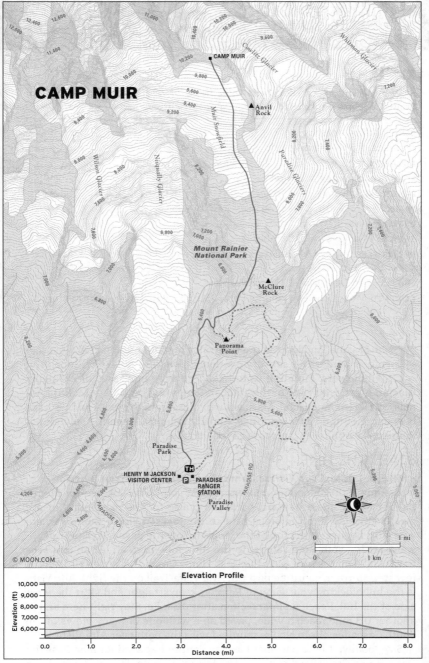

CAMP MUIR

12,400 12,600
12,000
11,400
11,000
10,200
10,400
10,300
10,000
9,600
Whitman Glacier
7,200
CAMP MUIR
Cowlitz Glacier
10,200
9,800
9,600
9,400
9,200
▲ Anvil Rock
8,200
7,400
9,400
8,600
Wilson Glacier
8,200
8,800
Nisqually Glacier
8,200
7,800
Paradise Glaciers
7,600
8,000
7,600
7,200
7,000
6,800
7,200
7,000
Mount Rainier National Park
6,600
▲ McClure Rock
6,000
6,600
7,000
6,800
Panorama Point
6,200
5,600
5,800
5,600
6,200
6,600
5,000
5,600
Paradise Park
4,400 4,600
4,000
HENRY M JACKSON VISITOR CENTER
TH
P
PARADISE RANGER STATION
PARADISE RD
5,200
5,800
4,200
Paradise Valley
4,600
4,800
5,000
PARADISE RD

© MOON.COM

0   1 mi
0   1 km

Elevation Profile

Elevation (ft): 10,000 / 9,000 / 8,000 / 7,000 / 6,000

Distance (mi): 0.0 1.0 2.0 3.0 4.0 5.0 6.0 7.0 8.0

View the Nisqually Glacier, waterfalls, fields of wildflowers, and a bevy of South Cascade peaks as Rainier towers overhead.

BEST: Wildflower Hikes

DISTANCE: 5.8 miles round-trip

DURATION: 3 hours

ELEVATION CHANGE: 1,400 feet

EFFORT: Moderate

TRAIL: Dirt, rock, pavement; be prepared for snow

USERS: Hikers

SEASON: Mid-June–mid-October

PASSES/FEES: 7-day national park pass, Mount Rainier Annual Pass, America the Beautiful Passes

MAPS: Green Trails Map 270S for Paradise

CONTACT: Mount Rainier National Park, 360/569-2211, www.nps.gov/mora

The Skyline Trail loop on the south side of Mount Rainier isn't just scenic, it borders on sensory overload. Meadows ablaze with colorful wildflowers. Plunging waterfalls. The deep crevasses of Nisqually Glacier. A majestic view of the Tatoosh Range and beyond to Mounts Adams, St. Helens, and Hood. Marmots whistling from the rocks and perhaps bear and mountain goat sightings. And all under the towering splendor of Rainier. No wonder this place is called Paradise.

START THE HIKE

▶ **MILE 0-1.0: Jackson Visitor Center to Glacier Vista Trail Junction**
In the late 1800s, eloquent conservationist John Muir lobbied for Mount Rainier to become a national park. His praise for the mountain's meadows is chiseled into the steps next to the **Jackson Visitor Center,** where your hike begins. At the top of the steps, follow the paved **Skyline Trail** upward, letting your lungs adjust to the thin, mile-high air. At an **intersection** 0.1 mile up the trail, pass the Dead Horse Creek and Waterfall Trails. A few steps farther, continue past the Alta Vista Trail on the right. **Alta Vista** is the hill blocking your view of Rainier; keep straight and skirt the west side of the hill. Reach an **intersection** after 0.3 mile. Stay right here and in another 0.3 mile reach a wide, paved area with one of many views of the South Cascades. (Here, you're reunited with the path over Alta Vista.)

Say goodbye to the pavement as you continue toward Rainier. Pass the Dead Horse Creek Trail again on the left in 0.3 mile, followed shortly by the **Glacier Vista Trail junction,** also on the left. The views of the Nisqually Glacier are spectacular from this side trail, but Skyline has glacier views, too, a little farther ahead.

▲ SKYLINE TRAIL LOOP

▶ **MILE 1.0-1.8: Glacier Vista Trail Junction to Panorama Point**
In 0.6 mile, pass the **Pebble Creek Trail** (the jumping-off point for Camp Muir) and then ascend along a steep, rocky slope for 0.2 mile to **Panorama Point.** Take some time here to look across Paradise to the Tatoosh Range, the Goat Rocks, and Mounts St. Helens, Adams, and Hood.

▶ **MILE 1.8-3.2: Panorama Point to Golden Gate Trail Junction**
Continue by following the **High Skyline Trail** to the left. In 0.4 mile pass another chance to join the Pebble Creek Trail shortly before the loop reaches its highest point (7,100 feet).

Rejoin the main **Skyline Loop** in 0.4 mile beyond the Pebble Creek intersection, then continue downward another 0.6 mile to the **intersection** with the Golden Gate Trail on the right. Golden Gate offers a shortcut back to the parking lot that shaves about a mile off your trip, but continue straight to see what else Skyline has in store.

▶ **MILE 3.2-3.9: Golden Gate Trail Junction to**
 Stevens-Van Trump Historical Monument
In 0.7 mile, shortly after stepping over the **Paradise River** and passing the Paradise Glacier Trail on the left, arrive at the **Stevens-Van Trump Historical Monument**. Erected in 1921, the monument is on the site where Hazard Stevens and P. B. Van Trump made camp before making the first documented summit of Rainier on August 17, 1870. Sluiskin, their Native American guide, reportedly waited here certain the men would perish.

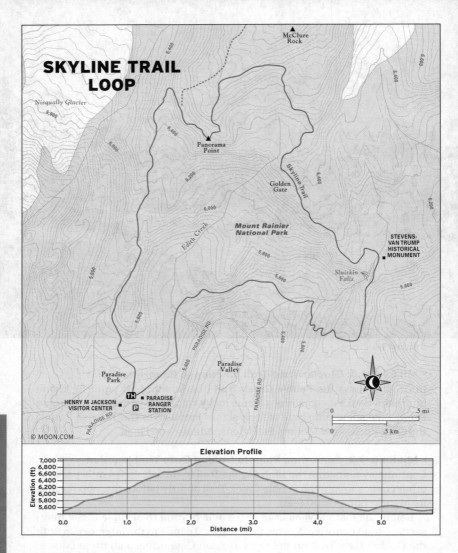

SKYLINE TRAIL LOOP

Elevation Profile

▶ MILE 3.9-5.3: Stevens-Van Trump Historical Monument to Myrtle Falls

Pass the Lakes Trail in 0.4 mile and then descend into the **Paradise Valley.** Spend the next 1 mile passing more side trails and wildflowers before crossing a bridge over **Myrtle Falls.** The falls viewpoint is just a few steps off the path on the left if you need one last postcard-worthy photo.

▶ MILE 5.3-5.8: Myrtle Falls to Parking Lot

Return to paved trail just beyond the **bridge** for the final 0.5 mile to the parking lot.

▲ SUNSET ON THE SKYLINE TRAIL LOOP

DIRECTIONS

From Highway 7 in Elbe, continue straight on Highway 706 for 13.6 miles to Mount Rainier National Park's Nisqually Entrance. Continue 17.5 miles inside the park to the large Paradise parking lot. Restroom facilities are located at the trailhead. The Jackson Visitor Center is open daily in summer and weekends and holidays in the winter. The Paradise Inn is typically open from May to mid-October.

GPS COORDINATES: 46.786070, –121.735881 / N46° 47.1642' W121° 44.1529'

BEST NEARBY BITES

Built as a service station in 1925, the **Copper Creek Inn** (35707 Rte. 706 E, Ashford, 360/569-2326, www.coppercreekinn.com, hours vary) restaurant opened in 1946 and has been a popular stop for Rainier visitors ever since. Skip to the dessert menu to find the most popular order: blackberry pie à la mode. From the trailhead, the 20-mile drive southwest takes less than 40 minutes via Paradise Road and Highway 706.

Skyline Trail Loop

MOUNT RAINIER

Grove of the Patriarchs and Silver Falls

MOUNT RAINIER NATIONAL PARK

Wander an easy forest path along the Ohanapecosh River to an island of giant trees and a four-story waterfall.

DISTANCE: 2.6 miles round-trip

DURATION: 2 hours

ELEVATION CHANGE: 400 feet

EFFORT: Easy

TRAIL: Dirt, bridges (one suspension bridge), boardwalk

USERS: Hikers

SEASON: May–October

PASSES/FEES: 7-day national park pass, Mount Rainier Annual Pass, America the Beautiful Passes

MAPS: Green Trails Map 269SX for Mount Rainier–Wonderland

CONTACT: Mount Rainier National Park, 360/569-2211, www.nps.gov/mora

Combine two short and easy hikes along different parts of the Eastside Trail to a pair of awe-inspiring destinations: an island of 1,000-year-old trees and a 40-foot waterfall.

START THE HIKE

▶ **MILE 0-1.2: Eastside Trail Loop**

Find the well-marked dirt path next to the parking lot restroom and follow the wide, gently descending **Eastside Trail** under a canopy of western red cedar, western hemlock, and Douglas fir. Walking along the **river,** you can see why it received its name: Ohanapecosh is believed to be a Taidnapam Indian word meaning "standing at the edge." As in, each summer Mount Rainier visitors flock to the Ohanapecosh River to stand at the edge of something beautiful. After 0.3 mile, reach an **intersection** and then descend to the right toward a narrow **suspension bridge.** Only one person should cross at a time so the span's undulations don't knock others off-balance.

On the other side of the bridge is an **island** surrounded by channels of the Ohanapecosh and packed with old-growth timber. Pass massive root wads from trees felled by the wind and nurse logs raising the next generation of evergreens on your way to a boardwalk loop visiting the island's giants. Twin century-old Douglas firs stand proud despite rotten cores. Some trees reach 200 feet into the sky and some have a circumference of more than 40 feet. The boardwalk loops around a colossal cedar that might be the park's most photographed tree.

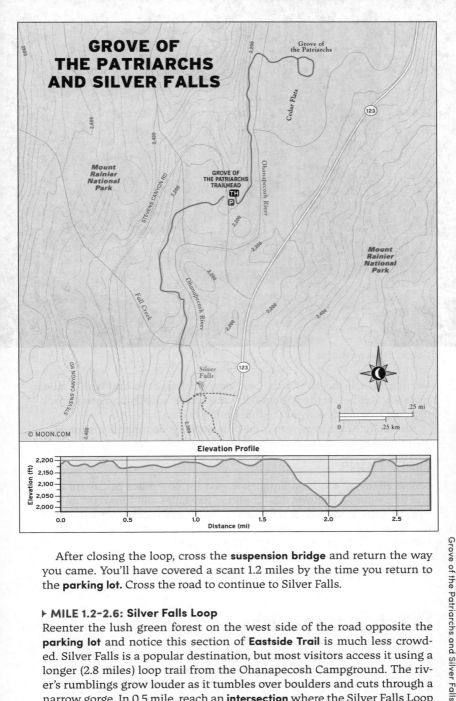

GROVE OF THE PATRIARCHS AND SILVER FALLS

Grove of the Patriarchs

Cedar Flats

123

Mount Rainier National Park

GROVE OF THE PATRIARCHS TRAILHEAD

Ohanapecosh River

Stevens Canyon Rd

Mount Rainier National Park

Fall Creek

Ohanapecosh River

Silver Falls

123

Stevens Canyon Rd

© MOON.COM

0   .25 mi
0   .25 km

Elevation Profile

After closing the loop, cross the **suspension bridge** and return the way you came. You'll have covered a scant 1.2 miles by the time you return to the **parking lot.** Cross the road to continue to Silver Falls.

▶ **MILE 1.2-2.6: Silver Falls Loop**

Reenter the lush green forest on the west side of the road opposite the **parking lot** and notice this section of **Eastside Trail** is much less crowded. Silver Falls is a popular destination, but most visitors access it using a longer (2.8 miles) loop trail from the Ohanapecosh Campground. The river's rumblings grow louder as it tumbles over boulders and cuts through a narrow gorge. In 0.5 mile, reach an **intersection** where the Silver Falls Loop bends back toward the campground. Go left on the **loop trail** and in another 0.1 mile pass a sign directing you to the **Silver Falls Overlook.** This is

▲ GROVE OF THE PATRIARCHS

worth a quick aside, but for the best view go straight. In another 0.1 mile, cross a bridge below the 40-foot falls and climb gradually up a switchback to a spot looking directly at the thundering cascade.

You can return the way you came or make the loop through the forest to visit the campground and the Ohanapecosh Hot Springs.

DIRECTIONS

Follow Highway 410 from Enumclaw east for 40.7 miles to Cayuse Pass and turn right on Highway 123. Continue 10.9 miles and turn right on Stevens Canyon Road. Park in the small lot just past the entry station. When the lot is full, cars park beyond the lot along Stevens Canyon Road. A restroom and water are available at the trailhead.

GPS COORDINATES: 46.758121, –121.557487 / N46° 45.4873' W121° 33.4492'

BEST NEARBY BITES

With a fence made of skis and old ski posters hanging on the walls, Packwood's **Cliff Droppers** (12968 U.S. Hwy. 12, Packwood, 360/494-2055, 11am-7pm daily) pays tribute to the nearby White Pass Ski Area while serving big burgers. Favorites include the one-third-pound bacon bleu cheese burger and the Canadian bacon-topped, two-third-pound Sasquatch burger. From the trailhead, the 13.5-mile drive southwest takes less than 25 minutes via Highway 123 and U.S. 12.

Hike up a forested ridge to a cliffside fire lookout with views of four iconic Cascade volcanoes: Rainier, Adams, St. Helens, and Hood.

BEST: Dog-Friendly Hikes
DISTANCE: 3.2 miles round-trip
DURATION: 2 hours
ELEVATION CHANGE: 1,400 feet
EFFORT: Moderate
TRAIL: Single track; short, steep rock slope at the top
USERS: Hikers, leashed dogs
SEASON: Mid-June–October
PASSES/FEES: None
MAPS: Green Trails Map 301 for Randle, USGS topographic map for Sawtooth Ridge
CONTACT: Gifford Pinchot National Forest, Cowlitz Ranger District, www.fs.usda.gov

START THE HIKE

▶ **MILE 0-0.7: Towhead Gap Trailhead to Mount Rainier Viewpoint**
The **Towhead Gap Trail** starts from the edge of Forest Road 8440 near a sign that reads "High Rock Trail 266." The task might seem daunting as you stand at the trailhead and look north to see High Rock Lookout perched precariously atop a cliff, but try to keep in mind that you'll be rewarded mightily for your work. The skinny dirt path starts with two quick **switchbacks** in the first 0.2 mile and then straightens out to continue the ascent along the tree-covered ridge. It doesn't take long before glimpses through the cedars and Douglas firs show the tops of green foothills, hints of the dramatic views to come. Keep a look out for deer and listen for chirping birds. Bears are sometimes spotted in this area.

After 0.4 mile, the trail steepens. You'll reach the top of the first pitch in another 0.1 mile, where a strategically placed **bench** awaits. The climbing only continues from here, but your eyes will inspire your thighs as you get your first peek of Mount Rainier about a hundred yards past the bench. Not much farther, Mount Adams and Mount St. Helens make their first appearances.

▶ **MILE 0.7-1.4: Mount Rainier Viewpoint to Johnnie T. Peters Memorial**
In 0.7 mile, the lookout can be seen through a wide opening in the trees. As you continue your ascent, you'll notice a **plaque** affixed to a rocky **overlook**. The plaque pays tribute to Johnnie T. Peters, who brought materials

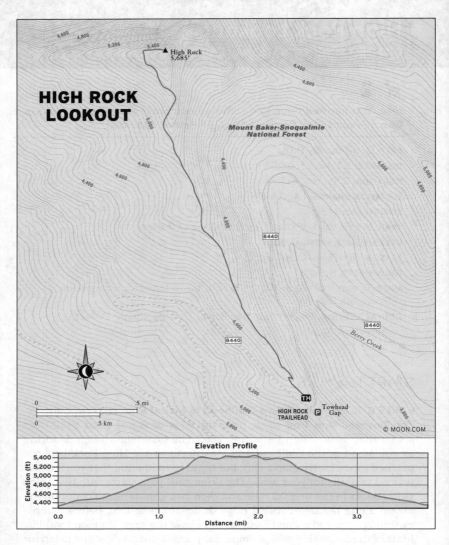

Elevation Profile

by mule from the town of Mineral to build this lookout and 10 others in 1930.

▶ **MILE 1.4–1.6: Johnnie T. Peters Memorial to High Rock Lookout**
From the **plaque,** it's less than 0.1 mile to the steep, exposed rocky **slope** that ascends to the lookout. You only need to climb about halfway up the slope for a 360-degree panorama view. Mount Rainier dominates to the north, while Adams, St. Helens, Hood, and the Goat Rocks fill out the view to the south. Far below, Cora Lake reflects the sunlight while the Nisqually River makes its way from Rainier to Puget Sound. You'll be hard-pressed to find a better view of Rainier outside of the national park.

Continue 0.1 mile to the top to see the 90-year-old **fire lookout,** though it's boarded up and no longer staffed. Watch your pets, kids, and step here.

▲ HIGH ROCK LOOKOUT

In addition to a 500-foot drop that makes many a little weak in the knees, vandalism and litter mean the threat of glass and other sharp objects hiding in the rocks.

Retrace your steps when you're ready to return to the trailhead.

DIRECTIONS

From Highway 7 in Elbe, continue east on Highway 706 for 10.1 miles through Ashford to Kernahan Road. Turn right on Kernahan Road and drive south 1.4 miles where the road turns left and becomes Skate Creek Road. Continue another 3.3 miles and turn right on Forest Road 84. There is no sign for the road approaching from this direction. Follow Forest Road 84 for 6.8 miles (staying left at the fork with Forest Road 8420) and then go right on Forest Road 8440. Continue another 2.6 miles to Towhead Gap, a level spot in the road with enough parking for a handful of vehicles. There are no toilets at the trailhead.

GPS COORDINATES: 46.666642, –121.891227 / N46° 39.9985′ W121° 53.4736′

BEST NEARBY BITES

In 1969, a logging truck weigh station was moved to Elbe from neighboring Ashford. In 1985, it was converted into **Scaleburgers** (54109 Mountain Hwy. E, Elbe, 360/569-2247, 11am-7pm daily), a burger stand that quickly became a favorite of hungry hikers. Try the especially popular Overload Burger. All seating is at outdoor picnic tables, but dogs are not permitted in the dining area. From the trailhead, the 24.5-mile drive northwest takes about 45 minutes via Skate Creek Road and Highway 706.

NEARBY CAMPGROUNDS

NAME	DESCRIPTION	FACILITIES	SEASON	FEE
Ohanapecosh Campground	on the Ohanapecosh River in the southeast corner of the park	188 RV and tent sites, restrooms	late May-late September	$20

Ohanapecosh Road, Packwood, Mount Rainier National Park, 877/444-6777, www.recreation.gov

NAME	DESCRIPTION	FACILITIES	SEASON	FEE
Cougar Rock Campground	situated near the confluence of the Paradise and Nisqually Rivers	173 RV and tent sites, restrooms	late May-late September	$20

Paradise Road, Longmire, Mount Rainier National Park, 877/444-6777, www.recreation.gov

NAME	DESCRIPTION	FACILITIES	SEASON	FEE
Mowich Lake	a ring of campsites near the park's biggest lake (Mowich) and longest trail (Wonderland)	10 walk-in tent sites, restrooms	early July-early October	none

Mowich Lake Road/Highway 165, Carbonado, Mount Rainier National Park, 360/569-2211, www.nps.gov/mora

NAME	DESCRIPTION	FACILITIES	SEASON	FEE
White River Campground	near the headwaters of the White River and a short drive (or a 3.3-mile uphill hike) from Sunrise	112 RV and tent sites, restrooms	late June-late September	$20

White River Road, Mount Rainier National Park, 360/569-2211, www.nps.gov/mora

NAME	DESCRIPTION	FACILITIES	SEASON	FEE
La Wis Wis Campground	in old-growth forest and with quick access to Mount Rainier National Park and the South Cascades	100 RV and tent sites, restrooms	late May-early September	$20

Forest Road 1272, Packwood, 877/444-6777, www.recreation.gov

NORTH CASCADES

Blanketed by evergreens, glaciers, and craggy peaks, the North Cascades is home to some of the nation's most breathtaking wilderness. A set of volcanoes—Mount Baker and Glacier Peak—and deep valleys stoke a spirit of adventure. Find ice caves, waterfalls, historic fire lookouts, and sweeping panoramas that include Puget Sound, the Olympics, and Canada. Marvel at beauty both natural and man-made (like the reservoirs created by massive dams on the Skagit River). Enjoy one of the few national parks that doesn't charge an entrance fee. Cross paths with mule deer, whistling marmots, and other creatures as you explore some of the Northwest's most stunning alpine terrain.

▲ ICE CAVE AT THE BASE OF BIG FOUR MOUNTAIN ▲ CEDAR BERRIES

1 Winchester Mountain
DISTANCE: 3.6 miles round-trip
DURATION: 2 hours
EFFORT: Moderate

2 Skyline Divide
DISTANCE: 6.8 miles round-trip
DURATION: 3.5 hours
EFFORT: Moderate

3 Table Mountain
DISTANCE: 3 miles round-trip
DURATION: 1.5 hours
EFFORT: Easy/moderate

4 Chain Lakes Loop
DISTANCE: 7.5 miles round-trip
DURATION: 4 hours
EFFORT: Moderate

5 Thunder Knob
DISTANCE: 3.6 miles round-trip
DURATION: 2 hours
EFFORT: Easy/moderate

6 Cascade Pass
DISTANCE: 7.4 miles round-trip
DURATION: 4 hours
EFFORT: Moderate

7 Maple Pass Loop
DISTANCE: 6.8 miles round-trip
DURATION: 4 hours
EFFORT: Moderate

8 Cedar Falls
DISTANCE: 3.5 miles round-trip
DURATION: 1.5 hours
EFFORT: Easy

9 Green Mountain
DISTANCE: 8.4 miles round-trip
DURATION: 5 hours
EFFORT: Moderate/strenuous

10 Mount Pilchuck
DISTANCE: 5.4 miles round-trip
DURATION: 3 hours
EFFORT: Moderate

11 Lake Twenty-Two
DISTANCE: 6.2 miles round-trip
DURATION: 3.5 hours
EFFORT: Moderate

12 Big Four Ice Caves
DISTANCE: 2.4 miles round-trip
DURATION: 1.5 hours
EFFORT: Easy

▾ STONE ARCH ON CHAIN LAKES LOOP TRAIL

NORTH CASCADES

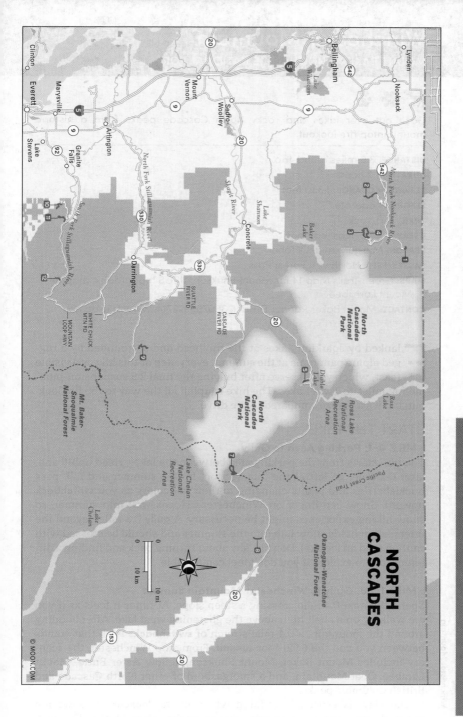

NORTH
CASCADES

© MOON.COM

1

Winchester Mountain
MOUNT BAKER–SNOQUALMIE NATIONAL FOREST

Gaze out over lakes and rocky North Cascade peaks from a historic mountaintop fire lookout.

DISTANCE: 3.6 miles round-trip
DURATION: 2 hours
ELEVATION CHANGE: 1,350 feet
EFFORT: Moderate
TRAIL: Dirt, rock
USERS: Hikers, leashed dogs
SEASON: Mid-July–mid-October
PASSES/FEES: Northwest Forest Pass
MAPS: Green Trails Map 14 for Mount Shuksan; USGS topographic map for Mount Larrabee
CONTACT: Mount Baker Ranger District, 360/599-2714, www.fs.usda.gov

F lanked by sparkling lakes at the trailhead and surrounded by a rugged alpine panorama at the summit, every step of this hike is a visible feast, which you deserve after braving the final 2.5 suspension-pummeling miles to Twin Lakes. The hike is uphill all the way to the fire lookout, but it's a breeze compared to the drive.

START THE HIKE

▶ MILE 0-1: Parking Area to Gully
The trail starts from the parking area between the lakes. Head uphill and, after 0.2 mile, go left at the intersection. In late summer and fall, pass huckleberries and plants changing to their fall colors as you **switchback** upward. Snow can linger on Winchester's slopes well into summer, so snow hiking experience might be necessary. A **gully** 0.8 mile beyond the intersection holds snow late into the summer and should be crossed with caution (and an ice axe). Don't be shy about turning back and finding a different trail to explore if you don't feel comfortable.

▶ MILE 1-1.8: Gully to Winchester Mountain Summit
Spend the next 0.4 mile crossing a steep slope. At times it feels as if you are walking on a shelf high above the glistening west lake. After bending around the mountain, a 0.4-mile stretch of **switchbacks** is all that stands between you and the 6,521-foot **summit.** From atop Winchester, the scenery includes Mount Baker, Mount Shuksan, Yellow Aster Butte, Mount Larabee, Goat Mountain, and a smorgasbord of other North Cascade and British Columbia peaks.

The view is especially striking when all the **lookout** windows are propped open and the structure accents rather than blocks the vista. Built in 1935, the Forest Service long ago stopped using the building and

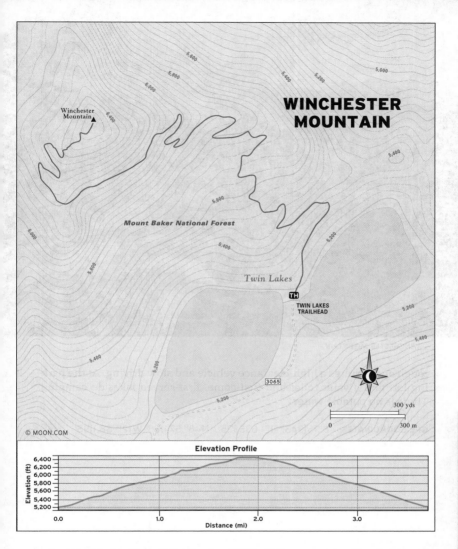

WINCHESTER MOUNTAIN

Winchester Mountain▲

Mount Baker National Forest

Twin Lakes

🚻 TWIN LAKES TRAILHEAD

3065

© MOON.COM

0 ——— 300 yds
0 ——— 300 m

Elevation Profile

scheduled it for demolition in the 1980s. Volunteers saved and restored the lookout. They continue to maintain the structure, which is available for camping on a first-come, first-served basis. Bears frequent the area, so make sure to secure all food and scented items. Even if you can't stay overnight, you'll want to spend some time on Winchester absorbing the tranquility and the endless view.

When you're ready to go, use the same trail to return to Twin Lakes.

DIRECTIONS

From I-5 in Bellingham, take exit 255 and head east on Highway 542 for 46 miles to Forest Road 3065/Twin Lakes Road, on the east side of a state Department of Transportation facility. Turn left and drive 7 miles to Twin Lakes. The 2.5 miles beyond the Yellow Aster Butte trailhead is especially

▲ WINCHESTER MOUNTAIN

rough and requires a high-clearance vehicle and slow driving. At the parking lot, find a vault toilet and first-come, first-served lakeside camping. There is no potable water.

GPS COORDINATES: 48.951943, –121.635325 / N48° 57.1166' W121° 38.1195'

BEST NEARBY BITES

La Fiamma Wood Fire Pizza (200 E. Chestnut St., Bellingham, 360/647-0060, www.lafiamma.com, hours vary) has been messing with perfection for two decades, and the result is one of the Northwest's most intriguing pizza menus. In addition to traditional offerings, try the eggs Benedict pizza or pizza topped with mashed potatoes (the Spuddy), shrimp (Finn) or mango chutney (Major Grigio). A walk-up window called the Pye Hole sells pizza by the slice. From the trailhead, the 56-mile drive west takes 1 hour, 45 minutes via Highway 542.

2

Skyline Divide

MOUNT BAKER-SNOQUALMIE NATIONAL FOREST

🦌 ❀ 🐾

Walk among wildflowers on a ridge that brings you face-to-face with Mount Baker while delivering views stretching from Puget Sound to Canada.

BEST: Wildflower Hikes
DISTANCE: 6.8 miles round-trip
DURATION: 3.5 hours
ELEVATION CHANGE: 2,500 feet
EFFORT: Moderate
TRAIL: Dirt, rock
USERS: Hikers, leashed dogs, pack llamas
SEASON: July–October
PASSES/FEES: Northwest Forest Pass
MAPS: Green Trails Map 13 for Mount Baker, USGS topographic map for Mount Baker, USGS topographic map for Bearpaw Mountain
CONTACT: Mount Baker Ranger District, 360/599-2714, www.fs.usda.gov

The ability to adjust the dial on the difficulty is just one of the things that makes this hike special. And popular. In fact, even hiking as little as 3.8 miles round-trip is far enough for the North Cascades' rugged beauty to knock your merino socks off.

START THE HIKE

▶ **MILE 0-1.9: Skyline Divide Trailhead to Ridge**
Starting from the busy trailhead, walk a few steps up the road and turn left into the forest. Climb among the firs on well-trodden trail. After 1.9 miles, enter the **Mount Baker Wilderness,** emerge from the evergreens, and try to keep your eyes from popping out of your head like a smitten cartoon character. Colorful fields of lupine, heather, daisies, asters, and other wildflowers carpet the ridge running above deep valleys. Mount Shuksan rises to the east and the glaciated slopes of Mount Baker dominate the view to the south. You don't have to go any farther to feel as if this was worth the trip. But the trail along the ridge urges you to continue with promises of more soul-stirring views.

▶ **MILE 1.9-2.5: Ridge to Second Knoll Fork**
Turning left takes you on a 0.25-mile side trip to the top of a knoll, but turning right allows you to wander the rolling ridge toward Mount Baker and Hadley Glacier. Turn right and in 0.4 mile reach a **fork** beneath the second knoll. Go right to skirt the knoll or left to crest it using a rougher trail. The paths reconnect on the other side. Cross the west slope of another knoll 0.2 mile farther.

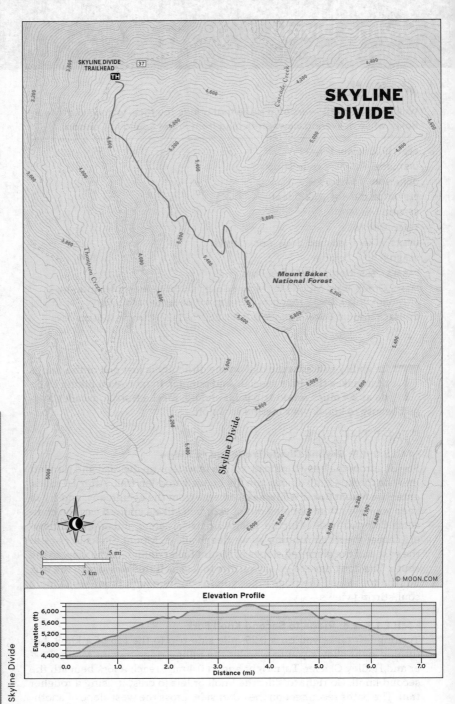

▲ SKYLINE DIVIDE TRAIL

▶ **MILE 2.5–3.4: Second Knoll Fork to Skyline Divide Ridge**
Go 0.5 mile more to a **fork** where the path on the left descends to Dead-horse Camp. Stay right to continue your walk across the sky. Climb 0.4 mile to a **broad spot** on the ridge (6,300 feet)—a perfect place to snap selfies, enjoy a picnic lunch, and let your gaze wander from Puget Sound to British Columbia while identifying peaks like Table, Winchester, and Yellow Aster Butte.

Be on the lookout for mountain goats, bears, and other wildlife in the area. Looking to the north, the trail you followed to get here traces the ridgetop. You'll return on this path back to your car.

DIRECTIONS

From I-5 in Bellingham, take exit 255 and head east on Highway 542 for 34.3 miles to Forest Road 39/Glacier Creek Road in Glacier. Turn right and then take an immediate left onto Forest Road 37. Follow this unpaved road for 12.6 miles to the trailhead. A vault toilet is located at the trailhead.

GPS COORDINATES: 48.88035, –121.86502 / N48° 52.821′ W121° 51.9012′

BEST NEARBY BITES
Chairlift seats hang outside and snowboards are mounted above the bar at **Chair 9 Woodstone Pizza and Bar** (10459 Mount Baker Hwy., Glacier, 360/599-2511, www.chair9.com, noon-close Mon.-Thurs., 11am-close Fri.-Sun.). The name and décor pay homage to Mount Baker's legendary skiing and snowboarding scene, but the thin-crust pizza and beer from Bellingham's Kulshan Brewing Company hit the spot year-round. From the trailhead, the 13-mile drive northwest takes about 15 minutes via Forest Road 37 and Highway 542.

3 Table Mountain
MOUNT BAKER–SNOQUALMIE NATIONAL FOREST

Scale the steep wall of Table Mountain and take in views of the Chain Lakes and the icy peaks of Baker and Shuksan.

DISTANCE: 3 miles round-trip
DURATION: 1.5 hours
ELEVATION CHANGE: 700 feet
EFFORT: Easy/moderate
TRAIL: Dirt, rock, potential late-season snow
USERS: Hikers
SEASON: July–mid-October
PASSES/FEES: Northwest Forest Pass
MAPS: Green Trails Map 14 for Mount Shuksan, USGS topographic map for Shuksan Arm
CONTACT: Mount Baker Ranger District, 360/599-2714, www.fs.usda.gov

Towering above Artist Point, Table Mountain is both alluring and intimidating. It might look like you should have packed rock-climbing shoes, but it is a nontechnical walk when it's free of snow. But that's not to say there aren't potential hazards.

START THE HIKE

▶ MILE 0-0.5: Parking Lot to Table Mountain Trail

After taking in the already stunning views from the boot-shaped parking lot, find the trailhead where the laces would be (on the north side of the lot). Start by walking about 100 yards on the **Chain Lakes Trail.** To get to the even better views, turn right on the **Table Mountain Trail;** in 0.2 mile, you'll begin the steep ascent. The trail hugs the side of the cliff and uses **rock steps** as it ascends almost 400 feet in 0.3 mile. Watch out for rocks kicked loose by hikers higher on the trail and holler "rock" to warn others should you knock a piece loose.

NORTH CASCADES

Table Mountain

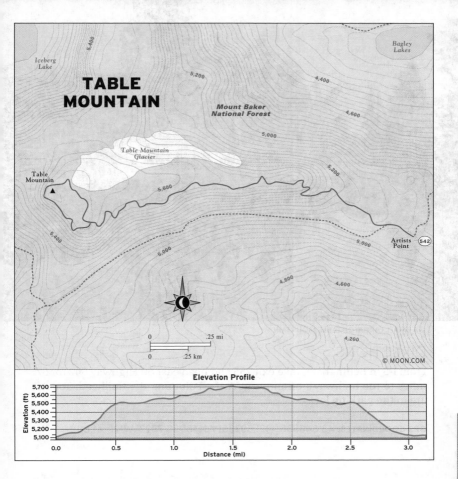

Elevation Profile

▸ MILE 0.5-1.5: Table Mountain Trail to Table Mountain Summit

On top of the **mesa-like peak**, a short spur to the right offers views of the Heather Meadows area and surrounding peaks. Turn left at this intersection and walk along the mostly flat plateau that formed when an ancient lava flow pooled into a lake of molten rock. Follow the path for 1 mile along the **south rim**, passing trees, patches of snow, and pools of water. On the west side of Table Mountain (its highest point at 5,746 feet), enjoy the bird's-eye view of the Chain Lakes and a 360-degree panorama of the North Cascades including Baker and Shuksan. Look for mountain goats, birds, and other wildlife.

▸ MILE 1.5-3: Table Mountain Summit to Parking Lot

Maps show a steep route descending to the Chain Lakes Trail, but it is treacherous, rarely used, and not recommended. Instead, when you've finished exploring the plateau, retrace your steps. If conditions don't allow or you aren't comfortable scaling Table Mountain, you can hike around it on the Chain Lakes Trail or make the easy 1.2-mile walk to Huntoon Point on the Artist Ridge Trail.

▲ A SMALL LAKE ATOP TABLE MOUNTAIN

DIRECTIONS

From I-5 in Bellingham, take exit 255 and head east on Highway 542 for 57 miles to the highway's terminus at Artist Point and the trailhead. Toilets are in the parking lot.

GPS COORDINATES: 48.846538, –121.693351 / N48° 50.7923' W121° 41.6011'

BEST NEARBY BITES

Milano's (9990 Mount Baker Hwy., Glacier, 360/599-2863, www.milanosrestaurantbar.com, 4pm-9pm Fri.-Sat., 4pm-8pm Thurs. and Sun., closed Mon.-Wed.) and its linguine topped with mussels, clams, and prawns draw a crowd. Bar Veneto shares the building and offers build-your-own tacos and gin, rum, vodka, and brandy from the owner's distillery, Paraty Spirits. From the trailhead, the 24-mile drive northwest takes 50 minutes via Highway 542.

Chain Lakes Loop
MOUNT BAKER-SNOQUALMIE NATIONAL FOREST

Visit a collection of alpine lakes while climbing ridges to views of Mount Baker and Mount Shuksan.

BEST: Summer Hikes
DISTANCE: 7.5 miles round-trip
DURATION: 4 hours
ELEVATION CHANGE: 1,800 feet
EFFORT: Moderate
TRAIL: Dirt, rocks, scree slopes
USERS: Hikers, leashed dogs
SEASON: Late July-mid-October
PASSES/FEES: Northwest Forest Pass
MAPS: Green Trails Map 14 for Mount Shuksan
CONTACT: Mount Baker Ranger District, 360/599-2714, www.fs.usda.gov

This stunning loop linking shimmering lakes, mountain views, and alpine meadows is only free of snow during the summer, so arrive at sunrise if you want to beat the crowds.

START THE HIKE

▶ **MILE 0-0.8: Bagley Lakes Trailhead to Bagley Lake**
There are several trailhead choices for this hike along the final stretch of the Mount Baker Highway, but for a grand loop on the **Chain Lakes Trail,** start at the **Bagley Lakes Trailhead** near the ski area. In the first 100 yards beyond the kiosk, stay right and cross a small dam on **Bagley Creek.** The trail bends left and spends a flat 0.7 mile tracing the shoreline of the first **Bagley Lake** and following the creek to the **second lake.** Look for sandpipers and ouzels around the water.

▶ **MILE 0.8-2.5: Bagley Lake to Herman Saddle**
At the outlet of the small second lake, an arched **stone bridge** crosses the creek and offers a stunning photo op with Table Mountain in the background. (It's also an opportunity to abbreviate the hike with a kid- and creaky-knee-friendly 1.5-mile loop.) Go straight past the bridge to continue along the lake, and in 0.2 mile the climbing begins. Marmots watch from the rocks as you ascend the open slope for 1.5 miles to Herman Saddle between Mazama Dome and Table Mountain. The view gets more majestic the higher you climb until, at the **saddle,** you can catch your breath and admire Mount Baker and Mount Shuksan, the Bagley Lakes, and, to the west, the next lakes you'll visit on this loop.

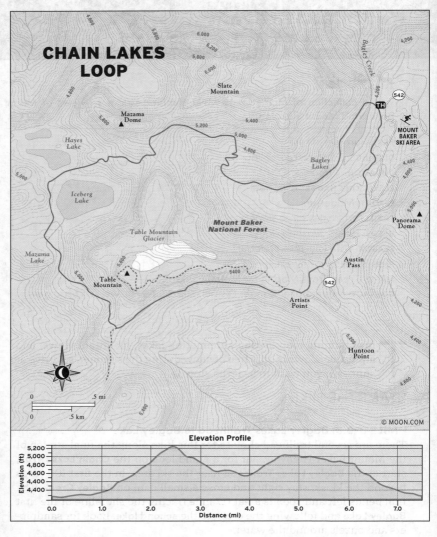

CHAIN LAKES LOOP

Elevation Profile

▶ **MILE 2.5-3.4: Herman Saddle to Hayes Lake Spur Trail**
Descend 500 feet in 0.7 mile on the west side of the saddle. Follow the
path over a strip of land between **Hayes and Iceberg Lakes.** The peaceful
alpine lakes invite visitors to stay, take a quick dip, and relax for a while. In
0.2 mile, pass the Hayes Lake Trail (a flat, 0.9-mile loop around Hayes Lake
that also visits Arbuthnot Lake) and a short, well-marked spur (on the left)
leading to a pit toilet overlooking Iceberg Lake.

▶ **MILE 3.4-5.7: Hayes Lake Spur Trail to Artist Point**
Continue south along the west side of Iceberg Lake, passing tiny **Mazama
Lake** (another options for a chilly swim) after 0.4 mile. Spend the next 0.8
mile ascending until you reach the **intersection** with the Ptarmigan Trail
at a gap between Table Mountain and Ptarmigan Perch. Go left to stay on

▲ CHAIN LAKES LOOP

the loop and walk 1.1 miles along the south slope of Table Mountain to **Artist Point,** enjoying views of the Swift Creek valley and Mount Baker along the way.

▶ MILE 5.7-7.5: Artist Point to Wild Goose Trail

At Artist Point is a large parking lot that will likely be packed with cars; the point's views of the North Cascades make it one of the most scenic summer driving destinations in the Northwest. Cross the lot and find the **Wild Goose Trail** next to the toilets. Take this trail, which crosses the highway and then descends—sharply at times, on log steps linked with cables—for 1 mile to the **Austin Pass Picnic Area** and the **Heather Meadows Visitor Center.** Should snow and ice make the trail unsafe, the shoulder of the road offers a more gradual descent. From the picnic area, follow the Wild Goose Trail 0.7 mile to complete the loop.

DIRECTIONS

From I-5 in Bellingham, take exit 255 and head east for 54 miles on Highway 542 to the Bagley Lakes Loop trailhead just above the Heather Meadows base area at Mount Baker Ski Area. Toilets are located at the trailhead.

GPS COORDINATES: 48.861551, -121.682533 / N48° 34.7448' W120° 28.7034'

BEST NEARBY BITES
Graham's Restaurant (9989 Mount Baker Hwy., 360/599-1933, noon-9pm Mon.-Fri., 8am-9pm Sat.-Sun.) pays tribute to Mount Baker's history as a filming location, with pictures of actors Clark Gable and Robert De Niro adorning the walls of the century-old building: Gable's *Call of the Wild* (1935) and De Niro's *The Deer Hunter* (1978) filmed scenes at Heather Meadows. According to locals, though, the real star at Graham's is the bacon meatloaf sandwich. From the trailhead, the 22-mile drive northwest takes 42 minutes via Highway 542.

🦌 ❁ 🐾 🚶

Admire man-made Diablo Lake from an overlook at the end of a short trail starting from a popular campground.

DISTANCE: 3.6 miles round-trip
DURATION: 2 hours
ELEVATION CHANGE: 600 feet
EFFORT: Easy/moderate
TRAIL: Dirt, rocks, pavement (in campground)
USERS: Hikers, leashed dogs
SEASON: Year-round
PASSES/FEES: None
MAPS: Green Trails Map 48 for Diablo
CONTACT: North Cascades Visitor Center, 206/386-4495 (mid-May–September); North Cascades National Park, 360/854-7200, www.nps.gov/noca

The family-friendly hike to a bluff overlooking Diablo Lake might be short, but a visit to this part of Ross Lake National Recreation Area doesn't have to be. The campground is a popular hub for those exploring this stunning landscape. From paddling and fishing on Diablo Lake to hiking and mountaineering, there is plenty to do.

START THE HIKE

▶ **MILE 0-0.5: Parking Lot to Highway 20 Bridge Viewpoint**

From the parking lot on the north side of the highway, walk the paved **driveway** into the **north campground**, making your way to the walk-in campsites and the clearly marked trailhead. The trail is immaculately maintained but not until after you make your way through an area reconfigured by prior flooding. Signs point the way and bridges cross channels carved by the creek. Walk toward campsite No. 11, crossing a bridge, then continue as the trail surface becomes smoother while traveling under hemlocks and Douglas firs and past moss-covered boulders. The trail climbs gently and 0.5 mile from the highway an opening in the trees frames a view of the Highway 20 bridge over the Thunder Arm of Diablo Lake.

▶ **MILE 0.5-1.3: Highway 20 Bridge Viewpoint**
  to Colonial Peak Viewpoint

Benches dot the next 0.4 mile, which brings you to a **clearing** with views of the steep, tree-covered slopes above the lake. Look south to see Colonial Peak and the glacier feeding Colonial Creek. Listen for woodpeckers as you pass a marsh in another 0.4 mile, and then continue upward under lodgepole pine to the top of the knob. This area is one of the best in the park for bird-watching. Get going early before the area is bustling with

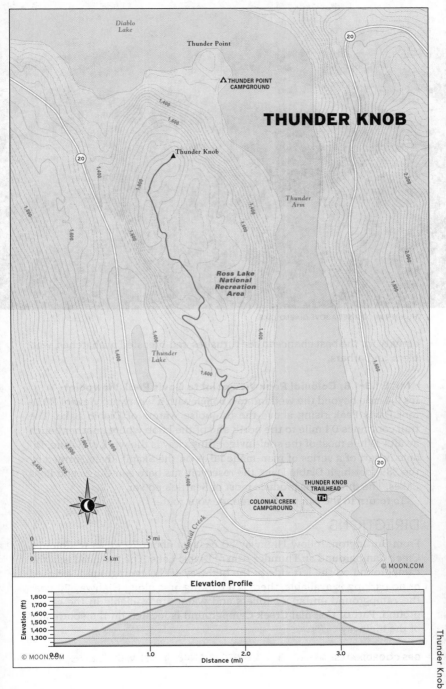

THUNDER KNOB

Thunder Point

Thunder Knob

Thunder Arm

Diablo Lake

Ross Lake National Recreation Area

Thunder Lake

Thunder Point Campground

Thunder Knob Trailhead

Colonial Creek Campground

Colonial Creek

© MOON.COM

Elevation Profile

© MOON.COM

▲ THUNDER KNOB RISES ABOVE DIABLO LAKE

activity for the best chance to see thrushes, red-breasted nuthatches, warblers, and others.

▶ **MILE 1.3–1.8: Colonial Peak Viewpoint to Davis Peak Viewpoint**
It's 0.4 mile beyond the wetland to a **bench** with a westward view of 7,051-foot Davis Peak rising above the turquoise waters of Diablo Lake. The trail continues 0.1 mile to the north end of the knob where another bench awaits. While most of the soul-invigorating view is the work of nature, Diablo is part of a series of man-made lakes on the Skagit River. Formed by the 389-foot-high Diablo Dam, the reservoir sits between Gorge and Ross Lakes. The three dams produce most of Seattle's power.

To return to the campground retrace your route.

DIRECTIONS

From Burlington, follow Highway 20 east for about 70 miles to Colonial Creek Campground on Thunder Arm of Diablo Lake. The trailhead is in the campground on the left side of the highway. If the campground is closed or no parking is available, there is a parking area along Highway 20 near the campground entrance. Toilets and water are available in the campground. Part of Colonial Creek Campground is located on the south side of the highway.

GPS COORDINATES: 48.690350, –121.097972 / N48° 41.421' W121° 5.8783'

Switchback your way through an old-growth forest to a mountain pass with views of the rocky and glaciated spires of the North Cascades.

DISTANCE: 7.4 miles round-trip
DURATION: 4 hours
ELEVATION CHANGE: 1,800 feet
EFFORT: Moderate
TRAIL: Dirt path
USERS: Hikers
SEASON: July–mid-October
PASSES/FEES: None
MAPS: Green Trails Map 80 for Cascade Pass
CONTACT: North Cascades National Park Wilderness Information Center, 360/854-7245, www.nps.gov/noca

START THE HIKE

▶ MILE 0-2.4: Loop Parking Lot to Switchbacks

The trail starts on the north side of the loop **parking lot,** but before you even get out of the car it is obvious this is a special place. Johannesburg Mountain rises sharply above the parking lot with glaciers clinging to its rocky cliffs. Ice and rock sometimes crash down the slopes, the rumble echoing through the basin.

Five steps into the hike, the path folds back 180 degrees for a taste of what's to come: thirty-four **switchbacks** in 2.4 miles. Think of them as your friend—they make a steep climb comparatively easy.

▶ MILE 2.4-3.7: Switchbacks to Cascade Pass

Making a game out of this daunting stretch can also make the trek easier. Feel free to use mine: at each switchback, name an athlete who wore the corresponding jersey number (1, Warren Moon; 2, Derek Jeter,

CASCADE PASS TRAIL ▶

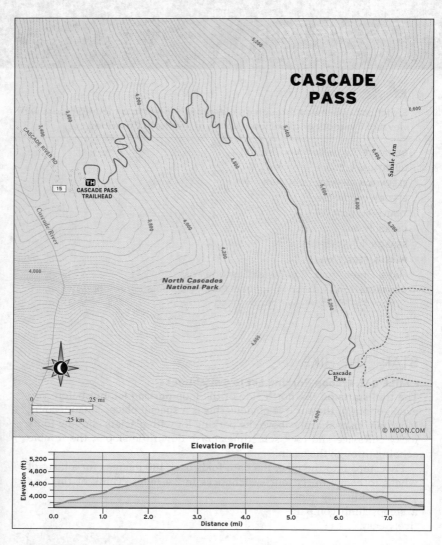

etc.). Before you know it, you will be making the **1.3-mile traverse** from Switchback 34 to the pass. It's during this traverse that you trade the dense woods for views of Johannesburg, Eldorado, Mix-up and other peaks.

At the **pass**, rest on one of the granite slabs arranged in a semicircle and check out the USGS benchmark disc. A path leads to a vault toilet. When gazing down into Pelton Basin, take in the effects of the last ice age, when massive continental glaciers covered much of the North Cascades. At 5,392 feet above sea level, Cascade Pass was used by Native Americans for generations to cross the North Cascades. Archaeologists have found stone tools and cooking hearths here dating back 9,000 years. Today, this area is one of the most easily accessed high-country adventures in the North Cascades.

Once you've had your fill of alpine views, return the way you came.

▲ PEAKS ABOVE CASCADE PASS

DIRECTIONS

From Burlington, follow Highway 20 east for about 57 miles to Marble-mount. When the highway bends left in town, continue straight and cross a steel bridge over the Skagit River on Cascade River Road. Follow the road for 19 miles to the Cascade Pass Trailhead parking lot. A vault toilet is at the trailhead.

GPS COORDINATES: 48.475443, –121.075064 / N48° 28.5266' W121° 4.5038'

Maple Pass Loop
OKANOGAN-WENATCHEE NATIONAL FOREST, RAINY PASS

PCT 🦌 ❄️ 🏞️ 🐾 ♿

Hike one of the North Cascades' classic trails through old-growth forest to ridge-top meadows above a glittering alpine lake.

BEST: Fall Hikes
DISTANCE: 6.8 miles round-trip
DURATION: 4 hours
ELEVATION CHANGE: 2,100 feet
EFFORT: Moderate
TRAIL: Dirt, rock
USERS: Hikers, wheelchair users (paved path to Rainy Lake), leashed dogs
SEASON: July-October
PASSES/FEES: Northwest Forest Pass
MAPS: Green Trails Map 49 for Mount Logan, Green Trails Map 50 for Washington Pass
CONTACT: Okanogan-Wenatchee National Forest, 509/996-4000, www.fs.usda.gov

START THE HIKE

▶ **MILE 0-1.4: Rainy Pass Trailhead to Lake Ann Trail Junction**
Starting at the **Rainy Pass Trailhead**, near where the Pacific Crest Trail makes its final highway crossing before the Canadian border, find the paved **Rainy Lake Trail** running behind the trailhead kiosk just south of the parking/picnic area loop. Look for the well-marked Maple Pass Trail behind the **kiosk** and start climbing. Take solace in knowing the climbing is more gradual heading this direction.

The **Maple Pass Trail** ascends through an old-growth forest of firs and hemlocks and, in late summer and fall, allows glimpses of the colorful foliage that lies ahead. Pass avalanche chutes with larger doses of color and a small waterfall before arriving at the **junction** with the Lake Ann Trail at 1.3 miles. The trail to the left reaches the lake in 0.6 mile, but stay right on the **Maple Pass Loop** and you'll get views of the lake in about 0.1 mile.

MAPLE PASS TRAIL ▶

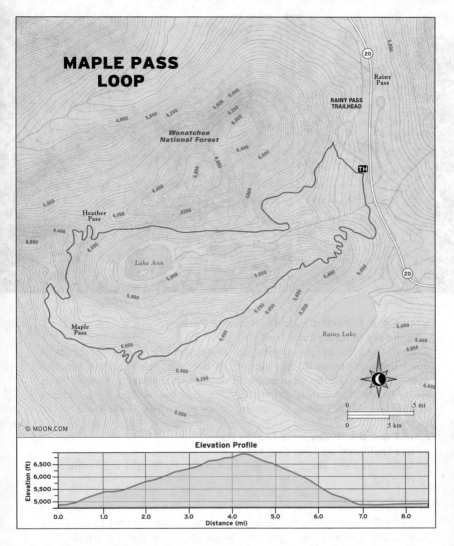

MAPLE PASS LOOP

Elevation Profile

The shimmering pool adorned with a tiny island continually lures your gaze as you make your way toward the ridge high above.

▶ MILE 1.4-4: Lake Ann Trail Junction to North Cascades National Park Boundary

One mile past the Lake Ann spur, a sign bolted to a tree welcomes you to **Heather Pass.** Keep straight and in 0.9 mile reach a marker indicating the boundary of **North Cascades National Park.** Most of the climbing is behind you at this point. Spend the next 0.7 mile strolling through ridge-top **meadows**, portions of which are roped off to prevent visitors from trampling fragile vegetation.

▲ MAPLE PASS

▶ **MILE 4-6.4: North Cascades National Park**
  Boundary to Rainy Lake Trail

Soak in the view before starting the steep, zigzagging descent down an **open slope.** Highway 20 is visible from here and the sound of vehicles sometimes breaks the silence, but it doesn't spoil the experience. Soon, Rainy Lake's blue waters are visible 1,500 feet below. The steep descent ends after 2.4 miles when you return to the paved **Rainy Lake Trail.**

▶ **MILE 6.4-6.8: Rainy Lake Trail to Rainy**
  Pass Trailhead and Parking Lot

To finish the loop, simply turn left and make the flat 0.4-mile walk back to your car.

DIRECTIONS

From Burlington, follow Highway 20 east for about 97 miles to the Rainy Pass picnic area and turn right into the parking area. The Rainy Lake, Maple Pass, and Pacific Crest Trails converge in this area. A restroom is located near the trailhead.

GPS COORDINATES: 48.515511, –120.735769 / N48° 30.9307′ W120° 44.1461′

BEST NEARBY BITES

Set on the bank of the Methow River in the Old West-themed town of Winthrop, the **Rocking Horse Bakery** (265 Riverside Ave., Winthrop, 509/996-4241, www.rockinghorsebakery.com, 7am-4pm daily) serves an array of breakfast pastries along with pizza, sandwiches, and salads. From the trailhead, the 35-mile drive west takes about 40 minutes via Highway 20.

Take an easy walk up a North Cascades valley to a place where Cedar Creek makes two sharp plunges.

BEST: Waterfall Hikes
DISTANCE: 3.5 miles round-trip
DURATION: 1.5 hours
ELEVATION CHANGE: 500 feet
EFFORT: Easy
TRAIL: Dirt, rock
USERS: Hikers, leashed dogs, mountain bikers, horseback riders
SEASON: May–early November
PASSES/FEES: Northwest Forest Pass
MAPS: Green Trails Map 50 for Washington Pass
CONTACT: Okanogan-Wenatchee National Forest, 509/996–4000, www.fs.usda.gov

Each season offers something different on the Cedar Creek Trail. Some make the long snowshoe via the closed North Cascade Highway in the winter to see the falls when they're frozen. Visit soon after the highway opens and snow is melting to find the creek thundering over the falls. Spring brings wildflowers. And autumn colors accent the journey when the falls have a smaller volume.

START THE HIKE

▶ **MILE 0–0.75: Cedar Creek Trailhead to Goat Peak Viewpoint**
The ambience improves quickly once you start hiking the **Cedar Creek Trail.** It's no surprise, really, considering the hike starts at a **gravel pit.** Starting from the **kiosk** at the southeast end of the gravel pit, the trail heads into the forest and immediately passes the Varden Lake Trail. Continue straight on the **Cedar Creek Trail** for a short bit of uphill before the trail settles into a gradually climbing valley walk. The forest of firs, spruce, and occasional cedars allows enough sunlight for wildflowers like lupine and scarlet paintbrush to grow. Look for deer and butterflies, but also be on the lookout for rattlesnakes.

Peek at peaks through the trees before, 0.75 mile into the hike, an **open spot** offers a view of the surrounding valley. Goat Peak and its rocky cliffs rise in the distance.

▶ **MILE 0.75–1.75: Goat Peak Viewpoint to Cedar Falls**
In 1 mile hear the roar of the falls cascading through a narrow canyon. The two tiers of the **falls** drop 40 and 55 feet, respectively. Exploring the area, you'll find **overlooks** with views of the falls, although there is not a

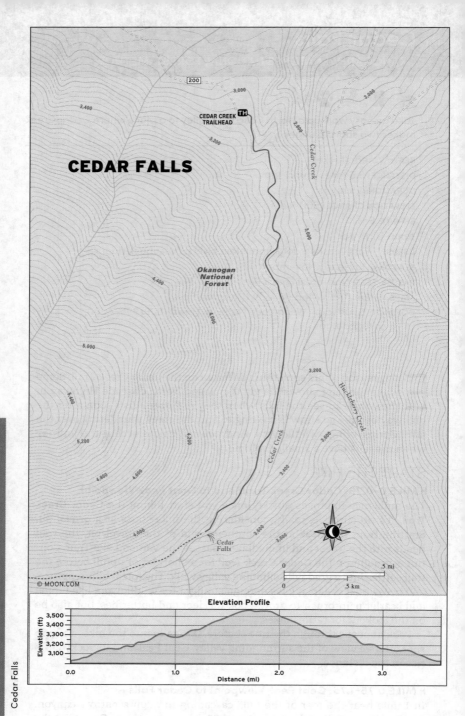

CEDAR FALLS

200

3,000

CEDAR CREEK
TRAILHEAD TH

3,200

Cedar Creek

2,800

3,000

3,400

*Okanogan
National
Forest*

4,400

4,000

5,000

3,200

Huckleberry Creek

5,400

4,200

5,200

3,600

Cedar Creek

3,400

4,800 4,600

*Cedar
Falls*

3,600 3,800

4,000

0   .5 mi

0   .5 km

© MOON.COM

Elevation Profile

3,500
3,400
3,300
3,200
3,100

Elevation (ft)

0.0   1.0   2.0   3.0

Distance (mi)

▲ CEDAR FALLS

viewpoint where you can squeeze both drops into one picture. Keep children and pets close and don't go near the edge of the exposed overlooks.

When you're ready to call it a day, retrace your route along Cedar Creek back to the trailhead.

DIRECTIONS

From Burlington, follow Highway 20 east for about 114 miles. Follow the Cedar Creek sign directing you to turn right on Forest Road 200. Drive 0.8 mile to the trailhead. A toilet is located at the trailhead parking area.

GPS COORDINATES: 48.57908, –120.47839 / N48° 34.7448' W120° 28.7034'

BEST NEARBY BITES

Nearly a century old, **The Mazama Store** (50 Lost River Rd., Mazama, 509/996-2855, www.themazamastore.com, 7am–6pm daily) sells pottery, soap, jewelry, and other items made by Methow Valley residents. Its fresh pastries, pies, pizza, and soup make it a popular stop for breakfast and lunch. From the trailhead, the 7-mile drive northeast takes about 20 minutes via Highway 20.

NORTH CASCADES

Cedar Falls

9

Green Mountain

MOUNT BAKER–SNOQUALMIE NATIONAL FOREST

Listen to whistling marmots, enjoy colorful wildflowers, and visit an old fire lookout while experiencing a far-reaching view of the North Cascades.

DISTANCE: 8.4 miles round-trip
DURATION: 5 hours
ELEVATION CHANGE: 3,300 feet
EFFORT: Moderate/strenuous
TRAIL: Dirt single track
USERS: Hikers, leashed dogs
SEASON: July–October
PASSES/FEES: Northwest Forest Pass
MAPS: Green Trails Map 80 for Cascade Pass
CONTACT: Darrington Ranger District, 360/436–1155, www.fs.usda.gov

The verdant journey along this beloved trail to one of Washington's most breathtaking views visits forest and grassy meadows. Experience for yourself how Green Mountain got its name.

START THE HIKE

▶ **MILE 0–1.5: Green Mountain Trailhead to Meadow**

The **well-marked trail** starts under a canopy of evergreens. The ascent, gradual at first, soon gets steeper. The shade won't last long, so carry plenty of water and sun protection as well as bug spray. After 1.5 miles, emerge from the trees and enter a lush **meadow** with a view of snowcapped peaks.

▶ **MILE 1.5–3: Meadow to Ponds**

The scenery only gets better as you continue. Hip-high leafy greenery lines the trail as you **switchback** upward for 1.5 miles before dropping about 100 feet to a **pair of ponds** at about 5,200 feet.

▶ **MILE 3–4.2: Ponds to Green Mountain Summit**

The trail gets steeper and the view more mesmerizing beyond the ponds as you climb 1,300 feet over the final 1.2 miles. Take your time and enjoy the columbine, glacier lilies, and bluebells

NORTH CASCADES

Green Mountain

HIKERS ON GREEN MOUNTAIN ▶

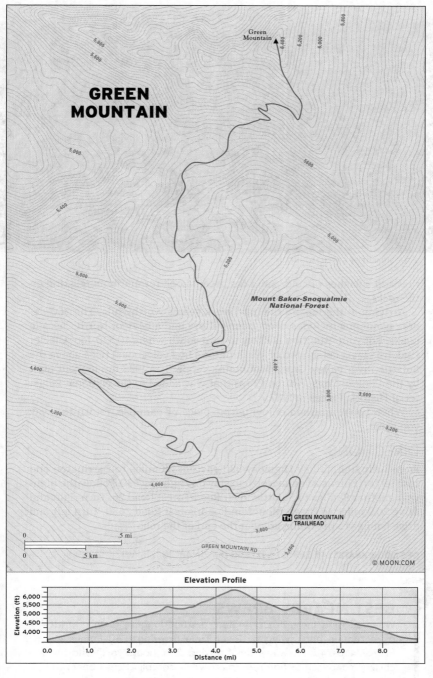

GREEN MOUNTAIN

Green Mountain

Mount Baker-Snoqualmie National Forest

GREEN MOUNTAIN TRAILHEAD

GREEN MOUNTAIN RD

0   .5 mi

0   .5 km

© MOON.COM

Elevation Profile

Elevation (ft): 6,000 / 5,500 / 5,000 / 4,500 / 4,000

Distance (mi): 0.0 1.0 2.0 3.0 4.0 5.0 6.0 7.0 8.0

▲ THE SUMMIT OF GREEN MOUNTAIN

that add splashes of color amid the green. Look for marmots relaxing on the rocks.

Arriving at the **top**, all the hard work seems worthwhile. The 360-degree panorama includes deep green valleys and a bevy of North Cascade peaks. But your attention is likely to turn south where 10,520-foot Glacier Peak (the least celebrated of Washington's five volcanoes) rises above the Suiattle River valley. Green Mountain's capper is a 1933 fire lookout built by the Civilian Conservation Corps that was added to the National Register of Historic Places in 1987.

When you're finished enjoying this piece of paradise, return the way you came.

DIRECTIONS

From Arlington, follow Highway 530 east for 28 miles to Darrington and turn left on Emens Avenue North to stay on Highway 530. Follow the highway another 8 miles to Suiattle River Road/Forest Road 26. Turn right and drive 20.2 miles to Green Mountain Road/Forest Road 2680. Turn left and drive 6 miles to the trailhead near the end of the road.

GPS COORDINATES: 48.269521, –121.236484 / N48° 16.1713' W121° 14.189'

BEST NEARBY BREWS

When passing through Darrington, a small logging town and ideal recreation hub, swing by **River Time Brewing** (660 Emens Ave. E., 267/483-7411, www.rivertimebrewing.com, hours vary) and try a chicken sandwich or flatbread pizza while sampling craft beers with names like Life Changer and Another Red Headed Stranger. From the trailhead, the 30-mile drive west takes about 90 minutes via Suiattle River Road/Forest Road 26 and Highway 530.

NORTH CASCADES

Green Mountain

10

Mount Pilchuck

MOUNT PILCHUCK STATE PARK

Perched on the edge of the Cascades, a historic fire lookout gives you a place to gawk at one of Washington's best views.

DISTANCE: 5.4 miles round-trip
DURATION: 3 hours
ELEVATION CHANGE: 2,300 feet
EFFORT: Moderate
TRAIL: Dirt, log and rock steps, short scramble over granite boulders
USERS: Hikers, leashed dogs
SEASON: July–early November
PASSES/FEES: Northwest Forest Pass
MAPS: Green Trails Map 109 for Granite Falls
CONTACT: Verlot Public Service Center, 360/691-7791, www.fs.usda.gov; Darrington Ranger District, 360/436-1155; Mount Pilchuck State Park, 360/793-0420, http://parks.state.wa.us

Some days it feels like you can see the entire state from the top of Mount Pilchuck. And some days it feels like the entire state has joined you on the trail. A short hike easily accessed from Seattle and with a three-volcano view, Mount Pilchuck is one of Washington's most popular trails.

START THE HIKE

▶ **MILE 0–1: Mount Pilchuck Trailhead to Mount Pilchuck State Park**
From the trailhead, start on what was once a ski area **service road.** In about 0.1 mile step over **Rotary Creek**; in another 0.2 mile, pass a weathered sign signaling your passage into 1,903-acre **Mount Pilchuck State Park.** Walk among cedars and firs and cross a **scree slope** in another 0.7 mile.

▶ **MILE 1–1.7: Mount Pilchuck State Park to Historic Chairlift**
A historical remnant sits trailside after another 0.7 mile. A large concrete foundation once anchored a **chairlift.** From 1951 to 1980, Pilchuck was home to a ski area.

▶ **MILE 1.7–2.7: Historic Chairlift to Mount Pilchuck Summit**
From here, there's 1 mile to go. The **summit** comes into view as the path's pitch increases on **slopes** covered with granite boulders and heather. The way is typically easy to find from summer until early November, making it an attraction for novice hikers eager to bag their first mile-high peak. However, this hike isn't without hazards. Snow can linger, sections of trail are exposed, and the final 100 feet or so to the lookout requires scrambling over large **granite boulders** (an impracticality for some children and pets).

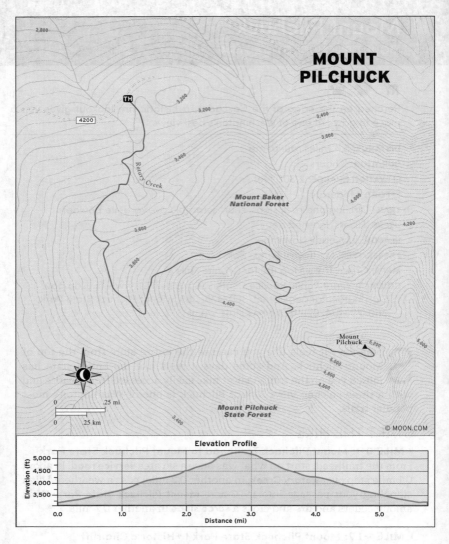

MOUNT PILCHUCK

TH

4200

Rotary Creek

Mount Baker National Forest

Mount Pilchuck

Mount Pilchuck State Forest

2,800
3,200
3,200
3,400
3,600
3,400
3,600
3,800
4,400
4,000
4,200
5,200
4,800
5,000
4,600
5,600
3,400

0   .25 mi
0   .25 km

© MOON.COM

Elevation Profile

Elevation (ft)

5,000
4,500
4,000
3,500

0.0   1.0   2.0   3.0   4.0   5.0

Distance (mi)

Poles, traction devices, and a willingness to turn around when conditions exceed your skill level are important.

A short scramble over the boulders and a climb up an eight-rung **ladder** places you on the deck of a historic **fire lookout** on the western edge of the Cascades. The view includes Mount Rainier, Mount Baker, Glacier Peak, and numerous other Cascade mountains. The Olympics, Puget Sound, Everett, and Seattle add to the scenery. Need help identifying what's what? Diagrams inside the lookout show the names of the surrounding peaks.

You won't want to leave this heavenly perch. Some unfurl sleeping bags and stake their claim to spots on the lookout floor. Others lie on boulders. When you do finally leave, use the same route for your descent.

▲ SUNSET ON MOUNT PILCHUCK

DIRECTIONS

From Seattle, follow I-5 north to exit 194 and follow U.S. 2 east. After 1.8 miles, follow the signs for Highway 204 and continue east toward Lake Stevens. After 2.1 miles turn left on Highway 9. In 1.6 miles turn right on Highway 92 and continue toward Granite Falls. Pass through three traffic circles as the road becomes 96th Street. At Alder Avenue turn left. This road becomes the Mountain Loop Highway.

In 10.8 miles, pass the Verlot Public Service Center on the left. Drive another mile and turn right onto Mount Pilchuck Road just after crossing a bridge. Follow the road 6.8 miles to the trailhead parking lot. The final mile of the road is not paved. A restroom is located at the trailhead.

GPS COORDINATES: 48.07029, −121.8145 / N48° 4.2174' W121° 48.888'

11

Lake Twenty-Two

MOUNT BAKER-SNOQUALMIE NATIONAL FOREST

🦌 ✿ 🏞 🐾

Hike past waterfalls and giant cedars on your way to the striking setting of Lake Twenty-Two.

BEST: Dog-Friendly Hikes

DISTANCE: 6.2 miles round-trip

DURATION: 3.5 hours

ELEVATION CHANGE: 1,350 feet

EFFORT: Moderate

TRAIL: Dirt path, rocks, talus slopes, boardwalks

USERS: Hikers, leashed dogs

SEASON: May-October

PASSES/FEES: Northwest Forest Pass

MAPS: Green Trails Map 109 for Granite Falls

CONTACT: Mount Baker-Snoqualmie National Forest, 360/436-1155, www.fs.usda.gov; Verlot Public Service Center, 360/691-7791

The trail and lake sit in the 790-acre Lake Twenty-Two Research Natural Area, a section of Mount Baker-Snoqualmie National Forest set aside in 1947 for the study of western red cedar, western hemlock, and various plants. The giant cedars are every bit the stars of this hike alongside the lake and waterfalls.

START THE HIKE

▶ **MILE 0-1.8: Trailhead to Three Fingers and Liberty Peaks Viewpoint**
From the South Fork Stillaguamish River on the opposite side of the Mountain Loop Highway to Twenty-Two Creek, the sound of moving water is constant as you walk under an evergreen canopy. The first 0.5 mile climbs gradually before giving way to switchbacks. After 0.5 mile of switchbacks, get your first of several looks at the **cascades.** The trail keeps climbing through old-growth forest and past ferns, salmonberry, violets, and trilliums for another 0.8 mile before reaching a **talus slope** with views of Three Fingers and Liberty Peaks to the north.

▶ **MILE 1.8-2.5: Three Fingers and Liberty Peaks**
   Viewpoint to Lake Twenty-Two
At 0.4 mile beyond the **talus slope,** the trail relents for a gentle 0.3-mile walk along the creek to the lake. Steep slopes rise above three sides of **Lake Twenty-Two** (2,400 feet elev.), creating a microclimate that supports subalpine vegetation usually found at higher elevations.

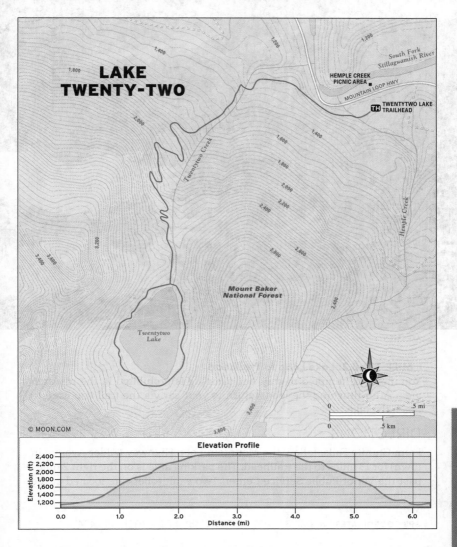

Elevation Profile

© MOON.COM

▸ **MILE 2.5–3.7: Lake Twenty-Two to Lake Loop**

At the lake, turn left on the **boardwalk** and take a few steps to a **bridge** crossing **Twenty-Two Creek.** This is arguably the best view at the lake, but you can gain a variety of perspectives by crossing the bridge and following the 1.2-mile **loop** around the water. Shortly into the loop, the boardwalk gives way to traditional trail.

Cross a **talus slope** before another short **boardwalk** on the lake's south side. Be aware of conditions if you hike the loop. Avalanches can crash down the rocky slopes early in the hiking season. Listen for frogs and scan the slopes for mountain goats. The clear lake is 53 feet deep and can be a good place for anglers to land rainbow trout.

▲ LAKE TWENTY-TWO

▶ MILE 3.7–6.2: Lake Loop to Trailhead

You might be tempted to stay, but camping is prohibited in the research area. After finishing the loop, return to your car via the trail you used to reach the lake.

DIRECTIONS

From Granite Falls, follow the Mountain Loop Highway (Alder Avenue in town) for 13 miles to the trailhead. The parking area is on the right 2 miles past the Verlot Public Service Center. Two vault toilets are located at the trailhead.

GPS COORDINATES: 48.077134, –121.74579 / N48° 4.628′ W121° 44.7474′

12

Big Four Ice Caves

MOUNT BAKER-SNOQUALMIE NATIONAL FOREST

🦌 ❀ ♨ 🐾 🚶 ♿

Scope out ice caves formed by melting snow at the foot of Big Four Mountain at the end of a family-friendly trail.

DISTANCE: 2.4 miles round-tip
DURATION: 1.5 hours
ELEVATION CHANGE: 250 feet
EFFORT: Easy
TRAIL: Gravel path, paved path, boardwalk
USERS: Hikers, wheelchair users, leashed dogs
SEASON: late June–September
PASSES/FEES: Northwest Forest Pass
MAPS: Green Trails Map 110 for Silverton
CONTACT: Verlot Public Service Center, 360/691-7791, www.fs.usda.gov; Darrington Ranger District, 360/436-1155.

Shortly before publication, the Forest Service removed the bridge over the Stillaguamish River and it is unclear when the bridge will be replaced. Hikers can still reach the caves if they ford the river, which is often about knee deep in summertime. Contact the ranger station for current conditions.

START THE HIKE

▶ **MILE 0-0.3: Information Kiosk to Pond**
Starting on the paved path left of the information kiosk, a walk to the **Big Four Ice Caves** immerses visitors in the wonders of nature. Salmonberries, ferns, and mossy trees line the trail that turns into a wooden boardwalk after 0.1 mile. Continue to pass nurse logs and uprooted trees for another 0.2 mile before reaching the intersection with a dirt path. Turn left and get your first glimpse of **Big Four Mountain** through the trees. In short order you'll pass a pond, a good place to linger and listen to birds and perhaps glimpse a beaver.

▶ **MILE 0.3-1: Pond to Forest Edge**
Another 0.1 mile brings you to an aluminum bridge spanning the **Stillaguamish River**, followed soon after by a wooden bridge over a creek. The 0.6 mile beyond the bridge cuts through the woods before the evergreen veil is lifted and the rocky slopes of the mountain can be viewed from top to bottom. Waterfalls look like tiny icicles as they cascade over the upper reaches of the peak. At the base of the mountain's avalanche chutes, water plunges into huge piles of melting snow, helping to carve the caves that lure so many visitors.

▶ **MILE 1-1.2: Forest Edge to Big Four Ice Caves**
A boulder-lined **cul-de-sac** marks the end of the trail in 0.2 mile. Here hikers will see warnings to go no farther. A boulder is engraved with the Forest

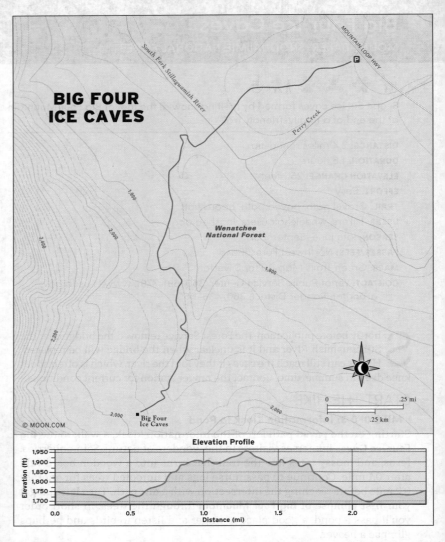

**BIG FOUR
ICE CAVES**

South Fork Stillaguamish River

Perry Creek

*Wenatchee
National Forest*

1,800

2,000

2,400

2,200

2,000

2,000

1,800

© MOON.COM

■ Big Four
Ice Caves

0   .25 mi

0   .25 km

Elevation Profile

Service logo and a description of the hazards of getting too close to the caves. Climbing atop the caves can be just as dangerous as exploring inside. Rangers don't always patrol this area, but they warn of avalanches, fissures in the snowfield, and falling rocks. Enjoy the ice caves from a distance.

When ready, return the way you came.

DIRECTIONS

From Granite Falls, follow the Mountain Loop Highway (Alder Avenue in town) east 25.2 miles and find the sign for the trailhead parking lot on the right. It is located 0.6 mile past a turnout for the Big Four Picnic Area, which offers alternate access to the ice caves trail. Three ADA restrooms are located at the trailhead.

GPS COORDINATES: 48.06598, –121.51048 / N48° 3.9588' W121° 30.6288'

NEARBY CAMPGROUNDS

NAME	DESCRIPTION	FACILITIES	SEASON	FEES
Verlot Campground	situated on the South Fork Stillaguamish River	25 RV and tent sites, restrooms	late April-late September	$18.34

Mountain Loop Highway, Verlot, Mount Baker-Snoqualmie National Forest, 877/444-6777, www.recreation.gov

NAME	DESCRIPTION	FACILITIES	SEASON	FEES
Newhalem Campground	located near Newhalem Creek and the Skagit River	107 RV and tent sites, restrooms	mid-May-mid-September	$16

Highway 20, Newhalem, North Cascades National Park, 360/854-7200, www.recreation.gov

NAME	DESCRIPTION	FACILITIES	SEASON	FEES
Colonial Creek Campground	two large camping areas set amid old-growth forest on Diablo Lake at the base of Colonial Peak	135 RV and tent sites, restrooms	year-round	$16

Highway 20, Diablo, North Cascades National Park, 877/444-6777, www.recreation.gov

NAME	DESCRIPTION	FACILITIES	SEASON	FEES
Douglas Fir Campground	under Douglas firs, hemlocks, and cedars on the North Fork Nooksack River	26 RV and tent sites, restrooms	late May-early September	$18.54-20.39

Mount Baker Highway, Glacier, Mount Baker-Snoqualmie National Forest, 360/419-5115, www.recreation.gov

NAME	DESCRIPTION	FACILITIES	SEASON	FEES
Klipchuck Campground	set in the woods along Early Winters Creek	46 RV and tent sites, restrooms	May-October	$12

Highway 20, Mazama, Okanogan-Wenatchee National Forest, 509/996-4000

CENTRAL CASCADES

The Central Cascades might be Washington's most convenient place to wander wilderness. Alpine lakes, towering waterfalls, and rocky mountaintops are all a day hike away in this region of the Cascades traversed by I-90, U.S. 2, and Highway 410. With an abundance of entry points, visitors can easily access the Alpine Lakes Wilderness and wander among cedars, Douglas firs, and, in fall, golden larches. But that's not all: Hikers can explore historical railroad routes and walk through a 2.3-mile tunnel; climb to a fire lookout with a view stretching from Mount Rainier north to Mount Baker and from eastern Washington west to the Olympics; or splash in a frigid lake and catch glimpses of mountain goats, deer, eagles, and other wildlife.

▲ SNOW LAKE

▲ FIRE LOOKOUT ON GRANITE MOUNTAIN

1 Wallace Falls
DISTANCE: 5.2 miles round-trip
DURATION: 2.5 hours
EFFORT: Easy/moderate

2 Lake Serene and Bridal Veil Falls
DISTANCE: 8.2 miles round-trip
DURATION: 5 hours
EFFORT: Moderate

3 Barclay Lake
DISTANCE: 4.4 miles round-trip
DURATION: 2.5 hours
EFFORT: Easy/moderate

4 Iron Goat Trail
DISTANCE: 5.9 miles round-trip
DURATION: 3.5 hours
EFFORT: Easy/moderate

5 Colchuck Lake
DISTANCE: 8.2 miles round-trip
DURATION: 4.5 hours
EFFORT: Moderate

6 Talapus and Olallie Lakes
DISTANCE: 5.6 miles round-trip
DURATION: 3 hours
EFFORT: Moderate

7 Granite Mountain
DISTANCE: 8.6 miles round-trip
DURATION: 5 hours
EFFORT: Strenuous

8 Snow Lake
DISTANCE: 6.8 miles round-trip
DURATION: 3.5 hours
EFFORT: Moderate

9 Palouse to Cascades State Park Trail: Snoqualmie Tunnel
DISTANCE: 5.2 miles round-trip
DURATION: 3 hours
EFFORT: Easy/moderate

10 Lake Ingalls
DISTANCE: 9.6 miles round-trip
DURATION: 4.5 hours
EFFORT: Moderate/strenuous

▾ TRAIL TO TALAPUS AND OLALLIE LAKES

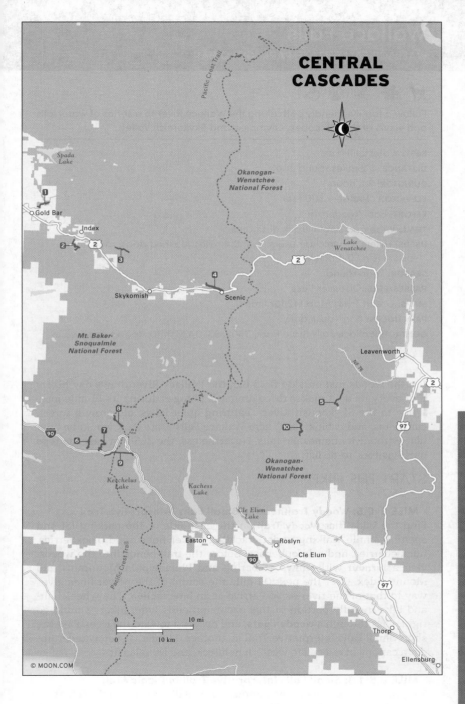

CENTRAL CASCADES

Follow a family-friendly path along the Wallace River to a series of waterfalls and views of the Cascades, Olympics, and Skykomish Valley.

BEST: Waterfall Hikes
DISTANCE: 5.2 miles round-trip
DURATION: 2.5 hours
ELEVATION CHANGE: 1,300 feet
EFFORT: Easy/moderate
TRAIL: Wide and single-track dirt paths
USERS: Hikers, wheelchair users (first 0.4 mile), leashed dogs, mountain bikers (first 0.4 mile)
SEASON: Year-round
PASSES/FEES: Discover Pass
MAPS: Green Trails Map 142 for Index
PARK HOURS: 8am–dusk daily
CONTACT: Wallace Falls State Park, 360/793-0420, http://parks.state.wa.us

I n the woods just outside Gold Bar, the Wallace River draws day hikers of every ilk as it makes three dramatic plunges during its 15-mile journey to the Skykomish River. Featuring quiet lakes, old-growth forest, campsites, and cabins, 1,380-acre Wallace Falls State Park would be popular without its namesake falls. Nevertheless, the 265-foot cascade tops most visitors' to-do list.

START THE HIKE

▸ **MILE 0-0.5: Woody Trailhead to Small Falls Interpretive Trail**
Find the wide, flat **Woody Trail** on the east side of the parking lot and spend 0.3 mile walking under crackling power lines amid blackberries, huckleberries, and salmonberries. Before the trail bends into the woods, visit a **turnout** with views of Baring and Philadelphia Mountains and Mount Index. Over the next 0.1 mile the sound of the power lines gives way to that of the river as you arrive at an **intersection**. The wheelchair- and bike-friendly portion of this excursion ends here; hikers should go right, pass through a **wooden gate,** and descend toward the river. Pass the short Small Falls Interpretive Trail in another 0.1 mile, as you wander under a canopy of red cedar, western hemlock, and Douglas fir.

▸ **MILE 0.5-1.8: Small Falls Interpretive Trail to Picnic Area**
Two side trails leading to the multiuse Greg Ball Trail are on the left at 0.5 and 1 mile beyond the Small Falls spur. Continue straight both times and,

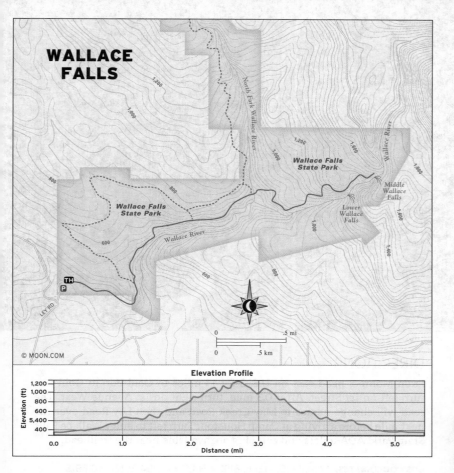

WALLACE FALLS

Wallace Falls State Park

Wallace Falls State Park

North Fork Wallace River

Wallace River

Wallace River

Middle Wallace Falls

Lower Wallace Falls

TH

P

LEY RD

0   .5 mi
0   .5 km

© MOON.COM

Elevation Profile

Elevation (ft)

1,200
1,000
800
600
5,400
400

0.0   1.0   2.0   3.0   4.0   5.0

Distance (mi)

after the second, descend to a **wooden bridge** spanning the North Fork Wallace River. The trail's first climbing of any significance awaits across the bridge, but don't worry: The climb is short and in 0.3 mile you'll arrive at a covered **picnic area** perfect for a break.

▶ **MILE 1.8–2.6: Picnic Area to Upper Falls Overlook**
The **lower falls viewing area** is 0.3 mile farther. Watch the river careen over cliffs at what's arguably the most impressive of the viewing areas. Scan the treetops and sky for bald eagles.

There's more to see, but the trail makes you work for these views. Climb (more steeply now) through the trees 0.3 mile to a view of the Skykomish Valley and the Olympics. Then continue 0.2 mile to the **upper falls overlook**.

You can extend your trip by exploring more of the park's 12 miles of trails, but retrace your steps for the most direct route back to the parking lot.

▲ WALLACE FALLS

DIRECTIONS

From Monroe, head east on U.S. 2 for 13 miles to Gold Bar. In Gold Bar, turn left on 1st Street. After 0.3 mile, turn right on 1st Avenue West. The road will change names to May Creek Road and then Ley Road over the next mile before arriving at Camp Houston. Turn left to enter Wallace Falls State Park. ADA toilets and camping are available near the trailhead.

GPS COORDINATES: 47.866990, -121.678192 / N47° 52.0194′ W121° 40.6915′

BEST NEARBY BITES

For many who love to the play in the mountains along U.S. 2, the **Sultan Bakery** (711 W. Stevens Ave., Sultan, 360/793-7996, 5:15am-7pm daily) is synonymous with the region. Start your adventure with a breakfast pastry or cap it with a large sandwich built on soft, fresh bread. Or do both. From the trailhead, the 7-mile drive west takes 14 minutes via U.S. 2.

Relax at the edge of a lake shimmering beneath the rocky slopes of Mount Index after visiting a massive seven-tiered waterfall.

BEST: Waterfall Hikes

DISTANCE: 8.2 miles round-trip

DURATION: 5 hours

ELEVATION CHANGE: 2,500 feet

EFFORT: Moderate

TRAIL: Dirt, steps, slippery rocks

USERS: Hikers, leashed dogs

SEASON: May-November

PASSES/FEES: Northwest Forest Pass

MAPS: Green Trails Map 142 for Index

CONTACT: Mount Baker-Snoqualmie National Forest, Skykomish Ranger District, 360/677-2414

Located just south of U.S. 2 and the confluence of the Skykomish River's north and south forks, this hike is ideal for people who love alpine lakes and giant waterfalls. In fact, one of the beauties of this trip is you don't have to venture all the way to the lake to be blown away. A round-trip to Bridal Veil Falls is 4.2 miles, a trip to the lake and back is 7.4 miles, and visiting both is 8.2 miles.

START THE HIKE

▶ **MILE 0-2.1: Old Logging Trail to Bridal Veil Falls**

From the parking lot, head south on an **old logging trail**. Pass alders, maples, Douglas firs, and hemlocks and step over creeks flowing toward the South Fork Skykomish over the next 1.7 miles. After descending some steps, turn right on the **spur for Bridal Veil Falls**. It's just 0.4 mile farther, but the way is steep and includes several sections of stairs. On warm summer days you might appreciate the spray from the falls as you arrive at the viewing areas. Other days, you might wish you packed a raincoat. Bridal Veil Creek fans out on the cliffs as it splashes down from Lake Serene. The falls drop nearly 1,300 feet over seven tiers. The entirety of the falls is too much to take in from any one spot, but you'll have no problem finding an impressive vantage point. Just be careful on the slippery rocks.

▶ **MILE 2.1-4.5: Bridal Veil Falls to Bridal Veil Falls Bridge and Lake Serene**

When you're finished marveling at the force of nature, descend 0.4 mile back to the **junction**. Turn right and, after 0.2 mile, cross the **Bridal Veil Falls bridge** to continue to Lake Serene. The most significant bit of climbing sits

Lake Serene and Bridal Veil Falls

CENTRAL CASCADES

135

LAKE SERENE AND
BRIDAL VEIL FALLS

▲ MOUNT INDEX

between the bridge and the lake. Spend 1.8 miles climbing **switchbacks** up 1,500 feet until the lake's stunning beauty finally comes into view.

▶ MILE 4.5-8.2: Lake Serene to Parking Lot

Lake Serene mirrors Index's sheer rock walls and invites you to stay and relax. Early in the season, when snow and ice still cling to the imposing cliffs of Mount Index, it's not uncommon for serenity to be interrupted by a loud crack as avalanches rumble down the slopes on the other side of the lake.

Despite this occasional drama, Lake Serene lives up to its name, even when it draws a crowd. Find room to sit on a shoreline boulder and do your own reflecting at the north end of the lake, where the path leads over the lake's outlet and passes a short spur trail leading to a view of the valley. When you've had your fill of serenity, ready your knees for the downhill return via the same trail.

DIRECTIONS

From Monroe, drive east for 20 miles on U.S. 2 and turn right on Mount Index Road just before a steel bridge crossing the South Fork Skykomish River. Drive 0.3 mile and turn right to access the parking lot. Vault toilets are in the parking lot.

GPS COORDINATES: 47.809189, –121.573693 / N47° 48.5513′ W121° 34.4216′

Lake Serene and Bridal Veil Falls

CENTRAL CASCADES

🦌 ❄ 🐾 🚶

Follow a family-friendly path along a creek to Barclay Lake at the foot of Baring Mountain.

DISTANCE: 4.4 miles round-trip
DURATION: 2.5 hours
ELEVATION CHANGE: 550 feet
EFFORT: Easy/moderate
TRAIL: Single track
USERS: Hikers, leashed dogs
SEASON: April–November
PASSES/FEES: Northwest Forest Pass
MAPS: Green Trails Map 143 for Monte Cristo
CONTACT: Mount Baker–Snoqualmie National Forest, Skykomish Ranger District, 360/677-2414, www.fs.usda.gov

START THE HIKE

If solitude is what you seek, consider saving this popular hike for a weekday in mid-spring or mid-fall.

▶ MILE 0–1.2: Parking Lot to Bridge

Starting from the southeast end of the parking lot, the trail dives immediately into the shade provided by a forest recovering from a previous clearcut. The path has mellow ups and downs as it follows Barclay Creek to the lake, but it is friendly for legs of all ages and is popular with backpackers, anglers, and families.

Walk among the cedars, Douglas firs, and western hemlocks on a path lined by salmonberry, ferns, and moss. After 1.2 miles reach a large **footlog bridge** with a handrail. Cross the creek and find the most substantial—but still gentle—climb.

BARCLAY LAKE ▶

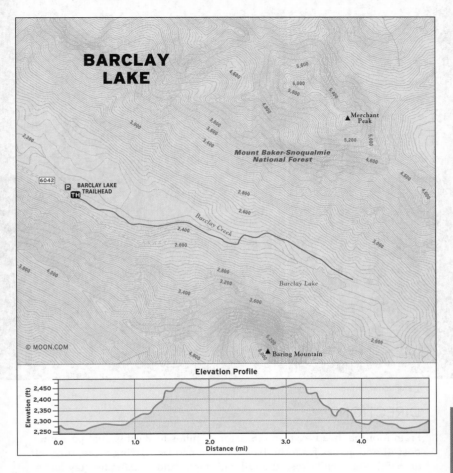

© MOON.COM

▶ MILE 1.2-1.7: Bridge to Barclay Lake

The incline won't slow you much, but the view might stop you in your tracks. Just a few hundred yards past the bridge, 6,129-foot Baring Mountain comes into view through the trees on the right side of the trail. At 0.5 mile past the bridge, get your first view of the blue waters of **Barclay Lake** glistening in the sunlight.

▶ MILE 1.7-2.2: Barclay Lake to Picnic Areas

While the trail continues for another 0.5 mile along the lake to a large camping spot and a spur trail leading to a vault toilet, you need not travel that far to find a spot to stop. Any of the trailside spots accessing the lake are ideal for picnicking, taking a dip, and enjoying Baring's towering splendor. This is a good place to introduce kids to alpine lake fishing. The lake is open year-round for rainbow trout fishing.

When you're finished playing at the lake, simply retrace your steps to return to the trailhead.

▲ BARING MOUNTAIN

DIRECTIONS

From Monroe, head east on U.S. 2 for 27 miles to Baring. Just past mile-post 41 and across from the Bavarian-themed Der Baring Store, turn left on 635th Place NE. Cross the railroad tracks and in 0.3 mile stay left as the road becomes Forest Road 6024. Continue 3.9 miles to the trailhead. A privy is located at the small parking area.

GPS COORDINATES: 47.792468, -121.459345 / N47°47.5481 W121°27.5607

BEST NEARBY BITES

Adam's Northwest Bistro & Brewery (104 N. Lewis St., Monroe, 360/794-4056, www.adamsnwbistro.com, hours vary) is a relaxed bistro serving local, sustainable foods. Chef Adam Hoffman left Seattle's fine-dining scene to open the restaurant, where bacon, salmon, and brisket are smoked in-house and the beer is brewed on-site. From the trailhead, the 30-mile drive northwest takes about 50 minutes via U.S. 2.

4 Iron Goat Trail

STEVENS PASS

Hear modern trains chugging over Stevens Pass while exploring the remnants
of the old Great Northern Railway

DISTANCE: 5.9 miles round-trip
DURATION: 3.5 hours
ELEVATION CHANGE: 800 feet
EFFORT: Easy/moderate
TRAIL: Dirt, boardwalk, short paved section
USERS: Hikers, wheelchair users, leashed dogs
SEASON: Late May–November
PASSES/FEES: Northwest Forest Pass
MAPS: Green Trails Map 176 for Stevens Pass
CONTACT: Mount Baker–Snoqualmie National Forest, Skykomish Ranger
District, 360/677-2414

I n 1893, when the Great Northern Railway pushed its way over Stevens
Pass and linked Seattle to Saint Paul, Minnesota, it was considered an
epic feat of engineering. Today, thanks to an epic feat of volunteering,
the remains of the route make for a riveting walking history lesson.

START THE HIKE

▶ **MILE 0-0.1: Red Caboose to Windy Crossover Trail Junction**
Starting from the **red caboose** at the **Iron Goat Trail Interpretive Site,** follow
a gentle uphill grade into the woods, continuing straight past the Windy
Crossover trail you'll use to finish this loop. This ADA-friendly section of
the trail is unpaved (after a short, paved stretch near the parking lot) and
surprisingly narrow considering its history.

▶ **MILE 0.1-0.3: Windy Crossover Trail Junction to Cement Wall**
In 0.2 mile (past the first of several white signs marked with the old rail
line mileage), reach the first long, tall **cement wall** lining the trail. The
walls, surreal in this natural setting, are remnants of snowsheds that covered the tracks and protected trains from avalanches. The trail is lined
with ferns, wildflowers, huckleberries, and nettles and is a good place to
view owls, woodpeckers, jays, and other birds, but it's the relics of the past
that set this hike apart.

▶ **MILE 0.3-1.8: Cement Wall to Twin Tunnels and Railroad Tie Bridge**
In 1 mile visit an **overlook** with a view of the current railway. A few steps
farther bring you to the **Twin Tunnels,** blasted through the granite in 1916.
You can't walk through these tunnels, but you can step inside and read
an interpretive sign. The trail skirts the tunnels and, over the next 0.2

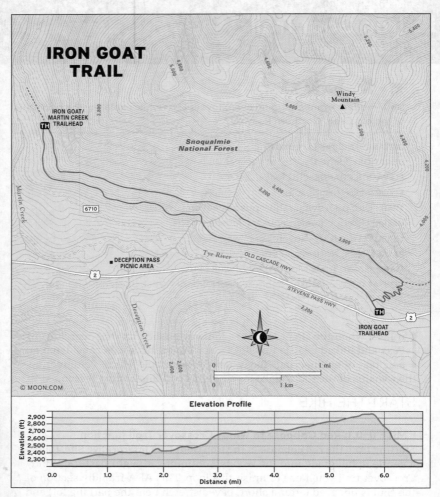

IRON GOAT
TRAIL

Iron Goat/
Martin Creek
Trailhead TH

Snoqualmie
National Forest

Windy
Mountain ▲

6710

DECEPTION PASS
PICNIC AREA

Tye River   OLD CASCADE HWY

Martin Creek

Deception Creek

STEVENS PASS HWY

2 200

IRON GOAT
TRAILHEAD TH

0   1 mi
0   1 km

© MOON.COM

Elevation Profile

mile, uses a **boardwalk** to pass through a narrow gulch. Cross a **bridge** made of railroad ties 0.1 mile farther. Go another 0.2 mile and you might feel a draft of cold air as you pass an adit (one of the tunnel's small ventilation shafts).

▶ MILE 1.8-3: Railroad Tie Bridge to Martin Creek Crossover

After 1 mile, near the Martin Creek trailhead, the ADA portion of the journey comes to an end as you turn right on the **Martin Creek Crossover** and ascend 0.2 mile to the upper portion of loop. At the mouth of **Tunnel 14,** turn right to follow a rougher, but still easily manageable dirt path. Pass salmonberries and ferns growing beneath Douglas fir and hemlock. Parts of the trail are overgrown, so take care to avoid tripping on unseen hazards.

▲ BRIDGE ON IRON GOAT TRAIL

▸ **MILE 3–4.2: Martin Creek Crossover to Reservoir**
After 1.2 miles on the upper trail pass the **Spillway Spur** on the left. The trail leads to a reservoir in a ravine below Windy Mountain.

▸ **MILE 4.2–5.9: Reservoir to Parking Lot**
Continue on the upper trail 1.2 miles to the **Windy Point Tunnel**. To finish the loop, turn right on the **Windy Crossover trail**. In a steep, switchbacking 0.5-mile stretch you'll give back all the vertical you slowly accumulated during your walk.

Turn left at the intersection toward the bottom to return to the parking lot.

DIRECTIONS

From Monroe, follow U.S. 2 east 43 miles to the Iron Goat Interpretive Site, located on the left side of the road about 9 miles east of Skykomish. Toilets, interpretive signs, and an old caboose are located at the trailhead.

GPS COORDINATES: 47.711262, –121.161761 / N47° 42.6757' W121° 9.7057'

BEST NEARBY BITES

Zeke's Drive-In (43918 U.S. 2, Gold Bar, 360/793-2287, 11am-7:30pm Mon.-Wed., 11am-8pm Thurs.-Sun.) opened in 1968 and is still a popular roadside burger stop. Menu highlights include two dozen flavors of shakes and the half-pound Honeymoon Special burger. From the trailhead, the 27-mile drive northwest takes about 30 minutes via U.S. 2.

5

Colchuck Lake

ALPINE LAKES WILDERNESS

Sample the granite grandeur of the Enchantments on a rugged trail climbing to one of the Northwest's most stunning alpine lakes.

BEST: Brew Hikes
DISTANCE: 8.2 miles round-trip
DURATION: 4.5 hours
ELEVATION CHANGE: 2,300 feet
EFFORT: Moderate
TRAIL: Roots, rocks, bridge, footlog
USERS: Hikers
SEASON: July–October
PASSES/FEES: Northwest Forest Pass; free day-use pass available at trailhead
MAPS: Green Trails Map 209S for The Enchantments
CONTACT: Okanogan-Wenatchee National Forest, Wenatchee River Ranger District, 509/548-2550, www.fs.usda.gov

As this trail dives immediately into dense forest, it's not obvious why the Enchantments are one of the most beloved hiking destinations in Washington. But it will all make sense when you reach the deep-blue water of Colchuck Lake reflecting the granite spires of Dragontail and Colchuck Peaks.

START THE HIKE

▶ **MILE 0-2.4: Stuart Lake Trail to Colchuck Lake Trail**
Each party is required to register at the trailhead kiosk and carry a free permit. Paperwork complete, follow the Stuart Lake Trail as it climbs gradually along Mountaineer Creek. Even when you can't see the creek, its burble keeps you company as you wander the thick forest and its pine trees and boulders the size of RVs. In 1.6 miles, cross the creek on a **footlog,** after which the trail steepens and the forest thins. Catch an occasional glimpse of the steep valley walls over the next 0.8 mile before arriving at a well-marked intersection; turn left on the Colchuck Lake Trail to keep climbing toward the lake.

▶ **MILE 2.4-4.1: Colchuck Lake Trail to Boulders**
In 0.1 mile use a **bridge** to cross Mountaineer Creek to a boulder field. Follow the path as it bends right and winds through the boulders, running briefly along the creek before reentering the forest and resuming the ascent. Over the next 1.6 miles the trail ascends **granite slopes** offering occasional views of the valley. The trail is rooted and rocky, adding to the challenge, but the payoff is well worth the effort.

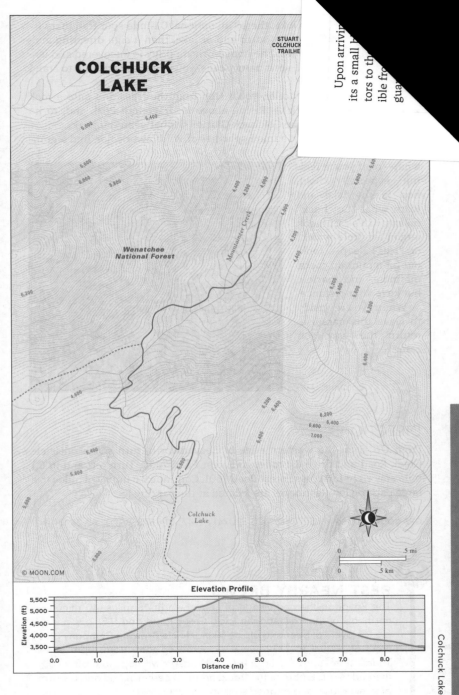

COLCHUCK LAKE

STUART
COLCHUCK
TRAILHE

Wenatchee
National Forest

Mountaineer Creek

5,000
5,400
5,600
6,000
5,800
6,200
4,400
4,200
4,000
4,200
4,400
5,200
5,400
5,600
6,200
6,400
5,800
4,600
6,200
6,400
5,400
5,600
5,400
5,800
5,600
5,800
6,200
6,400
6,600
7,000
6,800

Colchuck
Lake

Upon arrivin
its a small h
tors to th
ible fro
gua

© MOON.COM

0   .5 mi
0   .5 km

Elevation Profile

Distance (mi)									
0.0	1.0	2.0	3.0	4.0	5.0	6.0	7.0	8.0	

Elevation (ft): 5,500 / 5,000 / 4,500 / 4,000 / 3,500

...g at the **lake**, there's an optional 0.1-mile spur trail that vis-
...lue pool at the north end of lake, then a sign directing visi-
...e Colchuck toilet. The not-so-private privy is uncovered and vis-
...m the main trail, so, if nature calls, you might ask a friend to stand
...d.

Minutes beyond the toilet, you'll step from the trees and onto a rock slope overlooking the lake. Rising above is Dragontail Peak and, to its right, Colchuck Peak. The Colchuck Glacier sits between the peaks.

Explore the shoreline, admire splashes of wildflower color, find a granite slab and lie out for a nap—or, if you're feeling especially bold, hop in the lake and learn what "Colchuck" means. (It's Chinook jargon for "cold water" or "ice.") Keep a lookout for mountain goats, marmots, and marten, but keep your distance.

When you're ready to leave this paradise, return the way you came.

COLCHUCK LAKE ▸

DIRECTIONS

From U.S. 2 on the western edge of Leavenworth, turn south on Icicle Creek Road and drive 8.4 miles to Forest Road 7600. Turn left and in 0.1 mile stay right to access Forest Road 7601. Continue 3.6 unpaved miles to a large parking lot. Restrooms are located at the parking lot.

GPS COORDINATES: 47.527788, –120.820741 / N47° 31.6673′ W120° 49.2445′

BEST NEARBY BREWS

The Bavarian-themed village of Leavenworth, 13 miles (40 minutes) northeast of the trailhead via Icicle Creek Road and U.S. 2, is a utopia for lovers of beer and alpine hiking. **Icicle Brewing Company** (935 Front St., 509/548-2739, www.iciclebrewing.com, 11am-10pm Sun.-Thurs., 11am-11pm Fri.-Sat.) uses Yakima-grown hops to craft locally themed beers. Embrace the "fauxvarian" experience and add a warm pretzel or *landjaeger* (dried sausage) to your order.

6

Talapus and Olallie Lakes

ALPINE LAKES WILDERNESS

Take a dip in chilly Talapus or Olallie Lake at the end of a recently reconstructed family-friendly trail.

DISTANCE: 5.6 miles round-trip
DURATION: 3 hours
ELEVATION CHANGE: 1,250 feet
EFFORT: Moderate
TRAIL: New dirt paths, roots, boardwalk
USERS: Hikers, leashed dogs
SEASON: Mid-May–early November
PASSES/FEES: Northwest Forest Pass
MAPS: Green Trails Map 207 for Snoqualmie Pass
CONTACT: Mount Baker-Snoqualmie National Forest, Snoqualmie Ranger District, 425/888-1421, www.fs.usda.gov

The trail starts at the far end of the undersized parking lot, but odds are you'll start by walking a section of the dirt road if you don't arrive early on summer weekends. The shimmering lakes and relatively easy trail draw a crowd and it's not uncommon for parked cars to line the side of the road for a quarter mile or more. But as is the case with popular trails, there's good reason for the crowds.

START THE HIKE

▸ MILE 0-0.2: Parking Lot to Talapus Lake Trail

The **Talapus Lake Trail** is wide as it dives from the parking lot into a forest of Douglas fir. At 0.2 mile those with a keen eye and good memory might notice something is different: The Washington Trails Association, a legion of hardworking volunteers, unveiled a new section of trail here in 2017. The new route climbs gradually through the trees as it enters the Alpine Lakes Wilderness. The trail is made wide enough to handle heavy traffic while maintaining a route that's relatively easy to follow.

▸ MILE 0.2-1.7: Talapus Lake Trail to Talapus Lake

Walk 1.3 miles along gurgling **Talapus Creek** to an intersection with a sign pointing the way to the lakes. Go right to stay on the trail and cross a **footbridge** moments before arriving at **Talapus Lake,** 0.2 mile beyond the intersection.

▸ MILE 1.7-2.8: Talapus Lake to Olallie Lake

An obvious open space below the trail at 17.4-acre Talapus Lake is where most hikers stop. Hikers take turns posing for pictures on shoreline logs while others scout places to swim. The trail continues to the right of the lake and climbs gradually on rougher, root-strewn tread. After 0.8 mile

Talapus and Olallie Lakes

CENTRAL CASCADES

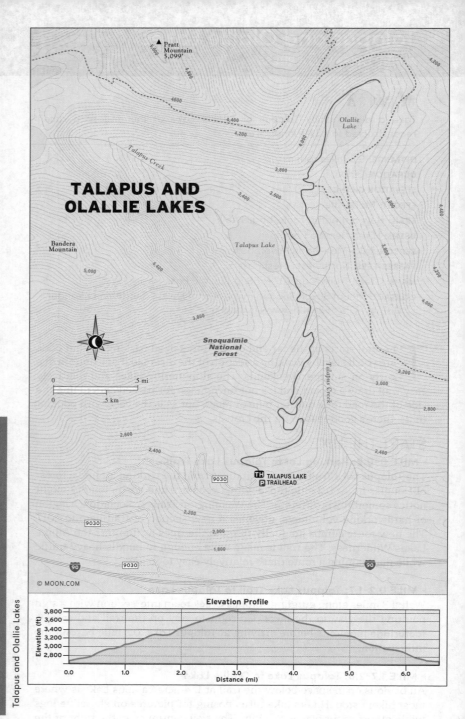

▲ TALAPUS LAKE

reach a **signed intersection** pointing the way to Olallie and Pratt Lakes. (Pratt is an option for extending your hike by about 6 miles round-trip.)

Turn left to follow the spur trail to **Olallie Lake.** In 0.3 mile, the 13.2-acre lake comes into view through the trees. A bit farther, a trailside clearing on the right offers access to the shoreline. This is a good place for day hikers to call their destination, but the trail does continue. A side trail to a toilet is a few steps farther, and campsites are available as the trail continues to the north end of the lake. Kids can take a dip in the lakes that by late summer are warm by Alpine Lakes Wilderness standards. (To be clear, that's still pretty chilly.) Fishing is permitted at both lakes and the state Department of Fish and Wildlife sometimes stocks Talapus with rainbow trout.

However you choose to enjoy the wilderness lakes, when it's time to go retrace your steps to the trailhead.

DIRECTIONS

From Seattle, follow I-90 east to exit 45. Turn left and follow Forest Road 9030 for 0.9 mile to an intersection with Mason Lake Road. Turn right to stay on Forest Road 9030 and continue 2.3 miles to the small parking lot. A vault toilet is located at the trailhead.

GPS COORDINATES: 47.401160, –121.518412 / N47° 24.0696' W122° 31.1047'

Granite Mountain

MOUNT BAKER-SNOQUALMIE NATIONAL FOREST

🦌 ❀ 🐾

Test your fitness and reward yourself with a sweeping view of the Cascades from an old fire lookout.

BEST: Fall Hikes
DISTANCE: 8.6 miles round-trip
DURATION: 5 hours
ELEVATION CHANGE: 3,800 feet
EFFORT: Strenuous
TRAIL: Dirt and rock trail
USERS: Hikers, leashed dogs
SEASON: Late June-early November
PASSES/FEES: Northwest Forest Pass
MAPS: Green Trails Map 207 for Snoqualmie Pass
CONTACT: Mount Baker-Snoqualmie National Forest, Snoqualmie Ranger District, 425/888-1421, www.fs.usda.gov

A classic hike for those who like their fall colors with a side of thigh burn, the route climbs relentlessly from I-90 to one of the best views on the Snoqualmie Pass corridor.

START THE HIKE

▶ **MILE 0-1: Pratt Lake Trailhead to Granite Mountain Trail**

Starting on the north side of the parking lot, follow the **Pratt Lake Trail** as it tilts upward, making sweeping switchbacks. After 1 mile, turn right on the **Granite Mountain Trail** (the Pratt Lake Trail continues straight).

▶ **MILE 1-2.4: Granite Mountain Trail to Meadow**

Granite Mountain Trail heads northeast for 0.4 mile before the switchbacks tighten and the assault on the valley wall gets more challenging. The trail pops in and out of the trees, offering glimpses of changing leaves if you visit in the fall. These open areas are an appreciated dose of variety, but the slopes bring an element of danger in early spring when snow and ice sometime linger high on the mountain. Granite Mountain is prone to avalanches; early-season hikers should have experience, proper equipment, and the latest avalanche forecasts (www.nwac.us).

After another 1 mile of switchbacks, start reaping the reward for your work as you step out of the trees. The **meadow** yields huckleberries and views of the valley and surrounding peaks. This is also where fall colors are most dazzling.

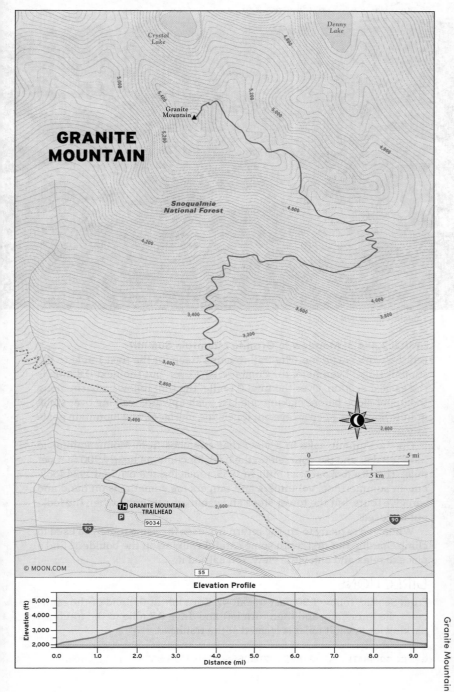

▲ GRANITE MOUNTAIN

▶ MILE 2.4–4.3: Meadow to Granite Mountain Summit

But the work isn't done. The trail remains steep for the next 1 mile to the summit ridge. Even here, the climbing isn't over, but the next 0.8 mile is the easiest section. Over the final 0.1 mile, the trail follows a basin along the upper slope before making one last push upward, walking over small granite boulders. Keep an eye out for eagles, marmots, and mountain goats as you hike.

On the summit, take in a view that stretches from Mount Rainier to Mount Baker and pat yourself on the back for climbing nearly 900 feet per mile. The **fire lookout** was built in 1955, replacing the original 1924 lookout. In summertime, volunteers and rangers are sometimes on hand and can give tours, but the tower steps and cabin are off-limits when the lookout is closed.

When you're ready to go, the return trip uses the same route you used to climb Granite. But first, with some careful walking on the boulders, find a place to relax and enjoy the view. You earned it.

DIRECTIONS

From Seattle, follow I-90 east to exit 47. Turn left at the end of the ramp, cross the interstate, and then turn left and drive 0.3 mile to the trailhead parking lot. A vault toilet is located at the trailhead.

GPS COORDINATES: 47.397826, –121.486560 / N48° 23.8696′ W121° 29.1936′

Hike the most popular trail in the Alpine Lakes Wilderness to a lake reflecting jagged Cascade peaks.

DISTANCE: 6.8 miles round-trip
DURATION: 3.5 hours
ELEVATION CHANGE: 1,800 feet
EFFORT: Moderate
TRAIL: Rocks, dirt trail
USERS: Hikers, leashed dogs
SEASON: Late June–early November
PASSES/FEES: Northwest Forest Pass
MAPS: Green Trails Map 207 for Snoqualmie Pass
CONTACT: Mount Baker-Snoqualmie National Forest, Snoqualmie Ranger District, 425/888-1421, www.fs.usda.gov

On sunny summer weekends, the large parking lot at Alpental ski area is nearly as packed as it is on powder days in winter. There are 615 miles of trails and more than 700 lakes in the Alpine Lakes Wilderness, and none receive more visitors than Snow Lake and its namesake trail. The steep, jagged faces of Roosevelt and Chair Peaks reflect in the 152.9-acre lake, creating the setting that lures so many.

START THE HIKE

▶ **MILE 0-1.7: Alpental Parking Lot to Source Lake Spur Trail**
Start with a quick climb up crib steps across the street from the northeast corner of the Alpental parking lot, then ascend gradually while traversing a slope above the South Fork Snoqualmie River.

For 1.7 miles pass through forest and cross avalanche chutes on your way to the intersection with the **Source Lake spur trail**. It's a gentle and peaceful walk in the summer, but winter avalanches have killed snowshoers on this trail.

▶ **MILE 1.7-2.4: Source Lake Spur Trail to Snow Lake Ridge**
At the intersection, turn right for 0.7 mile of **switchbacks** climbing to a ridge above Snow Lake. A sign bolted to a ridge-top tree welcomes visitors to the wilderness area. The ridge separates the watersheds of the south and middle forks of the Snoqualmie.

▶ **MILE 2.4-3.1: Snow Lake Ridge to Snow Lake Vista**
A quick trip to the left offers a view of the lake, but going right and staying on the trail delivers a stunning vista just as quickly. The next 0.7 mile descends almost 400 feet to the lake. A spur trail to the right leads to a pit toilet with a view of Snow Lake.

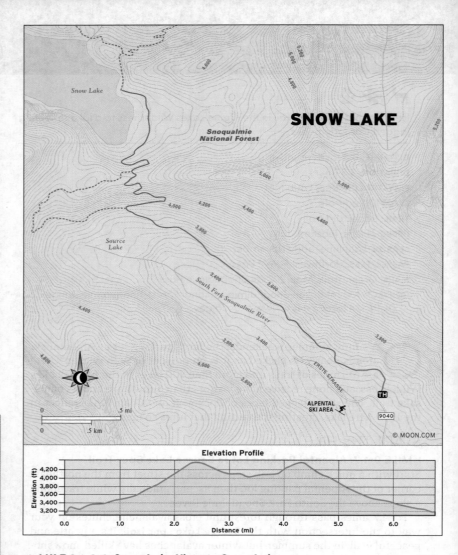

▶ MILE 3.1–3.4: Snow Lake Vista to Snow Lake

Follow the path along the edge of the lake for 0.25 mile to a large **open area**
overlooking the lake. Too glorious a spot to allow any one party to claim as
a campsite, this is a designated day-use area. Take a dip in the cold water
if you're feeling courageous or drop a line and try to land a rainbow trout.
Just know that the fishing is notoriously slow—views and mosquitoes are
the only sure things at Snow Lake.

Make the return trip via the same trail you used to access this Cascade
paradise.

▲ TRAIL TO SNOW LAKE

DIRECTIONS

From Seattle, follow I-90 east to Snoqualmie Pass and exit 52. Turn left on Highway 509, and in 0.2 mile continue straight on Erste Strasse. Continue 1.25 miles to the Alpental ski area parking lot. The well-marked trail starts across the road north of the parking lot. Vault toilets are located across the road from the trailhead.

GPS COORDINATES: 47.445273, −121.423740 / N47° 26.7164′ W121° 25.4244′

BEST NEARBY BITES AND BONUS

Located at the base of the Summit at Snoqualmie ski hills, **The Commonwealth** (10 Pass Life Way No. 1, Snoqualmie Pass, 425/434-0808, www.commonwealth906.com, hours vary) serves up locally sourced food. The 906 Burger is topped with white cheddar cheese, garlic aioli, and longhorn beef raised 50 miles down the road in Ellensburg. After you eat, head next door to check out Debbie Armstrong's 1984 Olympic gold medal at the **Washington State Ski & Snowboard Museum** (www.wsssm.org, free admission). From the trailhead, the 5.5-mile drive northeast takes 8 minutes via I-90.

Snow Lake

Palouse to Cascades State Park Trail: Snoqualmie Tunnel

SNOQUALMIE PASS

Delve into darkness while exploring a 2.3-mile-long retired railroad tunnel running under a ski area and the Pacific Crest Trail.

DISTANCE: 5.2 miles round-trip
DURATION: 3 hours
ELEVATION CHANGE: Negligible
EFFORT: Easy/moderate
TRAIL: Wide dirt trail through a dark tunnel
USERS: Hikers, wheelchair users, leashed dogs, mountain bikers, horseback riders
SEASON: May-October
PASSES/FEES: Discover Pass
MAPS: Green Trails Map 207 for Snoqualmie Pass
PARK HOURS: 6:30am-dusk daily
CONTACT: Lake Easton State Park, 509/656-2230, http://parks.state.wa.us

There are three things you can count on when exploring the 1914 Snoqualmie Tunnel: a cool escape from the summer heat, terrible views, and a hike unlike any other in Washington.

START THE HIKE

▶ **MILE 0-0.3: Cascades State Park Trailhead to Snoqualmie Tunnel**
The Palouse to Cascades State Park Trail runs along the west side of the parking lot. Turn right (north) on the trail previously known as the John Wayne Pioneer/Iron Horse State Park trail before it was renamed in 2018. The trail uses the right-of-way of the defunct Chicago, Milwaukee, St. Paul and Pacific Railroad (commonly referred to as the Milwaukee Road).

Reach the **tunnel** from the trailhead in a matter of minutes. It's just 0.3 mile until you're standing in front of the giant opening with huge doors on either side. A cool wind blows

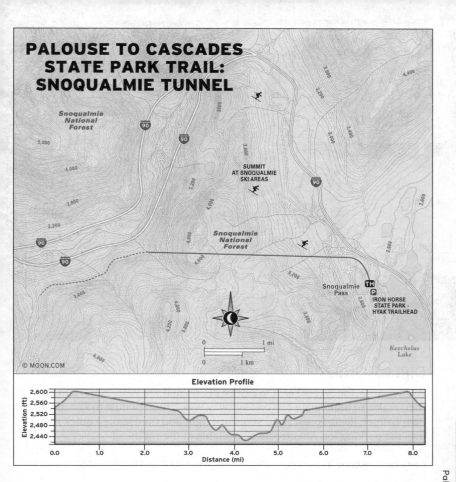

PALOUSE TO CASCADES STATE PARK TRAIL: SNOQUALMIE TUNNEL

© MOON.COM

Elevation Profile

from the tunnel. It's always chilly inside and sometimes moisture drips from the ceiling, so a jacket is a good idea.

Strong primary and secondary light sources are a must, not just so you can see where you're going, but so others can see you.

▶ **MILE 0.3–2.6: Snoqualmie Tunnel to Pacific Crest Trail Underpass**
Scan the walls with your headlamp as you walk, and notice the pinprick of light in the distance: That's the end of the tunnel 2.3 miles away and it's not as close as it looks. While there's not much to see, it's interesting to think about what's above you. You're cutting under part of the state's most popular ski area (Summit at Snoqualmie) and, toward the west end, you'll pass under the Pacific Crest Trail.

▶ **MILE 2.6–5.2: Pacific Crest Trail Underpass
to Cascades State Park Trailhead**
When your eyes adjust to the light after emerging from the far end of the tunnel, find a picnic table and a pit toilet. Relax here for a bit before returning the way you came.

▲ THE SNOQUALMIE TUNNEL

DIRECTIONS

From Seattle, follow I-90 east to exit 54 at Snoqualmie Pass. Turn right and then make an immediate left on Highway 906. Drive 0.4 mile to Keechelus Boat Launch Road/Forest Road 906. Turn right and then make a quick right into the parking lot. A restroom is available at the trailhead.

GPS COORDINATES: 47.391495, –121.392616 / N47° 23.4897' W121° 23.557'

BEST NEARBY BREWS

Hikers at mile 2,393 of the 2,650-mile Pacific Crest Trail must think it's a mirage: a brewery just a third of a mile off the trail. **Dru Bru** (10 Pass Life Way, Snoqualmie Pass, 425/434-0700, hours vary) uses Snoqualmie Pass water and Yakima-grown hops to craft a variety of European-inspired beers, but it doesn't serve food. Visitors are welcome to bring their own or have it delivered. From the trailhead, the 3-mile drive north takes 6 minutes via Highway 906.

Experience the striking contrast of golden larches against cobalt sky during a fall hike to an alpine pool cradled in a granite basin.

BEST: Fall Hikes
DISTANCE: 9.6 miles round-trip
DURATION: 4.5 hours
ELEVATION CHANGE: 2,700 feet
EFFORT: Moderate/strenuous
TRAIL: Dirt, scree, short scramble over boulders
USERS: Hikers
SEASON: July–October
PASSES/FEES: Northwest Forest Pass
MAPS: Green Trails Map 209 for Mount Stuart
CONTACT: Okanogan–Wenatchee National Forest, Cle Elum Ranger District, 509/852-1100, www.fs.usda.gov

Fall color zealots call it Larch Madness. It comes each autumn when these conifers create a golden spectacle so breathtaking it overshadows even the sight of a jagged peak mirrored in an alpine lake. Such is the case with the trail leading to Lake Ingalls. Even with a generous parking lot, cars line the roadside for over a mile on October weekends (summer weekends are busy, too). Arrive before sunrise for the best chance at finding a parking spot and long stretches of solitude on the trail.

START THE HIKE

▶ MILE 0–1.6: Trailhead Kiosk to Ingalls Way Trail

The North Fork Teanaway River cascades past the parking lot and Esmerelda Peaks rise above, setting the tone for a memorable hike. Start next to a trailhead kiosk reminding hikers that dogs aren't permitted beyond the wilderness boundary. Follow the **Esmerelda Basin Trail** above the river for 0.3 mile before turning right on **Ingalls Way Trail**. Trees and grass soon give way to scree over the next 1.3 miles as you climb to a junction. Continue straight (right leads to Longs Pass).

▶ MILE 1.6–3.6: Ingalls Way Trail to Ingalls Pass and Alpine Lakes Wilderness

The dirt trail follows the contour of the slope as it climbs at a gradual grade, the view of the surrounding peaks and Teanaway River basin growing more spectacular the higher you go. Finally, 1.7 miles beyond the Longs Pass junction, Mount Rainier appears to the southwest. Continue upward another 0.3 mile, a few switchbacks mitigating the steepness, to Ingalls Pass and the Alpine Lakes Wilderness.

CENTRAL CASCADES

Lake Ingalls

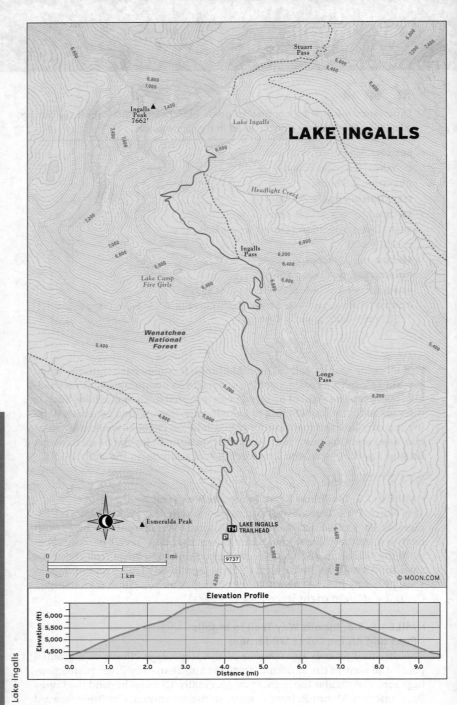

▲ LARCHES NEAR INGALLS LAKE

▶ MILE 3.6-4.8: Ingalls Pass and Alpine Lakes Wilderness to Ingalls Lake

Here, nature somehow turns the scenery dial up to 11. On the opposite side of the pass, larches dot the granite slopes of Headlight Basin and the Stuart Range's majestic namesake juts skyward in the distance. At an intersection on the pass, continue straight. The trail to the right shaves 0.25 mile off the trip to the lake but requires descending and then climbing out of the basin. Instead, take the flatter route around the basin and spend the next 1 mile snapping pictures of larches, picking your way through giant boulders, and passing campsites that will inspire you to come back and stay awhile. Mountain goats frequent the area; give them plenty of space. Wildflowers add bright patches of color in the spring and early summer.

When the trails intersect again on the opposite side of the basin, step over **Headlight Creek** and make the short 0.2-mile scramble over boulders to **Ingalls Lake.** Cradled in a basin below Ingalls Peak, the peaceful lakeside setting is the perfect place to kick back on a rocky slab and take a high-country nap.

▶ MILE 4.8-9.6: Ingalls Lake to Trailhead Kiosk

The return route is the same as your approach, although early birds are bound to find the descent takes longer as you constantly step aside to yield to the ascending masses. Give them a smile and be glad you set your alarm early enough to stay ahead of the madness.

DIRECTIONS

From I-90 in Cle Elum, take exit 85. Turn left on Highway 970/Sunset Highway, cross over I-90, and turn right to stay on the highway. Drive 7.6 miles and turn left (north) on Teanaway Road. After 7.3 miles the road bends right and becomes North Fork Teanaway Road. Drive another 5.8 miles

▲ LARCHES NEAR LAKE INGALLS

and, 0.1 mile beyond Twenty-Nine Pines Campground, turn right on Forest Road 9737. Continue 1.3 miles and turn left to stay on Forest Road 9737. The road ends at the trailhead after another 8.4 miles. A restroom is located on the west side of the parking lot.

GPS COORDINATES: 47.436773, –120.937097 / N47° 26.2064′ W120° 56.2258′

BEST NEARBY BITES

Situated in one of Cle Elum's oldest buildings, **Beau's Pizza, Pasta and Steak** (124 E. 1st St., 509/674-9798, www.beauspizzaandpasta.com, hours vary) offers weary hikers a place to enjoy a post-hike pizza and local microbrew while sitting next to a large fireplace. From the trailhead, the 31-mile drive south takes 70 minutes via Forest Road 9737 and Highway 970.

NEARBY CAMPGROUNDS

NAME	DESCRIPTION	FACILITIES	SEASON	FEE
Lake Wenatchee State Park	on the shore of Lake Wenatchee, a short drive from Leavenworth	197 RV and tent sites, restrooms	year-round	$12–50

21588 State Route 207, Coles Corner, 888/226-7688, www.washington.goingtocamp.com

NAME	DESCRIPTION	FACILITIES	SEASON	FEE
Money Creek Campground	in old-growth forest near a popular swimming spot on the South Fork Skykomish River	25 tent and RV sites, restrooms	early May–mid-September	$18.19–22

Old Cascade Highway, Skykomish, Mount Baker-Snoqualmie National Forest, 877/444-6777, www.recreation.gov

NAME	DESCRIPTION	FACILITIES	SEASON	FEE
Kachess Campground	ideal for family camping, located on the northwest shore of Kachess Lake, offers easy access to hiking and boating adventures	148 RV and tent sites, restrooms	June–mid-September	$21

Kachess Lake Road, Easton, Okanogan-Wenatchee National Forest, 877/444-6777, www.recreation.gov

NAME	DESCRIPTION	FACILITIES	SEASON	FEE
Beckler River Campground	amid thick forest on the banks of the Beckler River	27 RV and tent sites, restrooms	late May–mid-September	$16.37–18.37

Beckler Road, Skykomish, Mount Baker-Snoqualmie National Forest, 877/444-6777, www.recreation.gov

NAME	DESCRIPTION	FACILITIES	SEASON	FEE
29 Pines Campground	on the North Fork Teanaway River	59 RV and tent sites, restrooms	year-round	Discover Pass

Teanaway Road, Cle Elum, Teanaway Community Forest, 509/925-8510, www.dnr.wa.gov/teanaway

SOUTH CASCADES

Stretching from the Columbia River Gorge north to U.S. 12, the South Cascades is one of the quietest parts of the range despite its explosive reputation. Mount St. Helens's gaping crater and the blast zone from its 1980 eruption give visitors experiences they're hard-pressed to duplicate anywhere else. Tucked away and hard to spot from western Washington, Mount Adams is the state's second tallest (behind Rainier) and second most isolated volcano (behind Glacier Peak). A network of forest roads deliver access to lakes, views of the volcanoes and the Goat Rocks Wilderness, a subterranean adventure in a lava tube called Ape Cave, and some of Washington's most scenic terrain.

▲ MONITOR RIDGE

▲ PACKWOOD LAKE

◄ VIEW FROM TONGUE MOUNTAIN

1 Packwood Lake
DISTANCE: 8 miles round-trip
DURATION: 4 hours
EFFORT: Moderate

2 Tongue Mountain
DISTANCE: 3 miles round-trip
DURATION: 2 hours
EFFORT: Easy/moderate

3 Harry's Ridge
DISTANCE: 8 miles round-trip
DURATION: 4 hours
EFFORT: Moderate

4 Killen Creek
DISTANCE: 6.2 miles round-trip
DURATION: 3 hours
EFFORT: Moderate

5 Ape Cave
DISTANCE: 2.9 miles round-trip
DURATION: 2 hours
EFFORT: Easy

6 Monitor Ridge to Mount St. Helens Summit
DISTANCE: 10 miles round-trip
DURATION: 8 hours
EFFORT: Strenuous

7 Lava Canyon
DISTANCE: 5.8 miles round-trip
DURATION: 3 hours
EFFORT: Moderate

SUSPENSION BRIDGE IN LAVA CANYON

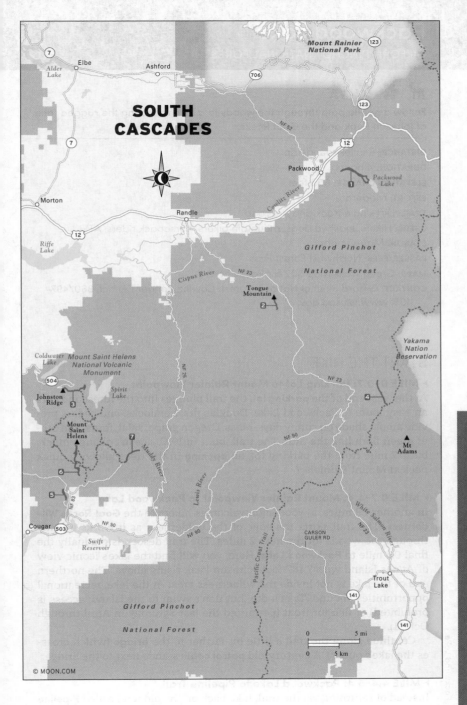

SOUTH CASCADES

167

🦌 ❀ 🐾 🚶

Follow a gentle path through the woods to a lake reflecting the rugged face of Johnson Peak and the Goat Rocks.

DISTANCE: 8 miles round-trip
DURATION: 4 hours
ELEVATION CHANGE: 600 feet
EFFORT: Moderate
TRAIL: Dirt single track and fire road
USERS: Hikers, leashed dogs, mountain bikers, horseback riders, ATVs
SEASON: May–October
PASSES/FEES: Northwest Forest Pass
MAPS: Green Trails Map 302 for Packwood
CONTACT: Gifford Pinchot National Forest, Cowlitz Ranger District, 360/497-1103, www.fs.usda.gov

START THE HIKE

▶ **MILE 0-0.7: Parking Lot to Mount Rainier Viewpoint**
At the west end of the **parking lot,** the trail plunges into the forest and cuts an easy route to Packwood Lake. Douglas firs, hemlocks, and cedars provide ample shade on sunny days. Moss, Oregon grape, salal, ferns, and other green flora line the trail. The trail, built in 1910, doesn't change much, but 0.7 mile from the parking lot, an **opening** in the trees allows a quick peek at Mount Rainier.

▶ **MILE 0.7-4.4: Mount Rainier Viewpoint to Packwood Lake**
In another 1.3 miles, a wood sign welcomes hikers to the **Goat Rocks Wilderness.** The trail skirts the edge of the wilderness as it works its way through the woods for the next 2 miles. The trail descends gradually the final 0.3 mile to **Packwood Lake.** Here, you will find the lake's iconic view of Agnes Island with 7,487-foot Johnson Peak rising above. The northern end of the lake is not inside the wilderness area. At the lake, recreational opportunities abound. Take a dip (but don't swim to the island; access is prohibited) or fish for trout (permitted the last Saturday in April through Oct. 31).

Continue along the trail a little bit farther to the **bridge** (which crosses the lake's outlet). A century-old **patrol cabin** stands next to the bridge.

▶ **MILE 4.4-5.4: Packwood Lake to Pipeline Trail**
Instead of returning via the trail, hike back on the old road called **Pipeline Trail.** From the **historic patrol cabin,** find the road running past the dam. When hiking in this direction the road offers more to see than the upper

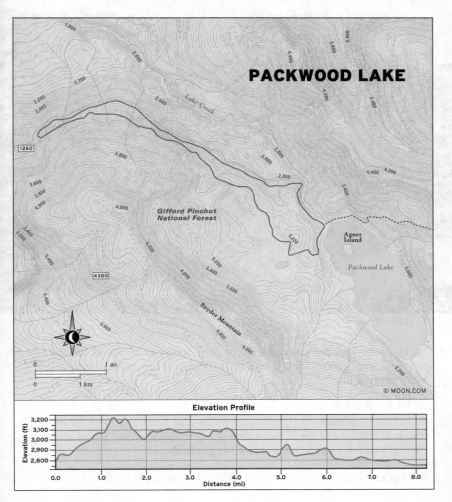

PACKWOOD LAKE

Lake Creek

Gifford Pinchot
National Forest

Agnes
Island

Packwood Lake

Snyder Mountain

1260

4380

0   1 mi

0   1 km

© MOON.COM

Elevation Profile

trail, including a section along the creek and views of Mount Rainier. At 0.3 mile a sign directs horse and foot traffic to go right and follow a trail that travels above the edge of the **creek's ravine** for 0.7 mile before rejoining the road.

▸ MILE 5.4–5.9: Pipeline Trail to Southern Face Mount Rainier Viewpoint

Walk another 0.5 mile where, at a bend in the road, you'll get a view of the southern face of Mount Rainier.

▸ MILE 5.9–8: Southern Face Mount Rainier Viewpoint to Parking Lot

Over the next 2.1 miles enjoy the flat, easy walk past occasional red columbine and other wildflowers. Notice the unmarked but heavily trodden **spur trail** on the left that is the final 200-foot uphill push to the parking lot. Don't worry if you miss this unmarked path: The Pipeline Trail continues a few hundred yards to the motorized trailhead. From there, either

▲ PACKWOOD LAKE

backtrack to look for the spur trail or continue walking about 100 yards to Forest Road 1260, turn left, and follow the road around the bend to the main parking lot.

DIRECTIONS

From U.S. 12 in Packwood, turn east on Snyder Road and drive 5.7 miles (the road changes to Forest Road 1260 along the way) on the paved road to the trailhead. A vault toilet is located at the trailhead.

GPS COORDINATES: 46.608709, –121.627365 / N46° 36.5225' W121° 37.6419'

BEST NEARBY BITES

The hunger you work up on the trail is quickly vanquished at Packwood's **Cruiser's Pizza** (13028 U.S. 12, 360/494-5400, 9am-9pm Mon.-Fri., 8am-10pm Sat., 8am-9pm Sun.). A large combo pizza is nearly nine pounds, with so much pepperoni, Canadian bacon, sausage, and mushrooms the servers say it barely fits in the oven. From the trailhead, the 6-mile drive southwest takes about 15 minutes via forest roads and U.S. 12.

2

Tongue Mountain

GIFFORD PINCHOT NATIONAL FOREST, RANDLE

Look for mountain goats on the rocky slopes of an easily accessed peak with an unobstructed view of Mount Adams.

DISTANCE: 3 miles round-trip
DURATION: 2 hours
ELEVATION CHANGE: 1,050 feet
EFFORT: Easy/moderate
TRAIL: Dirt single track, rock
USERS: Hikers, leashed dogs, mountain bikers, motorcyclists
SEASON: May-early November
PASSES/FEES: Northwest Forest Pass
MAPS: Green Trails Map 333 for McCoy Peak
CONTACT: Gifford Pinchot National Forest, Cowlitz Ranger District, 360/497-1103, www.fs.usda.gov

START THE HIKE

▸ **MILE 0-0.9: Forest Road 2904 to Tongue Mountain Lookout Trail 294A**

The 4,838-foot peak is easily accessed from Forest Road 2904. Find the Tongue Mountain Trail 294 sign on the east side of the road, opposite the Juniper Ridge Trail. The multiuse trail undulates—worn into rolling dirt waves by years of dirt bike traffic—as it gradually climbs through the forest. Get a reprieve in 0.9 mile at an **intersection** where you'll turn right on the Tongue Mountain Lookout Trail 294A. The trail has a traditional surface and is open only to hikers.

It shouldn't be a surprise that mountain goat sightings are common on this lightly used trail. Tongue Mountain was a traditional mountain goat hunting ground for the Taidnapam Indians. Keep your distance and give these creatures plenty of space. If a goat approaches, slowly move away; if that doesn't work, try to scare it off.

▸ **MILE 0.9-1.5: Tongue Mountain Lookout Trail 294A to Tongue's Fork**

In 0.3 mile, reach a short section of tight **switchbacks** that quickly climb above the trees and deliver views of Mount St. Helens. Ferns, vine maple, and huckleberries flank the path. In another 0.25 mile find yourself at the **tongue's fork,** a saddle between the two flat summits.

This might be as far as you choose to go. Reaching the top requires a short scramble in either direction. The summit is to the left (north), atop an imposing slope. Experienced hikers might find the short climb isn't as challenging as it looks, but it shouldn't be taken lightly. The easier scramble and best views are to the right (south), on the lower peak.

Tongue Mountain

SOUTH CASCADES

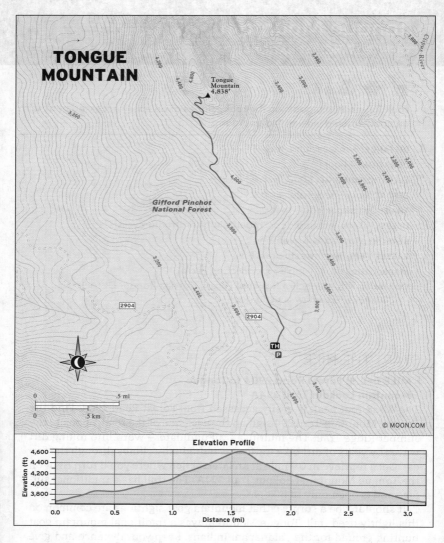

TONGUE MOUNTAIN

Tongue
Mountain
4,838'

Gifford Pinchot
National Forest

2904

2904

TH
P

Cispus River

1,800

0   .5 mi
0   .5 km

© MOON.COM

Elevation Profile

Mount Adams is in your face, the Cispus River is far below, and Mount Rainier looms to the north. (On the actual summit, Rainier is blocked by a small stand of evergreens.)

Mug for a picture or two (some goofy hikers snap apropos tongue-out selfies) before returning the way you came.

DIRECTIONS

From U.S. 12 in Randle, go south for 1 mile on Highway 131 and then bear left on Cispus Road/Forest Road 23. After 8.1 miles turn right to stay on Cispus Road and continue 0.9 mile to a Y-intersection. Bear left to access Forest Road 29. Drive 3.8 miles on the dirt road to Forest Road 2904 and turn

▲ VIEW FROM THE SUMMIT OF TONGUE MOUNTAIN

left. After 4 rough miles, find the trailhead on the left across from the Juniper Ridge trailhead. Restrooms and water are not available.

GPS COORDINATES: 46.3967, –121.76532 / N46° 23.802' W121° 45.9192'

BEST NEARBY BITES

In Randle, the **Mt. Adams Café** (9794 U.S. 12, Randle, 360/497-5556, 7am-7pm Sun.-Thurs., 7am-8pm Fri.-Sat.) is conveniently located to deliver that Angus burger and slice of pie you started craving during the final stretch of your hike. From the trailhead, the 17-mile drive northwest takes about 35 minutes via Forest Road 23 and Highway 131.

3

Harry's Ridge

MOUNT ST. HELENS NATIONAL VOLCANIC MONUMENT

🐐 ❀ ♿

Set your camera to panoramic mode if you're going to squeeze Mount St. Helens and Spirit Lake into one picture.

DISTANCE: 8 miles round-trip

DURATION: 4 hours

ELEVATION CHANGE: 1,000 feet

EFFORT: Moderate

TRAIL: Dirt, ash, short paved section

USERS: Hikers, wheelchair users

SEASON: Late June–mid-November

PASSES/FEES: Northwest Forest Pass (display at the observatory)

MAPS: Green Trails Map 332 for Spirit Lake

CONTACT: Johnston Ridge Observatory, 360/274-2140 (mid-May–late October), Mount St. Helens National Volcanic Monument, 360/449-7800, www.fs.usda.gov

START THE HIKE

▶ **MILE 0-0.4: Johnston Ridge Observatory to Boundary Trail**

From the **Johnston Ridge Observatory** (watching the observatory's short film about Mount St. Helens's 1980 eruption is a perfect way to start your hike), the moonscape of the blast zone unfurls between you and the volcano's gaping maw. Let the magnitude of one of North America's most destructive geological events sink in. Follow the paved, wheelchair-accessible **Eruption Trail** as it switchbacks to the top of a knoll. From here, those with a keen eye might look east and notice the destination, an old weather station atop Harry's Ridge.

Follow the paved path down the hill and past a **monument** with the names of those killed by the eruption. At 0.4 mile, as the paved trail bends back to the **parking lot** (a possible shortcut on your return trip), turn right on the **Boundary Trail,** leave the pavement, and follow the ash-covered path into the Mount Margaret Backcountry. This is where the ADA portion of the hike ends. Signs warn of a "minimum $100 fine" for straying off-trail. Shrubs and wildflowers display nature's resiliency, adding patches of color to the desolate landscape. Look for elk and black-tailed deer, which have returned to the area since the eruption.

▶ **MILE 0.4-1.8: Boundary Trail to Satan's Shortcut**

In 1.4 miles after leaving the pavement, pass an alternate route called Devil's Elbow. Erosion forced the closure of this path across steep slopes in 2018. Go straight following the detour I call **"Satan's Shortcut."**

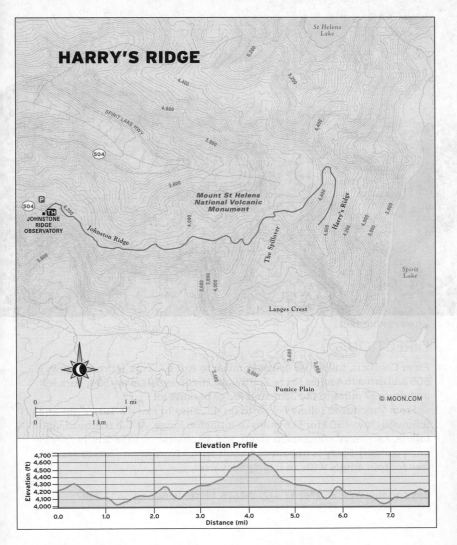

HARRY'S RIDGE

St Helens
Lake

SPIRIT LAKE HWY.

(504)

Mount St Helens
National Volcanic
Monument

JOHNSTONE
RIDGE
OBSERVATORY

Johnston Ridge

Harry's Ridge

The Spillover

Spirit
Lake

Langes Crest

Pumice Plain

© MOON.COM

0   1 mi
0   1 km

Elevation Profile

▶ **MILE 1.8-4: Satan's Shortcut to Harry's Ridge**

Half a mile farther, pass the Truman Trail (a 6.2-mile path to Windy Ridge) on your right and continue 0.9 mile to a **junction** at a saddle overlooking Spirit Lake. Turn right on **Harry's Ridge Trail** and spend the next 0.8 mile knocking out the steepest part of the journey. At the **high point**, look over massive Spirit Lake littered with logs left when the eruption blew away the once lush forest surrounding its shores. Mount St. Helens dominates the view to the south, but the glaciated peaks of Hood and Adams join the scenery.

The overwhelming sight urges you to stay for a while, but when it's time to go, travel back using the same trails.

▲ HARRY'S RIDGE TRAIL

DIRECTIONS

From Chehalis, follow I-5 south 15 miles to exit 63. Turn left on Highway 505 and drive 16.4 miles to the Spirit Lake Highway/Highway 504. Turn left and drive 37 miles to the Johnston Ridge parking lot.

From Vancouver, follow I-5 north for 48 miles to exit 49. Turn right and follow Highway 504 for 51.6 miles to Johnston Ridge. At the trailhead, find toilets, a seasonal concession stand, and an observatory ($8 adults, free 15 and younger). Entry is free for one adult with a Northwest Forest Pass and free for four adults with an interagency pass.

GPS COORDINATES: 46.276883, −122.216526 / N46° 16.613' W122° 12.9916'

BEST NEARBY BITES

The view alone is worth the stop at **Fire Mountain Grill** at 19 Mile House (15000 Spirit Lake Hwy., 360/957-1025, www.fmgrill.com, hours vary seasonally, closed winter). Overlook the North Fork Toutle River from the back porch while enjoying an elk burger and peach cobbler. From the trailhead, the 33-mile drive west takes about 40 minutes via Highway 504.

SOUTH CASCADES

Harry's Ridge

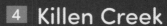

Get up close with Washington's second-tallest mountain, exploring its forests and colorful meadows and visiting the Pacific Crest Trail.

DISTANCE: 6.2 miles round-trip
DURATION: 3 hours
ELEVATION CHANGE: 1,500 feet
EFFORT: Moderate
TRAIL: Dirt, ash, rock
USERS: Hikers, leashed dogs, horseback riders
SEASON: Mid-July–October
PASSES/FEES: Northwest Forest Pass
MAPS: Green Trails Map 367S for Mount Adams
CONTACT: Gifford Pinchot National Forest, Mount Adams Ranger District, 509/395-3400, www.fs.usda.gov

W estern Washington's wet climate and eastern Washington's dry weather converge in the Mount Adams Wilderness, resulting in an ecological diversity that delights visitors. On the north side of 12,276-foot Mount Adams, the Killen Creek Trail cuts through a forest of Douglas fir and pine and visits meadows made colorful by wildflowers. While Mount Adams's southern slope extends like a long ramp inviting hikers to make the nontechnical climb to the summit, its north face is steep, daunting, and best left to experienced climbers—but it makes an impressive backdrop for your adventure.

START THE HIKE

▶ **MILE 0-2.2: Registration Kiosk to Meadow**
Starting from the climber's **registration kiosk** in the parking lot, head into the woods. Going above 7,000 feet requires a Cascade Volcano Pass, available at the kiosk. You'll only get to 6,200 feet on this hike, but you'll still have to fill out a registration form at a second kiosk (a few steps down the trail as you enter the 47,122-acre wilderness). The trail climbs gradually and consistently for the first 2 miles as it passes through the woods.

The path was made by Native Americans who picked berries in the area. In season, you might have opportunities of your own to sample huckleberries. Keep an eye out for elk and deer while admiring aster, lupine, and other wildflowers. As you continue, Mount Adams comes into view, a majestic reward for your work. Expect a few short, steep sections over the next 0.2 mile before arriving at a **large meadow.**

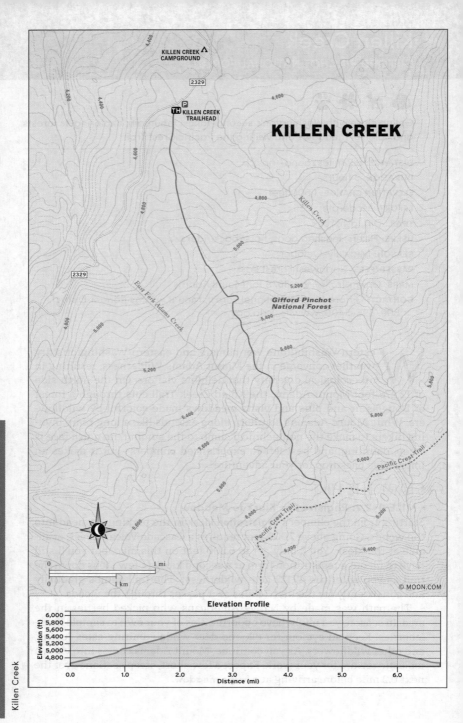

KILLEN CREEK
CAMPGROUND

2329

KILLEN CREEK
TRAILHEAD

KILLEN CREEK

Killen Creek

*Gifford Pinchot
National Forest*

East Fork Adams Creek

2329

Pacific Crest Trail

Pacific Crest Trail

0   1 mi
0   1 km

© MOON.COM

Elevation Profile

Elevation (ft)

6,000
5,800
5,600
5,400
5,200
5,000
4,800

0.0   1.0   2.0   3.0   4.0   5.0   6.0

Distance (mi)

▲ KILLEN CREEK TRAIL

▶ MILE 2.2–3.1: Meadow to Pacific Crest Trail Junction

After another 0.9 mile that climbs gradually, the trail flattens and a battered placard atop a weathered post welcomes you to the 2,650-mile **Pacific Crest Trail.** Here, find a place to relax and enjoy the surroundings.

When you're ready, retrace your route.

DIRECTIONS

From U.S. 12 in Randle, go south for 1 mile on Highway 131 and then bear left on Cispus Road/Forest Road 23. After 8.1 miles continue straight to remain on Forest Road 23 for 22.4 miles. Turn left on Forest Road 2329. Follow Forest Road 2329 for 4.8 miles to the trailhead.

From White Salmon, go north on Highway 141 for 20.3 miles to the town of Trout Lake and then continue straight on Mount Adams Road. In 1.3 miles continue straight on Forest Road 23. After another 23.2 miles turn right on Forest Road 2329. Follow Forest Road 2329 for 4.8 miles to the trailhead. A vault toilet is at the trailhead.

GPS COORDINATES: 46.288471, –121.552446 / N46° 17.3083′ W121° 33.1468′

Ape Cave
MOUNT ST. HELENS NATIONAL VOLCANIC MONUMENT

🐾

Go on an underground adventure at the foot of Mount St. Helens by scrambling through one of the longest lava tubes in the United States.

DISTANCE: 2.9 miles round-trip

DURATION: 2 hours

ELEVATION CHANGE: 400 feet

EFFORT: Easy

TRAIL: Boulder fields, uneven terrain inside an unlit cave, ladder, stairs, single track

USERS: Hikers

SEASON: May–November

PASSES/FEES: Northwest Forest Pass

MAPS: Green Trails Map 332S for Mount St. Helens National Volcanic Monument

CONTACT: Mount St. Helens National Volcanic Monument, 360/449-7800, www.fs.usda.gov.

The Ape Cave formed about 1,900 years ago when Mount St. Helens erupted with glowing orange lava rather than its more common explosive eruptions. The lava flowed into and through a stream drainage for about a year. The lava cooled on the surface and sides, and when the lava stopped flowing the 13,042-foot lava tube (believed to be the third longest in the United States) was left behind.

START THE HIKE

▶ **MILE 0-0.1: Visitors Center to Cave Floor**

This underworldly hike starts on a paved path beside the **visitors center** at the north end of the parking lot. Shoe brushes are trailside to clean your boots. Cleaning your gear before and after entering the cave helps protect bats from the deadly white-nose syndrome.

At 0.1 mile, reach a set of **stairs** that descend into a large pit. You can walk down the first set of steps and still have plenty of light to appreciate the subterranean setting. But by the bottom of the second staircase you'll need a trustworthy headlamp. The Forest Service recommends carrying three sources of light and extra batteries. Sturdy shoes, warm clothing (it's 42 degrees year-round in the cave), and lightweight gloves with good grip are also a good idea. Even with gloves, however, try not to touch the slick walls. This slime is a food source for cave life and takes years to grow.

▶ **MILE 0.1-1: Cave Floor to Upper Cave and Lava Fall**

Once on the cave's floor you'll have two options. A **sign** bolted to the wall points right to the easier and shorter lower cave, a 0.75-mile, out-and-back walk that's a fun option for kids. Go left, past the stairs, to explore the

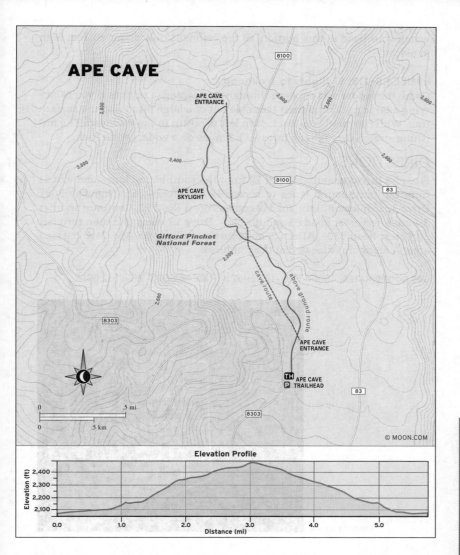

APE CAVE

Elevation Profile

upper cave. The 88-foot-wide **Big Room** is a few steps away and a good place to appreciate this geological wonder.

Beyond the Big Room, traveling the upper cave requires a little extra work. You'll climb over 27 large **boulder piles** called breakdown. These boulders fell from the walls and ceiling after the ancient eruption subsided.

About 0.9 mile into the upper cave, reach an 8-foot-tall **"Lava Fall."** This basalt wall might require a little teamwork to scale. A notch is chiseled about halfway up the left side of the wall to help cavers.

▶ **MILE 1-1.6: Lava Fall to Skylights**
Another 0.4 mile brings you to the first of two **skylights** at the upper end of the lava tube. Continue 0.2 mile farther to the exit. Should you want to explore a little more, you can go another 500 feet to the end of the cave;

watch your head in this portion, as the ceiling is only about six feet high in places.

▸ MILE 1.6-2.9: Skylights to Trailhead

Climb the **ladder** and squeeze through an opening (a tight fit if you're carrying a large pack) and then scramble out of a large pit to find the surface trail. With the pit at your back, turn left to return to the trailhead. The finishing stretch through the forest is 1.3 miles on a wide, gentle path.

DIRECTIONS

From I-5 in Woodland, use exit 22 from the southbound lanes and exit 21 from the northbound lanes to access Lewis River Road (Highway 503). Drive 30.6 miles until the road becomes Forest Road 90. Continue another 3.4 miles to Forest Road 83 and turn left. Drive 1.7 miles and then turn left on Forest Road 8303. After 0.9 mile, turn right into the Ape Cave parking area. A restroom is located at the trailhead.

GPS COORDINATES: 46.108338, -122.211523 / N46° 6.5003' W122° 12.6914'

APE CAVE SIGN ▸

BEST NEARBY BITES

Woodland's **Fat Moose Bar and Grill** (1382 Lewis River Rd., 360/225-7944, www.fatmoosebarandgrill.com, 11am-10pm Mon.-Thurs., 11am-1am Fri.-Sat., 9am-8pm Sun.) can prepare a box lunch before your adventure, quell your hunger with a burger and brew, or test your alimentary limits. The Undertaker Burger is about seven inches tall and includes two pounds of hamburger, eight slices of ham, and four eggs. It's $25, but it comes with a pound of french fries and a pitcher of soda. Finish it all in less than 30 minutes and it's free. From the trailhead, the 37-mile drive southwest takes about 50 minutes via Highway 503/Lewis River Road.

Monitor Ridge to Mount St. Helens Summit

MOUNT ST. HELENS NATIONAL VOLCANIC MONUMENT, COUGAR

Scramble up snowfields and a rocky ridge to the crater rim of a volcano that blew its top in 1980.

DISTANCE: 10 miles round–trip
DURATION: 8 hours
ELEVATION CHANGE: 4,500 feet
EFFORT: Strenuous
TRAIL: Dirt, steep snow slopes, boulders, ash
USERS: Hikers
SEASON: Mid-May–October
PASSES/FEES: Northwest Forest Pass, climbing permit ($22 per person)
MAPS: Green Trails Map 364S for Mount St. Helens Climbing
CONTACT: Mount St. Helens National Volcanic Monument, 360/449-7800, www.fs.usda.gov

This is a challenging hike, but it's easier than it used to be. Prior to the morning of May 18, 1980, Mount St. Helens was a symmetrical stratovolcano standing 9,677 feet above sea level. But, that morning, the most disastrous eruption in U.S. history blew away the mountain's north face and shortened the summit elevation to 8,337 feet. If those facts don't do it already, the sheer magnitude of the event that created the 2-mile-wide crater is likely to blow your mind once your reach the top.

START THE HIKE

▶ **MILE 0-2.1: Ptarmigan Trailhead to Loowit Trail**

The hiking begins on the **Ptarmigan Trail** at Climber's Bivouac on the mountain's south side, but your journey needs to start in front of a computer on March 18 at 7am PDT, when permits go on sale. To limit visitor impact on the peak, climbing permits are limited to 100 per day May 15-October 31, when climbing is most popular. The first-come, first-served permits ($15 per person plus $6 per transaction) sell out within minutes at www.recreation.gov. But, often, hikers can buy passes from other hikers at www.purmit.com.

The Ptarmigan Trail starts by climbing through an evergreen forest where you might hear birds chirp and see squirrels scurrying up trees. Views are scarce at first, but after about 1.5 miles you'll get glimpses of the **rocky ridge** you're about to climb. Over the next 0.6 mile the trail steepens and offers a view of Mount Adams before it intersects with the Loowit Trail.

A pit toilet (the only one on this trip) is located near the **intersection.** The 28-mile Loowit Trail loops around the mountain. Cross the Loowit

▲ DESCENDING MOUNT ST. HELENS

Trail and soon you'll step out of the trees and find yourself staring up the steep slopes of Mount St. Helens. A **sign at 4,800 feet above sea level** reminds hikers that this is as far as you can go without one of those coveted climbing permits.

▶ MILE 2.1–4.9: Loowit Trail to Monitor Ridge

From here, pick your way up the boulders to access **Monitor Ridge.** Posts placed along the ridge help hikers navigate the next 2.8 miles to the crater rim. Sometimes, forward progress is hard to come by as ash makes the climb reminiscent of scaling an enormous sand dune.

While it's not a bad option to work your way from post to post while scrambling over boulders, many find it more comfortable to leave the rocks and make their way upward on the snowfields. With the absence of trail, enjoy the options but be sure to regularly confirm the route: It's hard to get off course during the slow uphill push, but relatively easy to do on the descent. Gaiters help keep ash and snow out of your boots. Gloves can protect your hands from abrasive surfaces. Trekking poles will help with balance and take some of the stress off your knees during the long descent. In winter, spring, and early summer, conditions might require crampons and an ice axe.

▶ MILE 4.9–5: Monitor Ridge to Mount St. Helens Summit

The final few steps to the **rim** are visually stunning. Mount Rainier and Spirit Lake come into view. And, below you, the volcano's new lava dome rises from the crater floor. It is important to keep your feet on solid ground at the summit. Cornices form on the crater rim and sometimes block the view. A short walk along the rim usually yields an opening.

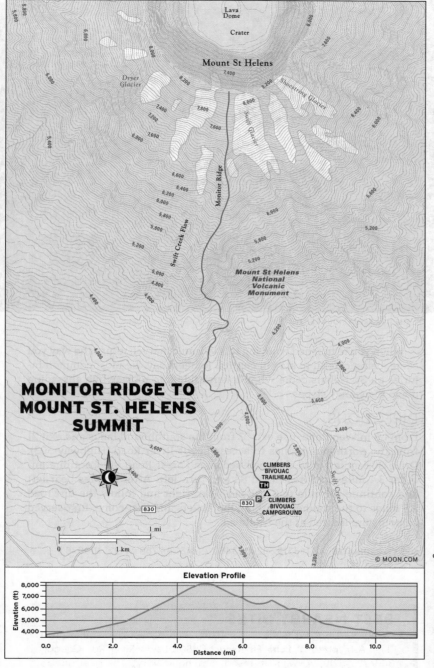

MONITOR RIDGE TO MOUNT ST. HELENS SUMMIT

Lava Dome

Crater

Mount St Helens

Dryer Glacier

Shoestring Glacier

Swift Glacier

Monitor Ridge

Swift Creek Flow

Mount St Helens National Volcanic Monument

CLIMBERS BIVOUAC TRAILHEAD

TH

P

830

CLIMBERS BIVOUAC CAMPGROUND

830

Swift Creek

0   1 mi

0   1 km

© MOON.COM

Elevation Profile

Elevation (ft)

8,000
7,000
6,000
5,000
4,000

0.0   2.0   4.0   6.0   8.0   10.0

Distance (mi)

▲ THE VIEW FROM MOUNT ST. HELENS

When you're finished enjoying this volcanic marvel, return the way you came, being careful to stay in control. Rangers say the most common injuries on St. Helens come when hikers slide into rocks while glissading down the snowy slopes.

DIRECTIONS

From I-5 in Woodland, use exit 22 from the southbound lanes and exit 21 from the northbound lanes to access Lewis River Road (Highway 503). Drive 30.6 miles until the road becomes Forest Road 90. Continue another 3.4 miles to Forest Road 83 and turn left. After 3 miles bear left and continue 0.4 mile to 830 Road. Turn right and follow the dirt road 2.5 miles to the trailhead parking lot. Toilets and first-come, first-served camping are located at the trailhead.

GPS COORDINATES: 46.146315, –122.183460 / N46° 8.7789' W122° 11.0076'

BEST NEARBY BITES

Celebrate bagging this iconic volcano with a beer and a thin-crust "Kick Ash" pizza at **Lone Fir Resort** (16806 Lewis River Rd., Cougar, 360/238-5210, www.lonefirresort.com, hours vary). The beer on tap comes from Northwest breweries. From the trailhead, the 14-mile drive southwest takes less than 30 minutes via Forest Road 83 and Highway 503.

🦌 ❀ 💦 🏃 ♿

Cross a suspension bridge and descend a 30-foot ladder while exploring a narrow canyon scoured by the 1980 eruption of Mount St. Helens.

DISTANCE: 5.8 miles round-trip
DURATION: 3 hours
ELEVATION CHANGE: 1,600 feet
EFFORT: Moderate
TRAIL: Paved trail, dirt trail, exposed sections, ladders, stairs, suspension bridge
USERS: Hikers, wheelchair users
SEASON: Late May–November
PASSES/FEES: Northwest Forest Pass
MAPS: Green Trails Map 364 for Mount St. Helens
CONTACT: Mount St. Helens National Volcanic Monument, 360/449-7800, www.fs.usda.gov

Lava Canyon Trail 184 is a three-layer hike with each level a little more challenging than the last. Start with a paved wheelchair-friendly section and work your way up to a better-watch-your-step stretch that sometimes feels like a shelf hanging on the canyon wall.

START THE HIKE

▶ **MILE 0-0.3: ADA Trailhead to Muddy River Views**
The paved **ADA trail** starts on the south side of the parking lot and descends a grade steep enough to give pause to some wheelchair users. Benches are available along the path that quickly delivers views of the **Muddy River.** Interpretive signs on this 0.3-mile section tell the story of how the river carved the canyon and how ancient lava flows created large volcanic rock formations. The 1980 Mount St. Helens eruption scoured away trees, leaving a dingy gray canyon that's since recovered its green.

▶ **MILE 0.3-0.7: Muddy River Views to Suspension Bridge**
The ADA path continues to a **waterfall viewing area,** but if you plan to hike farther turn right just before the viewing area (you'll visit it on your return) and use the **steel bridge** to cross the river. On the east side, turn left and walk down cement steps, a metal staircase, and a rocky path for 0.4 mile to a **suspension bridge** that moves with each step. Cross it back to the west side of the canyon and find an option to turn left to return to the parking area, or turn right for the hike's most challenging layer.

▶ **MILE 0.7-2.95: Suspension Bridge to Smith Creek Trail**
Turning right, descend the exposed trail hugging the edge of the canyon with a steep drop to the river on the right. In 0.5 mile the trail is interrupted

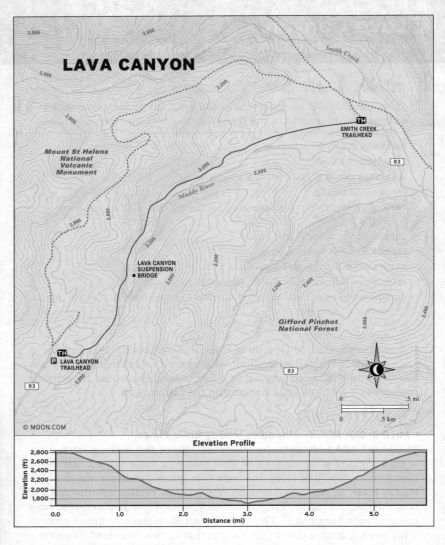

LAVA CANYON

Mount St Helens
National
Volcanic
Monument

SMITH CREEK
TRAILHEAD

Muddy River

LAVA CANYON
SUSPENSION
BRIDGE

Gifford Pinchot
National Forest

LAVA CANYON
TRAILHEAD

© MOON.COM

Elevation Profile

by a **cliff**. A 30-foot **ladder** allows you to continue into the heart of the canyon. Pass a spur trail 0.25 mile beyond the ladder. (This 0.3-mile round-trip side trail uses a ladder to ascend a rock formation called The Ship and deliver views up the canyon.) Continue 1.5 miles beyond **The Ship spur** to the **intersection** with the Smith Creek Trail. Along the way, emerge from older forest into an area with trees so small it seems like a Christmas tree farm. The intersection is where you'll turn back, but first head right a few steps on the **Smith Creek Trail** to view the confluence of Smith Creek and the Muddy River.

▶ **MILE 2.95-5.8: Smith Creek Trail to ADA Trailhead**
When you're ready to return, head back the way you came. At the **suspension bridge**, continue straight to explore the west side of the **intermediate**

▲ LOWER LAVA CANYON TRAIL

loop and visit the **waterfall viewing area.** This 0.3-mile section of the **Lava Canyon Loop** will deposit you back on the **ADA trail** for a 0.3-mile stroll back to the parking lot.

DIRECTIONS

From I-5 in Woodland, use exit 22 (southbound) and exit 21 (northbound) to access Lewis River Road (Highway 503). Drive 30.6 miles until the road becomes Forest Road 90. Continue another 3.4 miles to Forest Road 83 and turn left. After 3 miles bear right and continue 7.5 miles to the trailhead. A toilet is located at the trailhead.

GPS COORDINATES: 46.165722, -122.088385 / N46° 9.9433' W122° 5.3031'

BEST NEARBY BITES

The Cougar Bar and Grill (16849 Lewis River Rd., 360/238-5252, 10am–9pm Mon.–Thurs., 10am–10pm Fri., 8am–10pm Sat.–Sun.) pays tribute to local soldiers past and present with framed images hanging above the bar. The Volcano Burger topped with jalapeno and chipotle mayo is popular among visitors, but the restaurant is best known for its halibut. The staff says some customers make the 130-mile round-trip drive from Portland each week just for the popular dish. From the trailhead, the 18-mile drive southwest takes about 30 minutes via Forest Road 83 and Highway 503.

NEARBY CAMPGROUNDS

NAME	DESCRIPTION	FACILITIES	SEASON	FEE
Iron Creek	situated on the Cispus River and easily accessed from Randle and Highway 12	98 RV and tent sites, restrooms	late May-early September	$20
Forest Road 25, Randle, 877/444-6777, www.recreation.gov				
Takhlakh Lake Campground	a lakeside campground with views of Mount Adams	54 tent sites, restrooms	late June-late September	$18
Takhlakh Loop Road, Randle, 877/444-6777, www.recreation.gov				
Kid Valley Campground	in the woods along North Fork Toutle River with easy access to Mount St. Helens	30 RV and tent sites, restrooms	year-round	$20-30
9360 Spirit Lake Highway, east of Toutle, 360/274-9060, www.kidvalley.com				
Lower Falls Campground	a forested camp with trails leading to the Lewis River and several waterfalls	43 RV and tent sites, restrooms	late May-late September	$15
Forest Road 90, Mount Adams, Gifford Pinchot National Forest, 509/395-3400, www.recreation.gov				
Swift Forest Camp	on the Swift Reservoir just outside Mount St. Helens National Volcanic Monument	93 tent and RV sites, restrooms	late April-September	$18
280 Road, Cougar, 360/238-5251, www.pacificcorp.com				

WASHINGTON COAST

The Pacific Ocean is the artist responsible for much of the beauty on Washington's coast. With the help of constant wind, it carved the sea stacks adorning Point of Arches and chiseled the famous hole into the rocky wall at Rialto Beach. It reflects radiant sunsets and, for a few hours each day, it retreats to unveil tide pools teeming with life. Whether visitors come to watch birds wheeling in the sky, skip rocks, or wander long, secluded beaches, the wild coast is one of Washington's most-loved wonders.

▲ BANANA SLUG

▲ GULLS ON RIALTO BEACH

1   Cape Flattery
DISTANCE: 1.5 miles round-trip
DURATION: 1 hour
EFFORT: Easy

2   Point of Arches via Shi Shi Beach
DISTANCE: 9 miles round-trip
DURATION: 4.5 hours
EFFORT: Moderate

3   Ozette Triangle
DISTANCE: 9.3 miles round-trip
DURATION: 4.5 hours
EFFORT: Moderate/strenuous

4   Hole-in-the-Wall
DISTANCE: 3 miles round-trip
DURATION: 1.5 hours
EFFORT: Easy

5   North Head Trail
DISTANCE: 3.8 miles round-trip
DURATION: 2 hours
EFFORT: Easy

▾ SEA STACKS AT OZETTE TRIANGLE

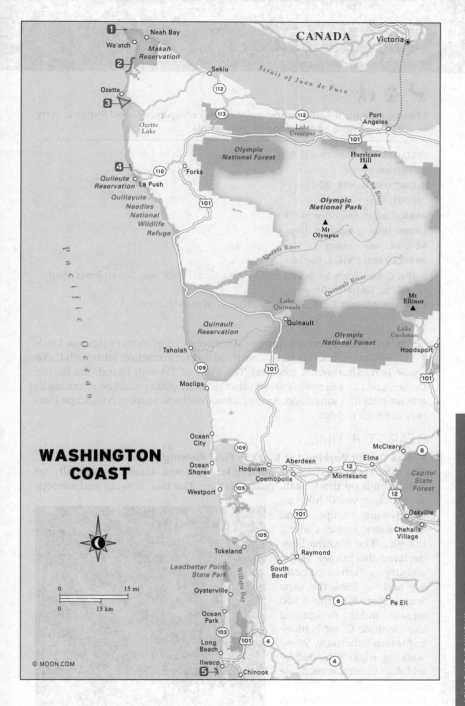

WASHINGTON COAST

CANADA

Victoria

Neah Bay
Wa'atch
Makah Reservation
Sekiu
Strait of Juan de Fuca
Port Angeles
Hurricane Hill
Elwha River

Ozette
Ozette Lake

Olympic National Forest

Lake Crescent

Olympic National Park

Mt Olympus

Quileute Reservation
La Push
Forks

Quillayute Needles National Wildlife Refuge

Queets River

Quinault River

Mt Ellinor

Lake Cushman

Taholah
Quinault Reservation

Lake Quinault
Quinault

Olympic National Forest

Hoodsport

Moclips

Ocean City

Ocean Shores
Hoquiam
Aberdeen
Montesano
Cosmopolis

McCleary
Elma

Capitol State Forest

Westport

Oakville

Chehalis Village

Tokeland
Raymond
South Bend
Pe Ell

Leadbetter Point State Park

Willapa Bay

Oysterville

Ocean Park

Long Beach
Ilwaco
Chinook

P a c i f i c   O c e a n

0   15 mi
0   15 km

© MOON.COM

1

Cape Flattery

MAKAH INDIAN RESERVATION, NEAH BAY

🦌 🐾 🚶

Stand on the northwesternmost point of the contiguous United States and try to catch a glimpse of a sea lion or gray whale.

DISTANCE: 1.5 miles round-trip
DURATION: 1 hour
ELEVATION CHANGE: 200 feet
EFFORT: Easy
TRAIL: Dirt, stairs, boardwalk
USERS: Hikers, leashed dogs
SEASON: Year-round
PASSES/FEES: Makah Recreation Pass
MAPS: Green Trails Map 99S for Olympic Coast Beaches, Green Trails Map 98S for Cape Flattery
CONTACT: Makah Tribe, 360/645-2201, www.makah.com

Cape Flattery comprises the northwest tip of the contiguous United States, but it is not a contrived tourist attraction (although there is no shortage of tourists). The view of Tatoosh Island, the Pacific Ocean, and the sea caves carved into the rocky cliffs would be stunning at any latitude and longitude. As far as easy walks to scenic spots, Cape Flattery is tough to beat.

START THE HIKE

▶ **MILE 0-0.5: Parking Lot Kiosk to First Viewing Area**
The hike starts next to the **parking lot kiosk** and descends gradually on a path built by the Makah Indian Nation. The trail is wide and smooth at first but you'll hike on boardwalks, steps, and some rooty sections along the way. The Makahs have declared this corner of the country a nature sanctuary and, in 1994, the cape was included in the 3,300 square miles designated the Olympic Coast National Marine Sanctuary. Wood walking sticks whittled by a Makah artist are available at the trailhead. They're free to borrow or $5 to keep.

WASHINGTON COAST

Cape Flattery

TREE ON CAPE FLATTERY ▶

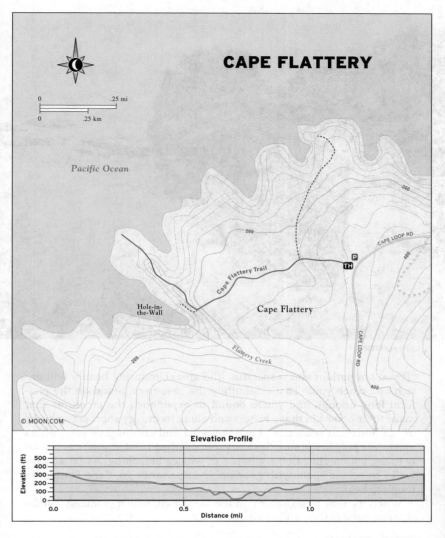

CAPE FLATTERY

Pacific Ocean

Cape Flattery Trail

Hole-in-the-Wall

Cape Flattery

Flattery Creek

CAPE LOOP RD

© MOON.COM

Elevation Profile

On the left about 0.5 mile down the trail, a boardwalk leads about 20 yards to a **platform** overlooking a rugged beach and sea stacks to the south.

▶ MILE 0.5-0.75: First Viewing Area to Third Viewing Area

Continue a few steps straight beyond the intersection to reach the **second viewing area.** Step down to a **perch** with views of caves notched into the cliffs.

The third and final viewing area is 0.25 mile farther. Climb a two-step ladder onto an **elevated wooden deck** and gaze west toward Tatoosh Island and a deactivated lighthouse that once directed ships to the entrance of the Strait of Juan de Fuca. At various times, tribal fishermen, whale and seal hunters, and the U.S. Coast Guard and Navy used the island, named for a former Makah chief. A sign at a nearby trailhead says,

▲ CAPE FLATTERY

"If you are patient and respectful, (the area's) enduring beauty will enrich and teach you." That's definitely the case here. Stand on the platform long enough and you're bound to experience the creatures that make their homes in these waters and along its craggy shores. The barks of sea lions and seals rise above the wind and crashing waves. Puffins and otters play in the surf. Seabirds soar overhead and, if you're especially lucky, you might catch a glimpse of whales breaching. As far as easy walks to scenic spots with geographic importance go, Cape Flattery is tough to beat.

When it's time to go, return on the same trail, which gradually climbs 200 feet back to the parking lot.

DIRECTIONS

From Neah Bay, follow Highway 112/Bayview Avenue until it bends left and becomes Fort Street. Turn right on 3rd Street after 0.1 mile, then left on Cape Flattery Road after less than 0.1 mile. Drive 7.8 miles (the road becomes Cape Loop Road after 3.2 miles) to the parking lot. Toilets are located at the trailhead.

GPS COORDINATES: 48.384880, -124.715790 / N48° 23.0928' W124° 42.9474'

2

Point of Arches via Shi Shi Beach

MAKAH INDIAN RESERVATION, OLYMPIC NATIONAL PARK

Explore the tide pools and towering sea stacks of what might be Washington's most striking beach.

BEST: Winter Hikes
DISTANCE: 9 miles round-trip
DURATION: 4.5 hours
ELEVATION CHANGE: 200 feet
EFFORT: Moderate
TRAIL: Dirt trail, beach
USERS: Hikers
SEASON: Year-round
PASSES/FEES: Makah Recreation Pass
MAPS: Green Trails Map 99S for Olympic Coast Beaches, Green Trails Map 98S for Cape Flattery
CONTACT: Olympic National Park, Wilderness Information Center, 360/565-3100, www.nps.gov/olym

Part of the longest stretch of wild coastline in the contiguous United States, the trek to Point of Arches on the south end of Shi Shi Beach (pronounced "Shy Shy") is a bucket list trip for many hikers, especially those with a passion for nature photography. Time your visit for low tide or sunset, and you'll see why.

START THE HIKE

Be aware that reaching Shi Shi requires walking an often-muddy trail through the woods and making a short but steep descent. While easiest to walk at low tide when there is wet, hard-packed sand at the edge of the surf, Shi Shi is passable at high tide. Always pay attention to the tide, so you don't find yourself stranded beyond the point.

▶ **MILE 0-2.1: Makah Tribal Land to Olympic National Park**
The walk starts on Makah tribal land. At 0.3 mile from the parking lot, you'll cross an A-frame **bridge.** The next 1.8 miles are along a wide, flat, and well-marked path under Sitka spruce and Douglas fir. You can skirt huge puddles in drier months, but for much of the year you should expect to get your boots muddy.

▶ **MILE 2.1-2.2: Olympic National Park to Shi Shi Beach**
At 2.1 miles, a sign welcomes you to **Olympic National Park.** Here, the trail drops more than 100 feet in 0.1 mile before emerging from the trees onto the sandy **Shi Shi Beach.** To the south, the sea stack skyline of Point of Arches rises in the distance, but it's still a ways before you get there. Pass

patches of green and brown kelp washed ashore by the sea. Watch herons and sea lions wade in the surf and coyotes, deer, raccoons, and other animals skitter across the tree line.

▶ MILE 2.2–3.5: Shi Shi Beach to Petroleum Creek

After 1.3 miles, step over **Petroleum Creek.** You'll see tents dotting the beach by the dozens. If you want to join them, you'll need to pay for overnight parking and a backcountry permit, and pack your food in a required bear canister. Contact Olympic National Park's Wilderness Information Center (www.nps.gov/olym) for more information.

▶ MILE 3.5–4.5: Petroleum Creek to Point of Arches

After 1 mile along the beach, you'll reach the **Point of Arches.** At low tide, walk around the point (designated a National Natural Landmark in 1971) and explore tide pools teeming with colorful starfish and sea anemones. Admire the towering sea stacks and arches, the handiwork of the pounding surf and perpetual wind. Stay for one of the most awe-inspiring (and most photographed) sunsets in Washington.

When you're ready, retrace your steps.

DIRECTIONS

From Neah Bay, follow Highway 112/Bayview Avenue until it bends left and becomes Fort Street. Turn right on 3rd Street after 0.1 mile, then left on Cape Flattery Road after less than 0.1 mile. Drive 2.4 miles and turn left on Hobuck Road. After about a mile, bear right following the signs to the fish hatchery. Drive 0.3 mile and then turn left on Makah Passage. Drive 0.8 mile and then turn right on Tsoo-Yess Beach Road. Drive 2 miles and turn left on Fish Hatchery Road. Drive 0.2 mile and find the trailhead on the right. A restroom with a comically loud foot-pump sink is located at the trailhead.

GPS COORDINATES: 48.29375, –124.66524 / N48° 17.625' W124° 39.9144'

SHI SHI BEACH ▶

BEST NEARBY BITES

Cap off a day of seaside play by retracing your driving route about 7 miles (15 minutes) northeast to Neah Bay, where you can enjoy a thin-crust, smoked-on-site salmon pizza and a slice of pie at **Linda's Wood Fired Kitchen** (1110 Bayview Ave., 360/640-2192, hours vary).

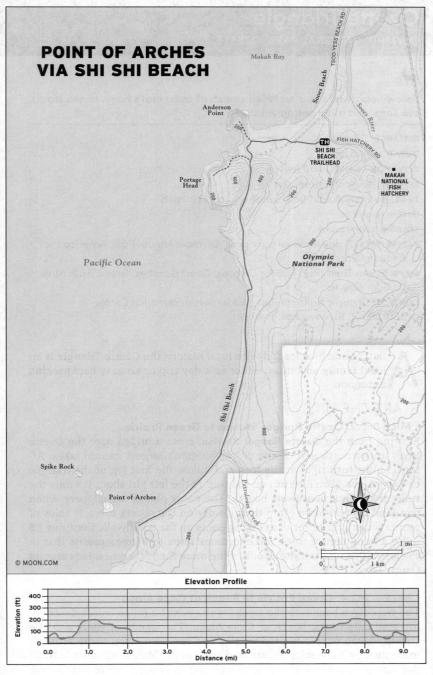

POINT OF ARCHES
VIA SHI SHI BEACH

Makah Bay

TSOO-YESS BEACH RD

Sooes Beach

Sooes River

Anderson
Point

TH
SHI SHI
BEACH
TRAILHEAD

FISH HATCHERY RD

MAKAH
NATIONAL
FISH
HATCHERY

Portage
Head

Olympic
National Park

Pacific Ocean

Shi Shi Beach

Petroleum Creek

Spike Rock

Point of Arches

0   1 mi

0   1 km

© MOON.COM

Elevation Profile

Elevation (ft)

400
300
200
100
0

0.0   1.0   2.0   3.0   4.0   5.0   6.0   7.0   8.0   9.0

Distance (mi)

Follow boardwalks to a secluded stretch of coast that's home to sea stacks, sea lions, and tribal petroglyphs.

DISTANCE: 9.3 miles round-trip

DURATION: 4.5 hours

ELEVATION CHANGE: 400 feet

EFFORT: Moderate/strenuous

TRAIL: Boardwalk, dirt trail, sandy and rocky beach

USERS: Hikers

SEASON: Year-round

PASSES/FEES: 7-day national park pass, Olympic Annual Pass, America the Beautiful Passes

MAPS: Green Trails Map 99S for Olympic Coast Beaches, Green Trails Map 130S for Ozette

CONTACT: Olympic National Park, Wilderness Information Center, 360/565-3130, www.nps.gov/olym

A flat, scenic hike loaded with local history, the Ozette Triangle is an ideal family adventure either as a day trip or an easy backpacking excursion.

START THE HIKE

▶ **MILE 0-2.2: Ozette Ranger Station to Green Prairie**

Starting from the **Ozette Ranger Station,** cross a bridge over the Ozette River at the north end of one of Washington's largest natural lakes. After 0.1 mile, turn right at the fork and follow the first leg of the triangle to Cape Alava. (You'll return on the trail to the left.) In about 0.3 mile the trail's trademark **boardwalk** begins. The cedar planks are slippery when wet (and it's wet more often than it's dry on the coast); the soft soles of tennis shoes grip better than hiking boots on the boardwalk. Continue 1.8 miles among spruce trees and enormous ferns to a green **prairie** that in the late 1800s was the site of one of the more than 30 homesteads around Ozette Lake.

▶ **MILE 2.2-3.4: Green Prairie to Beach at Cape Alava**

The trail dives back into the trees for the next 1.2 miles before descending gradually to the beach at **Cape Alava.** Thousands of years ago, the Ozette Makah people hunted whales and sea lions here; many artifacts unearthed by archaeologists are on display at the Makah Museum in Neah Bay. Camping is allowed here with a permit and bear canister (visit www.nps.gov/olym for more information).

Turn left and walk south on the **rocky beach.** Look for starfish in the tide pools and watch your step on rocks covered with slippery algae and

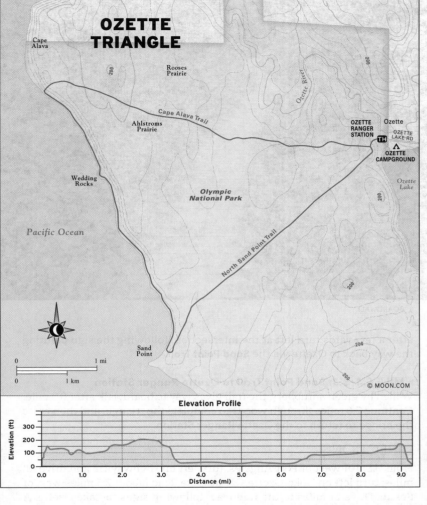

Elevation Profile

seaweed. Sea stacks and offshore islands appear from the morning fog and are home to cormorants, puffins, and gulls. Seals, bald eagles, and peregrine falcons make frequent appearances.

▶ MILE 3.4–6.4: Beach at Cape Alava to Sand Point

The beach leg of the triangle is 3 miles. About halfway is an area known as the **Wedding Rocks.** Take time to examine the large boulders for petroglyphs. You can find an orca, seal, and face etched in the rocks, but they're easy to miss if you don't look for them.

At **Sand Point** (another camping spot) it's clear how this place got its name: the rocky beach gives way to soft, barefoot-inviting sand. Look for a black and red disc mounted to a tree. Find the trail under the disc and

▲ BOARDWALK

after a few yards turn left at the intersection, following the sign pointing the way back to Ozette via the **Sand Point Trail.**

▶ MILE 6.4–9.3: Sand Point Trail to Ozette Ranger Station
Walled by green shrubbery, the trail gives way to boardwalk after 0.3 mile. Continue 2.6 miles through woods to complete the triangle and then cross the bridge to return to the Ozette Ranger Station.

DIRECTIONS

From U.S. 101 west of Port Angeles, turn left on Highway 112 and drive 48 miles; turn left on Hoko-Ozette/Ozette Lake Road (about 2.5 miles west of Sekiu). Drive 21 miles to the trailhead, following signs to Lake Ozette. A ranger station, campground, lake access, and toilets are located near the trailhead.

GPS COORDINATES: 48.153633, –124.668654 / N48° 9.218′ W124° 40.1192′

Hole-in-the-Wall

OLYMPIC NATIONAL PARK, RIALTO BEACH

Take a short, easy walk along the Pacific Ocean to a sea arch that allows you to walk through a bluff at low tide.

DISTANCE: 3 miles round-trip

DURATION: 1.5 hours

ELEVATION CHANGE: Negligible

EFFORT: Easy

TRAIL: Beach

USERS: Hikers, leashed dogs (only to Ellen Creek)

SEASON: Year-round

PASSES/FEES: 7-day national park pass, Olympic Annual Pass, America the Beautiful Passes

MAPS: Green Trails Map 99S for Olympic Coast Beaches, Green Trails Map 130S for Ozette

CONTACT: Olympic National Park, Wilderness Information Center, 360/565-3100, www.nps.gov/olym

START THE HIKE

▶ MILE 0-0.7: Rialto Beach to Ellen Creek

The magic of **Rialto Beach** is obvious as soon as you step foot the sand at the end of the short path at the north end of the parking lot. James Island is visible to the south at the mouth of the Quillayute River. Your journey, however, will take you north on a beach lined with sea stacks and enormous driftwood logs.

After 0.7 mile, cross **Ellen Creek.** While Rialto Beach is one of the few places in Olympic National Park where dogs are allowed, they aren't allowed beyond the creek. A permit (www.nps.gov/olym) is needed to use one of the campsites scattered along the tree line between Ellen Creek and Hole-in-the-Wall.

▶ MILE 0.7-1.5: Ellen Creek to Hole-in-the-Wall

On a clear day, the rocky bulkhead that is your destination is visible for the 0.8 mile beyond the creek. When sea stacks appear from the fog and the ocean subsides, revealing a secret passageway, it seems appropriate that Rialto Beach was named by a famous magician. In the early 1900s, Claude Alexander Conlin, "The Crystal Seer," had a home in the area. He is frequently credited with coining the beach's name, which was often used by theaters of that era.

Pause to skip flat, smooth rocks and to snap pictures of the towering sea stacks and explore the tide pools and enjoy the relaxing sound of waves lapping at the shore. Gulls and bald eagles soar overhead, while

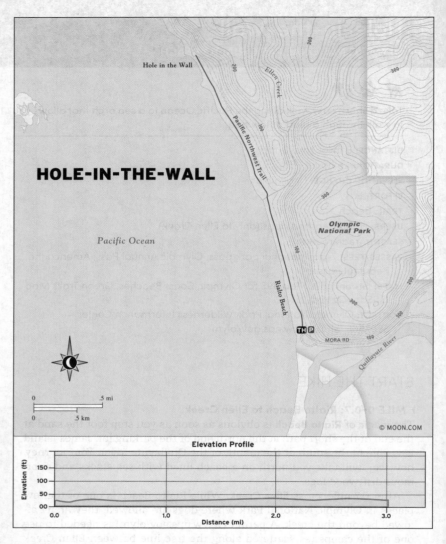

HOLE-IN-THE-WALL

Hole in the Wall

Ellen Creek

Pacific Northwest Trail

Pacific Ocean

Olympic National Park

Rialto Beach

TH P

MORA RD

Quillayute River

0   .5 mi

0   .5 km

© MOON.COM

Elevation Profile

Elevation (ft): 150, 100, 50, 00

Distance (mi): 0.0, 1.0, 2.0, 3.0

guillemots and scoters play in the surf. Just south of Hole-in-the-Wall, a pit toilet is located near what the park service calls the "split rock."

Ideally, you timed your hike to arrive at low tide when the **Hole-in-the-Wall** is usually exposed enough for you to scamper through. The sea arch, chiseled by wind and the sea, is one of the jewels of Washington's wild coast. Even at high tide, you can scramble atop the bluff on a short but steep trail. Find the trail under a black and red disc mounted to a tree.

Follow the beach south to your vehicle when you're ready to return.

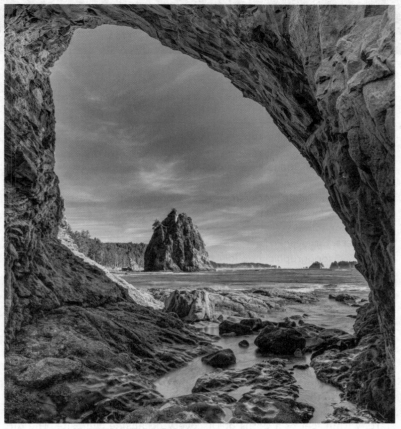

▲ SEA STACKS NEAR HOLE-IN-THE-WALL

DIRECTIONS

From Forks, drive north 1.5 miles on U.S. 101 and turn left on Highway 110. Drive 7.8 miles and turn right on Mora Road. After another 5 miles, arrive at the Rialto Beach parking lot. A toilet is located at the parking lot.

GPS COORDINATES: 47.920983, –124.637986 / N47° 55.259' W124° 38.2792'

BEST NEARBY BITES

La Push is less than a mile south of the trailhead, but you'll have to make an 11-mile (18-minute) drive on Mora and La Push Roads to cross the Quillayute River and reach **River's Edge Restaurant** (41 Main St., 360/374-0777, 8am-8pm daily). Try the fresh salmon or a burger while enjoying the coastal view through enormous picture windows.

🦌 🐾 🚶

Take a hike brimming with history to a sweeping view of the Pacific and a century-old lighthouse.

DISTANCE: 3.8 miles round-trip
DURATION: 2 hours
ELEVATION CHANGE: 300 feet
EFFORT: Easy
TRAIL: Wide and single-track dirt sections, wooden steps, roots, pavement
USERS: Hikers, leashed dogs.
SEASON: Year-round
PASSES/FEES: Discover Pass
MAPS: USGS topographic map for Cape Disappointment
PARK HOURS: 6:30am-dusk daily
CONTACT: Cape Disappointment State Park, 360/642-3078, http://parks.state.wa.us

START THE HIKE

▶ **MILE 0-0.2: North Head Trail to Railroad Tie Steps**

Start your exploration on the north side of the road where a sign welcomes you to the **North Head Trail.** With Sitka spruce towering overhead and the Pacific nowhere to be seen, you might be surprised that this hike starts within feet of a Corps of Discovery oceanside campsite. The dirt trail is flat for the first 0.2 mile as it cuts through the forested wetland to steps fashioned from railroad ties.

Marvel at giant trees as you wander the old-growth forest, but don't spend too much time looking up: Big trees mean big, gnarly roots, and there are plenty of these tripping hazards along the way. The trail can also be quite muddy at times.

▶ **MILE 0.2-1.6: Railroad Tie Steps to Parking Lot**

In another 0.9 mile, steps descend to a **bridge** crossing a creek and then ascend the opposite side. A few hundred yards farther, look for the Pacific through the trees. You aren't likely to regret walking even as the trail brings you to a **parking lot** in 0.5 mile that would have shaved a couple miles off the trip.

▶ **MILE 1.6-1.9: Parking Lot to Lighthouse**

From the lot, pass the **lighthouse keepers' residences** ($154-437/night, www.washington.goingtocamp.com) and follow a wide service road 0.3 mile to the **North Head Lighthouse** and a dramatic coastal view. Built in 1898, the beacon is still active. The lighthouse was deemed necessary when ship captains approaching from the north complained the rocky

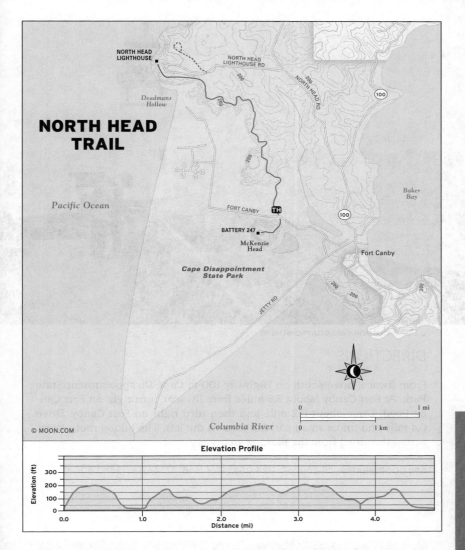

NORTH HEAD TRAIL

North Head Lighthouse

North Head Lighthouse Rd

Deadmans Hollow

Pacific Ocean

Fort Canby

Battery 247

McKenzie Head

Baker Bay

Fort Canby

Cape Disappointment State Park

Jetty Rd

Columbia River

© MOON.COM

0   1 mi
0   1 km

Elevation Profile

headland blocked the nearby Cape Disappointment Lighthouse (the oldest in the state). Lighthouse tours ($2.50 adults, free children 17 and under) start every 20 minutes most days. The view to the south includes tree-covered McKenzie Head where you started the hike.

Return the way you came to complete the hike.

For bonus views, take a short walk on the wide dirt path that ascends McKenzie Head. The well-marked trail starts from the small parking area on the south side of Fort Canby Road. Along the way, get a glimpse of the black and white Cape Disappointment Lighthouse, and atop the hill explore a World War II coastal defense battery. Scramble to the top of the battery for the best view.

▲ LIGHTHOUSE ON CAPE DISAPPOINTMENT

DIRECTIONS

From Ilwaco, drive south on Highway 100 to Cape Disappointment State Park. At Fort Canby (about 5.5 miles from Ilwaco), turn right on Fort Canby Road. Drive about 0.2 mile and then turn right on Fort Canby. Drive 0.4 mile and find a small parking area on the left. The hiking route starts across the street from the parking area.

GPS COORDINATES: 46.285737, –124.063346 / N46° 17.1442' W124° 3.8008'

BEST NEARBY BITES

It would be a shame to visit the Long Beach Peninsula without sampling locally gathered oysters, clams, salmon, and other seafood. There are plenty of good post-hike dining options, including **Drop Anchor Seafood** (900 Pacific Ave. S, Long Beach, 360/642-4224, www.dropanchorseafood.com, 11am-8pm daily) and the **Pickled Fish** (409 Sid Snyder Dr., Long Beach, 360/642-2344, www.pickledfishrestaurant.com, 8am-10pm Mon.-Thurs., 8am-11pm Fri.-Sun.). From the trailhead, the 5-mile drive to Ilwaco takes about 15 minutes via Highway 100. Long Beach is about 3.3 miles (9 minutes) farther north via U.S. 101 and Highway 103.

NEARBY CAMPGROUNDS

NAME	DESCRIPTION	FACILITIES	SEASON	FEE
Cape Disappointment State Park	located on the Pacific Ocean in a setting brimming with history	310 RV and tent sites, restrooms	year-round	$12–50
244 Robert Gray Drive, Ilwaco, 888/226-7688, www.washington.goingtocamp.com				
Hobuck Beach Resort	on the Makah Indian Reservation steps from the Pacific Ocean	210+ RV and tent sites, restrooms	year-round	$25–40
2726 Makah Passage, Neah Bay, 360/645-2339, www.hobuckbeachresort.com				
Mora Campground	sheltered by coastal forest on the Quillayute River and just minutes from the beach	94 RV and tent sites, restrooms	year-round	$15
Mora Road, 2 miles east of Rialto Beach, 360/565-3130, www.nps.gov/olym				
Ozette Campground	located near Lake Ozette and the Ozette Triangle trailhead	15 tent and RV sites, restrooms	year-round	$20
Hoko-Ozette Road, Ozette, Olympic National Park, 360/565-3130, www.nps.gov/olym				
Kalaloch Campground	popular campground with sites overlooking the Pacific Ocean	170 RV and tent sites, restrooms	year-round	$22
Kalaloch Campground F Road, Kalaloch, Olympic National Park, 360/962-2271, http://recreation.gov				

OLYMPIC NATIONAL PARK

Olympic National Park routinely ranks among the nation's 10 most visited national parks, and it's easy to see why. With beaches, rain forests, churning rivers, cobalt lakes, and a secluded mountain range, this is one of America's most diverse parks. Its beauty is enhanced by the surrounding Olympic National Forest and nearby protected areas like the Dungeness National Wildlife Refuge. Waterfalls, the lush Hoh and Quinault Rain Forests, and sweeping mountaintop views are available for even casual day hikers. Meanwhile, those seeking more challenging adventures have plenty of options for leaving the crowds behind and exploring deep into the wilderness.

▲ SIGNS ON DUNGENESS SPIT

▲ QUINAULT RAIN FOREST NATURE TRAIL LOOP

◀ LAKE IN GRAND VALLEY

1 Dungeness Spit
DISTANCE: 10.2 miles round-trip
DURATION: 5 hours
EFFORT: Moderate/strenuous

2 Hurricane Hill
DISTANCE: 3.4 miles round-trip
DURATION: 2 hours
EFFORT: Easy/moderate

3 Klahhane Ridge
DISTANCE: 5.4 miles round-trip
DURATION: 3 hours
EFFORT: Moderate

4 Hall of Mosses and Hoh River Trail
DISTANCE: 6.7 miles round-trip
DURATION: 3.5 hours
EFFORT: Easy/moderate

5 Grand Valley
DISTANCE: 9.3 miles round-trip
DURATION: 5 hours
EFFORT: Moderate/strenuous

6 Mount Townsend
DISTANCE: 8 miles round-trip
DURATION: 4 hours
EFFORT: Moderate/strenuous

7 Quinault Loop
DISTANCE: 4 miles round-trip
DURATION: 2 hours
EFFORT: Easy

8 Staircase Rapids and Shady Lane
DISTANCE: 4.2 miles round-trip
DURATION: 2 hours
EFFORT: Easy

9 Mount Ellinor
DISTANCE: 3.4 miles round-trip
DURATION: 2.5 hours
EFFORT: Moderate

10 Lena Lake
DISTANCE: 6.8 miles round-trip
DURATION: 3 hours
EFFORT: Moderate

▾ LENA LAKE

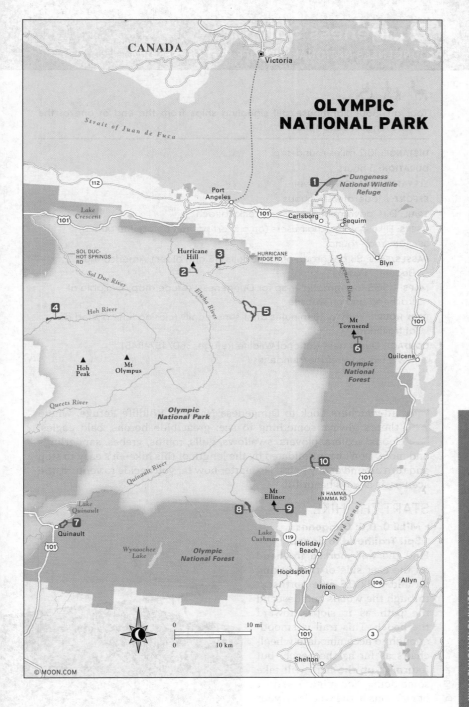

CANADA

● Victoria

Strait of Juan de Fuca

OLYMPIC NATIONAL PARK

112

Port Angeles

Lake Crescent

101

101 Carlsborg   Sequim

1 Dungeness National Wildlife Refuge

Blyn

101

SOL DUC-HOT SPRINGS RD

Sol Duc River

Hurricane Hill **3**

2

HURRICANE RIDGE RD

Elwha River

Dungeness River

4

Hoh River

5

Mt Townsend **6**

Olympic National Forest

Quilcene

101

▲ Hoh Peak

▲ Mt Olympus

Queets River

Olympic National Park

Quinault River

10

101

N HAMMA HAMMA RD

Mt Ellinor **9**

8

Lake Quinault

7

Quinault

101

Wynoochee Lake

Olympic National Forest

Lake Cushman

119 Holiday Beach

Hood Canal

Hoodsport

Union   **106**   Allyn

3

101

Shelton

0   10 mi

0   10 km

© MOON.COM

Tour an 1850s lighthouse still signaling ships from the end of one of the world's longest sand spits.

DISTANCE: 10.2 miles round–trip

DURATION: 5 hours

ELEVATION CHANGE: 130 feet

EFFORT: Moderate/strenuous

TRAIL: Dirt, pavement, sandy and rocky beach

USERS: Hikers, wheelchair users (on a short portion before the beach)

SEASON: Year–round

PASSES/FEES: $3 per group of four adults (16 and older), America the Beautiful Passes

MAPS: USGS topographic map for Dungeness; refuge map available at trailhead and on website

PARK HOURS: 7am to 30 minutes after sunset daily (closing time posted daily at trailhead)

CONTACT: Dungeness National Wildlife Refuge, 360/457-8451, www.fws.gov/refuge/dungeness

B ird-watchers flock to Dungeness National Wildlife Refuge, where there's always something to see: great blue herons, bald eagles, loons, scoters, plovers, swallows, gulls, robins, grebes, sanderlings and more. Don't be intimidated by the length of this hike—it's easy to stop and turn around at any point. No matter how far you decide to venture, the scenery is always beautiful.

START THE HIKE

▶ **MILE 0-0.5: Dungeness Spit Trailhead to Beach**

Find the **well-marked trailhead** on the east side of the parking lot and walk 0.5 mile northeast through the woods and descend the path as it slopes toward the **beach.** This trail is smooth enough to accommodate wheelchairs as far as the beach, but returning up the path will take some doing. You might see deer or raccoons in the woods on your way to trailside overlooks with

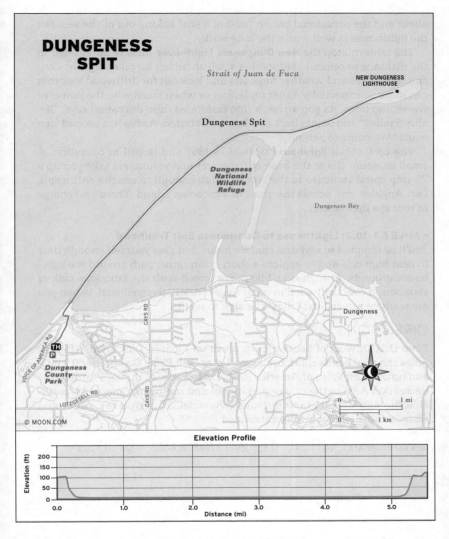

DUNGENESS SPIT

Strait of Juan de Fuca

NEW DUNGENESS LIGHTHOUSE

Dungeness Spit

Dungeness
National
Wildlife
Refuge

Dungeness Bay

Dungeness

CAYS RD

VOICE OF AMERICA RD

TH
P
Dungeness
County
Park

LOTZGESELL RD

CAYS RD

0   1 mi

0   1 km

© MOON.COM

Elevation Profile

Elevation (ft)

200
150
100
50
0

0.0   1.0   2.0   3.0   4.0   5.0

Distance (mi)

telescopes to aid viewing one of the world's longest sand spits. The narrow spit, reaching nearly 5 miles into the Strait of Juan de Fuca, is formed by currents depositing sediment from rivers and coastal erosion.

On the **beach**, a **sign** states, "Birds only beyond this sign." The area hosts up to 25,000 shorebirds during their spring migration and about half that many in summer and fall. While most of the spit (and all of attached Graveyard Spit) is closed to humans, the west-side beach is open year-round.

▶ MILE 0.5–5.1: Beach to Lighthouse

Reaching the lighthouse requires 4.6 miles of **beach,** but it doesn't have to be your destination. Just a few steps on the beach will be enough to enjoy the waves lapping at your feet and the sight of sanderlings scampering about and the occasional brown head of a seal poking out of the sea. But the lighthouse is well worth the long walk.

The lantern atop the **New Dungeness Lighthouse** flickers far enough in the distance to remind visitors this stroll shouldn't be taken lightly. Consult tide tables and weather forecasts and look out for driftwood logs that can move unexpectedly either underfoot or when faced with the power of waves and tides. As you arrive, a sign fashioned from driftwood says, "Reality 5 miles" and points back to where you started. Above it, a second sign reads "Welcome to Serenity."

The 63-foot-tall **lighthouse** opened in 1857 and is still in operation. A small museum sits at the base of the tower and volunteers take you up a 75-step spiral staircase to the lantern, high enough to see the entire spit, Port Angeles, and across the strait to Vancouver Island. There's no charge to tour the lighthouse.

▶ **MILE 5.1–10.2: Lighthouse to Dungeness Spit Trailhead**
You'll be tempted to stay and chat for hours, but give yourself enough time to beat high tide and to explore a short interpretive path around the lighthouse grounds. At high tide, hikers are forced with the laborious task of clambering over driftwood in order to get back to the trailhead. When you are ready to return, just follow the sign to reality.

DIRECTIONS

From U.S. 101 west of Sequim, turn north on Kitchen-Dick Road. After 3.2 miles the road bends right, becoming Lotzgesell Road. Go another 0.2 mile and turn left on Voice of America Road. Drive 1.1 miles through Dungeness Recreation Area to the refuge parking lot and trailhead. Camping is available through Clallam County Parks (www.clallam.net/parks). Water and restrooms are available at the trailhead.

GPS COORDINATES: 48.141341, –123.190549 / N48° 8.4805' W123° 11.4329'

BEST NEARBY BITES

After hiking along the Salish Sea, get a taste of its bounty at **Salty Girls Sequim Seafood Co.** (210 W. Washington St., 360/775-3787, www.saltygirlsseafood.com, hours vary). The oyster bar has local beer on tap and a menu that includes oysters (raw or baked), steamed clams, and Dungeness crab from Olympic Peninsula suppliers. From the trailhead, the 7-mile drive southeast takes about 15 minutes via Sequim–Dungeness Way.

🦌 ❀ 🚶 ♿

Get serious bang for your buck on this easy hike with mile-high views of the Strait of Juan de Fuca, British Columbia, and Cascade and Olympic peaks.

DISTANCE: 3.4 miles round-trip

DURATION: 2 hours

ELEVATION CHANGE: 700 feet

EFFORT: Easy/moderate

TRAIL: Dirt, pavement

USERS: Hikers, wheelchair users

SEASON: June–October, snowshoeing in winter

PASSES/FEES: 7-day national park pass, Olympic Annual Pass, America the Beautiful Passes

MAPS: Green Trails Map 134S for Elwha North–Hurricane Ridge

CONTACT: Olympic National Park Wilderness Information Center, 360/565-3130, www.nps.gov/olym

[handwritten: an amazing veiw, time & date were perfect]

[handwritten margin note: 06 Tues 6/30/2015 4:35PM 5hr]

This is a perfect hike for people of all ages, and as a result it's often crowded, which takes a toll on the trail and makes parking difficult. The park is in the middle of a **rehabilitation project,** so check availability before you go. During construction, the hike starts at **Picnic Area B,** with a 0.3-mile serpentine path through the trees to reach the main trail.

START THE HIKE

▶ **MILE 0–0.4: Parking Lot to Hurricane Hill Path**

You'll start getting views of the Bailey Range before you even open your car door. At the primary parking lot, signs point the way to the wide, **paved path**. From here, there's hardly a step that doesn't have a good view. Purple bells-of-Scotland and other wildflowers add color. Mountain goats and even bears sometimes meander across surrounding slopes. Rabbits, grouse, deer, and marmots make

VIEW FROM HURRICANE HILL ▶

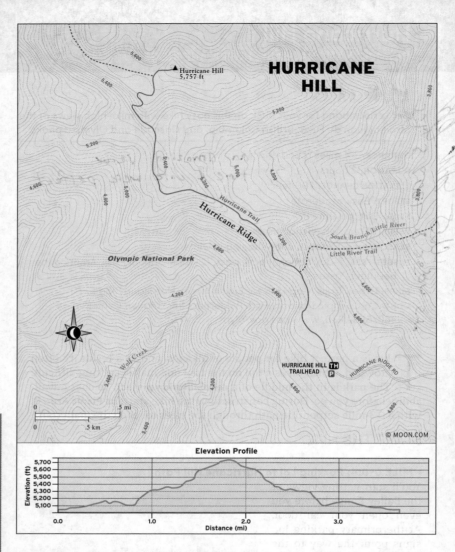

Elevation Profile

© MOON.COM

more frequent appearances. After 0.4 mile, pass a **turnoff** for the **Little River Trail**.

▶ **MILE 0.4-1.5: Hurricane Hill Path to Junction**

In another 0.7 mile, find yourself looking up at the steepest section of the trail. Don't worry—sweeping **switchbacks** make easy work of the 200-foot climb over the next 0.4 mile.

▶ **MILE 1.5-1.7: Junction to Hurricane Hill Viewpoint**

After climbing you'll reach a **junction;** keep straight and follow the path as it bends right, offering several hilltop paths over the next 0.2 mile. Finally, you'll be 5,761 feet above the Strait of Juan de Fuca, enjoying a 360-degree panorama that includes Port Angeles, Vancouver Island, and the peaks of

▲ MOUNTAIN GOATS ON HURRICANE HILL

the Cascades, Olympics, and British Columbia. Take some selfies and explore a battered USGS benchmark on the rocks nearby.

If you can pull yourself away from the view, make your way back to your car the same way you came.

DIRECTIONS

From U.S. 101 in Port Angeles, turn south on Race Street and drive about 1.8 miles (the road changing to Mt. Angeles Road along the way) to the Olympic National Park visitors center. Bear right just beyond the visitors center onto Hurricane Ridge Road and drive 18 miles to Hurricane Ridge. Drive through the parking lot and continue 1.3 miles to the trailhead. (In 2020, the hike will start at Picnic Area B, 1.2 miles beyond the Hurricane Ridge parking lot.) Toilets are located at the trailhead.

GPS COORDINATES: 47.976311, –123.517537 / N47° 58.5787′ W123° 31.0522′

Wonderful climate, beautiful wildlife and views, clear walkway.. easy fave

BEST NEARBY BREWS

Near the Port Angeles ferry terminal, **Barhop Brewing** (124 W. Railroad Ave., 360/797-1818, hours vary) serves rotating house beers and artisan pizza cooked in its stone oven. The brewer describes the beer as "aggressive California-style ales, with a Northwest twist, using fresh Northwest ingredients." Can't beat that. From the trailhead, the 21-mile drive north takes less than 45 minutes via Hurricane Ridge Road and U.S. 101.

OLYMPIC NATIONAL PARK

Hurricane Hill

Climb steep slopes adorned with wildflowers to a ridge overlooking the Strait of Juan de Fuca, Canada, and the Olympics.

DISTANCE: 5.4 miles round-trip
DURATION: 3 hours
ELEVATION CHANGE: 1,700 feet
EFFORT: Moderate
TRAIL: Dirt trail, exposed slopes, rock
USERS: Hikers
SEASON: Mid-June-October
PASSES/FEES: 7-day national park pass, Olympic Annual Pass, America the Beautiful Passes
MAPS: Green Trails Map 134S for Elwha North-Hurricane Ridge
CONTACT: Olympic National Park Wilderness Information Center, 360/565-3130, www.nps.gov/olym

START THE HIKE

▶ MILE 0-0.6: Switchback Trailhead to Trail Intersection

The **Switchback Trail**'s name gives away what's in store as you depart the tiny roadside parking area next to a cascading creek. This trailhead, with a sign clearly marking the trail, is one of four in the park with trails leading to skyscraping Klahhane Ridge. This is the shortest trail, but it's also the steepest. You may spot bears, deer, mountain goats, and marmots, but keep your distance. An **intersection** appears at a switchback 0.6 mile into the hike.

▶ MILE 0.6-1.6: Trail Intersection to Klahhane Ridge

A sign points left to Hurricane Ridge (a mellower 2.5-mile hike); you can make an escape here if you wish, but you'll get more breathtaking views if you turn right and continue climbing **Klahhane Ridge.** The view improves with each step over the next 1 mile. Avalanche lilies, lupine, scarlet paintbrush, and other wildflowers color the slopes in summer. Mount

VIEW FROM KLAHHANE RIDGE ▶

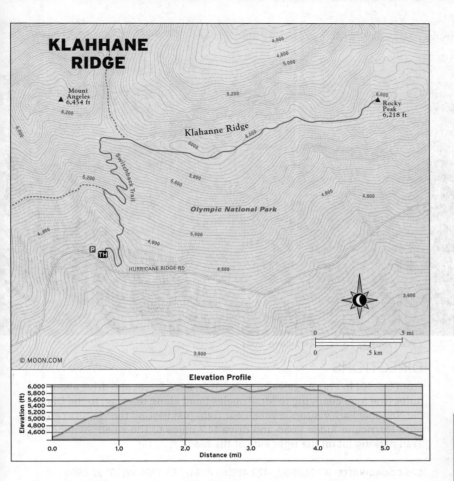

KLAHHANE RIDGE

Mount
Angeles
6,454 ft

Rocky
Peak
6,218 ft

Klahanne Ridge

Switchback Trail

Olympic National Park

P TH

HURRICANE RIDGE RD

0 .5 mi

0 .5 km

© MOON.COM

Elevation Profile

Olympus is visible to the south, and below you can see cars and hardy cyclists ascending Hurricane Ridge Road. The climbing ends as you arrive at a **saddle** between two rocky peaks. Here, the view doubles in grandeur with the additions of the Strait of Juan de Fuca and Victoria on Vancouver Island.

▶ MILE 1.6–2.7: Klahhane Ridge to High Point

From the **saddle**, you can turn left to descend to Heather Park, but I recommend going right for a real treat. The thrill of strolling across the sky is likely to encourage even those with tired legs to push on a little farther.

Over the next 1.1 miles, stroll across the basalt rocks of **Klahhane Ridge,** enjoying views of Port Angeles's Ediz Hook and Sequim's Dungeness Spit reaching into the strait 6,000 feet below. You'll make a final short climb and arrive at a **high point** ideal for a break. This is a good place to turn back. Beyond this point, the trail starts descending to Lake Angeles.

For the return trip, retrace your path across the ridge and head back down the **Switchback Trail.** Your knees are likely to be less cranky about the steep descent if you use trekking poles.

▲ PORT ANGELES SEEN FROM KLAHHANE RIDGE

DIRECTIONS

From U.S. 101 in Port Angeles, turn south on Race Street and drive about 1.8 miles (the road changing to Mt. Angeles Road along the way) to the Olympic National Park visitors center. Bear right just beyond the visitors center onto Hurricane Ridge Road and drive 14.7 miles to the small Switchback Trail parking lot on the right side of the road.

GPS COORDINATES: 47.986502, −123.461159 / N47° 59.1901' W123° 27.6695

BEST NEARBY BITES

In Discovery Bay, stop at the giant wood-carved hamburger sitting in front of **Fat Smitty's** (282624 U.S. 101, 360/385-4099, www.fatsmittys. com, 10:30am-7pm daily). The Smitty Burger that headlines the menu isn't as big as the sculpture, but it is gargantuan in its own right. The most expensive wallpaper on the peninsula is courtesy of visitors who decorate dollar bills and pin them to the walls and ceiling. Every five years a Boy Scout troop removes the money (more than $26,000 in 2017), which is donated to the Scouts and other local organizations. From the trailhead, the 51-mile drive east takes about 1 hour, 15 minutes via Hurricane Ridge Road and U.S. 101.

Wander beneath blankets of moss hanging from towering trees as you follow family-friendly trails through the Hoh Rain Forest.

BEST: Spring Hikes
DISTANCE: 6.7 miles round-trip
DURATION: 3.5 hours
ELEVATION CHANGE: 300 feet
EFFORT: Easy/moderate
TRAIL: Dirt trail, bridge crossings
USERS: Hikers, wheelchair users
SEASON: Year-round
PASSES/FEES: 7-day national park pass, Olympic Annual Pass, America the Beautiful Passes
MAPS: Green Trails Map 133S for Seven Lakes Basin–Mount Olympus
CONTACT: Hoh Rain Forest Visitor Center, www.nps.gov/olym

This route combines the very popular Hall of Mosses loop with a taste of the less traversed Hoh River Trail, the entirety of which stretches 17.3 miles to Glacier Meadows beneath Mount Olympus, the highest peak on the Olympic Peninsula. On summer afternoons, Olympic National Park uses meter lights to control traffic as visitors flock from around the globe to experience the Hoh's lush, green wonderland. Get here early to avoid the crowds.

START THE HIKE

▶ **MILE 0-0.9: Visitors Center to Hall of Mosses**
Starting from the visitors center, walk about 0.1 mile to an **intersection** and sign directing you left toward the **Hall of Mosses.** The 0.8-mile Hall of Mosses loop lives up to its name as you quickly find yourself immersed in green. Ferns and other plants cover the forest floor, trees with bizarre root formations line the path, and sheets of moss hang from branches. Make sure to make the 200-foot side trip to the **Maple Grove.**

▶ **MILE 0.9-3.8: Hall of Mosses to Hoh River Trail**
After completing the loop, return to the first intersection and continue straight for 0.1 mile to the **Hoh River Trail.** As **Mineral Creek** cascades down a moss-covered cliff on its way to the river, it creates a lovely setting and a good destination for those wanting to sample the trail. Reach the falls by walking the mostly flat, neatly groomed Hoh River Trail for 2.8 miles. Along the way, listen to chirping birds and the churning Hoh River while keeping a lookout for Roosevelt elk.

Hall of Mosses and Hoh River Trail

OLYMPIC NATIONAL PARK

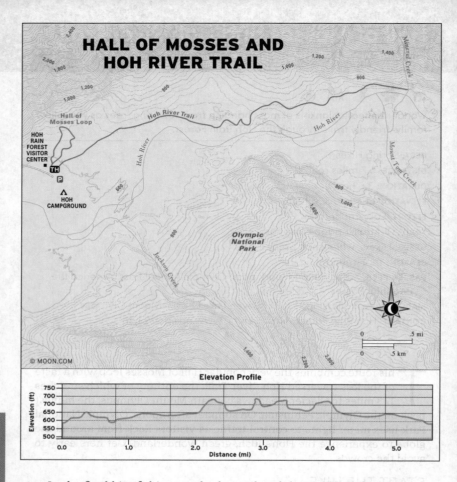

HALL OF MOSSES AND HOH RIVER TRAIL

Elevation Profile

In the final bit of this stretch, the trail undulates a bit before coming to a **bridge** crossing Mineral Creek. The falls are visible through the vegetation. On the far side of the crossing, a well-worn social trail leads up the slope to the base of the falls. However, rangers prefer visitors stay off this path to protect the undergrowth.

▶ **MILE 3.8–6.7: Hoh River Trail to Visitors Center**
From here you can continue deeper into the rain forest or turn back to return 2.9 miles to the visitors center.

▲ MINERAL CREEK FALLS

DIRECTIONS
From U.S. 101 (12 miles south of Forks and 90 miles north of Hoquiam) turn east on Upper Hoh Road and drive 18 miles to the Hoh Rain Forest Visitor Center parking lot. Restrooms and camping are available.

GPS COORDINATES: 47.860490, –123.934749 / N47° 51.6294' W123° 56.0849'

BEST NEARBY BITES
Looking out over Kalaloch Creek and the Pacific Ocean, it's hard to beat the view at **Creekside Restaurant** (157151 U.S. 101, 866/622-9928, www.thekalalochlodge.com, hours vary). The restaurant partners with local farms and businesses to produce delicious, hearty fare. Try the dry-rubbed salmon or the bacon, lettuce, tomato, and avocado sandwich. From the trailhead, the 39-mile drive southwest takes about 55 minutes via Upper Hoh Road and U.S. 101.

🦌 ❋

Watch marmots play, relax beside a pristine lake, and gaze at Mount Olympus while hiking through the aptly named Grand Valley.

BEST: Wildflower Hikes

DISTANCE: 9.3 miles round-trip

DURATION: 5 hours

ELEVATION CHANGE: 2,500 feet

EFFORT: Moderate/strenuous

TRAIL: Dirt trail, log crossing, loose rock, rock steps

USERS: Hikers

SEASON: Mid-July–mid-October

PASSES/FEES: 7-day national park pass, Olympic Annual Pass, America the Beautiful Passes

MAPS: Green Trails Map 134S for Elwha North–Hurricane Ridge

CONTACT: Olympic National Park Wilderness Information Center, 360/565-3130, www.nps.gov/olym

START THE HIKE

▸ **MILE 0–0.2: Parking Lot to Badger Valley Trail**

Make your way to the eastern edge of one of the highest parking lots in the Olympics (elev. 6,100 feet). This hike starts at **Obstruction Point,** which would be a fulfilling destination for most hikes—but on this trail it's just the beginning. Admire the view of the snowcapped Olympics and the lush green valleys below before following the signs left to **Badger Valley and Deer Park.** Yes, the sign points right for a more direct trip to Grand Lake, but Badger Valley offers a gentler, more knee-friendly descent; you'll finish the loop on the other trail. In 0.2 mile, you'll reach an unmarked **intersection** on the slope beneath Obstruction Point. Turn right at the intersection to drop into the valley on the switchbacking **Badger Valley Trail.**

▸ **MILE 0.2–3.1: Badger Valley Trail to Badger Creek**

The trail is steep at first but soon mellows. After 1 mile, keep straight, passing the Elk Mountain Trail. Over the next 1.9 miles enjoy the peaceful beauty of the valley as you walk along the gurgling **Badger Creek** through sections of forest. Butterflies flutter about scarlet paintbrush, bluebells-of-Scotland, lupine, and other summer wildflowers. The grass alongside the trail sometimes grows waist-high. You may even glimpse a bear.

▸ **MILE 3.1–5.9: Badger Creek to Grand Pass Trail**

You'll cross **Badger Creek** on some stable logs before reaching the first uphill section. Climb for 0.4 mile, cross a bridge over **Grand Creek,** and

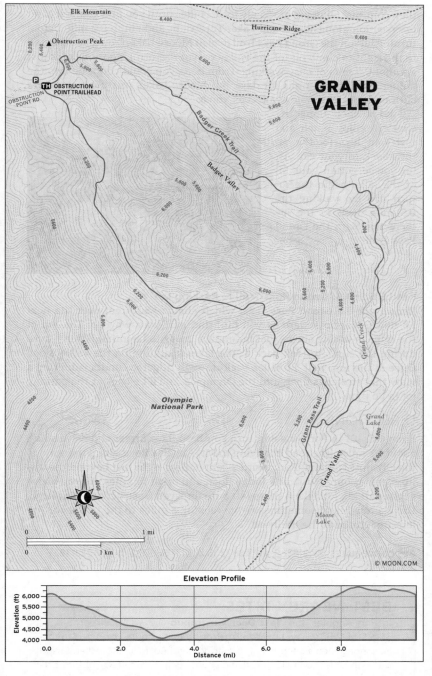

then continue climbing gradually for 1.2 miles until you find yourself at an intersection alongside **Grand Lake.** Turn right and climb 0.2 mile before turning left on the **Grand Pass Trail** to visit Moose Lake. (You'll use the trail to the right to climb out of the valley on your return.) Moose Lake is just another 0.5 mile of easy walking. From here, you could continue into the wilderness, linking trails for days, but Moose Lake's pristine waters and surrounding steep valley walls beg you to stay.

Find a spot along the shore to enjoy lunch and rest your legs for the return back to your car. After you've gotten your fill of the lake, begin the return trip by walking the 0.5 mile back to the **intersection** with the Grand Pass Trail.

GRAND LAKE ▸

▸ **MILE 5.9–9.3: Grand Pass Trail to Parking Lot**

Return via the **Grand Pass Trail,** which climbs 1,500 feet over the next 1.8 miles. Marmots stare as you huff and puff your way up. The top of the ridge is visible above, just far enough away to be intimidating. Pause during the climb to look back at the lakes sparkling on the valley floor. Once at the top, walk 1.6 miles back through ridgetop tundra, admiring a view that stretches deep into the Olympics. You'll be back at the parking lot in no time.

DIRECTIONS

From U.S. 101 in Port Angeles, turn south on Race Street and drive south about 1.8 miles (the road changing to Mt. Angeles Road along the way) to the Olympic National Park visitors center. Bear right just beyond the visitors center onto Hurricane Ridge Road and drive 18 miles. As you arrive at the parking lot, take a sharp left onto unpaved Obstruction Point Road. Drive a rough and sometimes nerve-racking 8 miles to the trailhead. Toilets are located at the trailhead.

GPS COORDINATES: 47.918386, –123.382303 / N47° 55.1032′ W123° 22.9382′

BEST NEARBY BITES

In Port Angeles, the **Next Door Gastropub** (113 W. 1st Street, Ste. A, 360/504-2613, www.nextdoorgastropub.com, hours vary) is a favorite among locals because of its outdoor seating, local ingredients, and a burger selection with creative options such as a coffee-rubbed bacon cheeseburger called Not Your Average Joe. From the trailhead, the 27-mile drive north takes less than 90 minutes via Hurricane Ridge Road and U.S. 101.

6

Mount Townsend

OLYMPIC NATIONAL FOREST

Wander upward past waterfalls, rhododendrons, and wildflowers to a peak with views of the Olympics, Cascades, and the Strait of Juan de Fuca.

DISTANCE: 8 miles round-trip
DURATION: 4 hours
ELEVATION CHANGE: 3,000 feet
EFFORT: Moderate/strenuous
TRAIL: Dirt, rock
USERS: Hikers, leashed dogs
SEASON: June–November
PASSES/FEES: None
MAPS: Green Trails Map 136 for Tyler Peak
CONTACT: Olympic National Forest, Hood Canal Ranger District,
360/765-2200, www.fs.usda.gov

Mount Townsend gives away a million-dollar view for free—unless you count the toll it takes on your legs. A view stretching from Vancouver Island to Seattle and the Cascades awaits atop the broad 6,280-foot peak. You just have to climb 3,000 feet to get there.

START THE HIKE

▶ **MILE 0-1.6: Mount Townsend Upper Trailhead to Townsend Creek**
Starting from the **upper trailhead,** follow the path at the west end of the parking lot as it climbs into the woods. The sound of Townsend Creek splashing toward the Big Quilcene River welcomes you as you approach a series of **switchbacks.** Pass hemlocks, Douglas fir, cedar, and rhododendrons (typically blooming in May and June), and maybe cross paths with a deer or smaller critters as you continue upward. After 1.5 miles, you get your first glimpse of what makes this hike special as you step from the trees and get a view of the upper slope. Cross **Townsend Creek** beneath a tiny cascade and find another stack of switchbacks in 0.1 mile.

▶ **MILE 1.6-3: Townsend Creek to Silver Lakes Trail Intersection**
In another 1.1 miles, a sign points right to continue climbing (but if you're ready for a break, take a quick 50-yard detour to the left and enjoy tiny Windy Lake). The **switchbacks** continue, passing the **intersection** with the Silver Lakes Trail in another 0.3 mile.

▶ **MILE 3-4: Silver Lakes Trail Intersection to Mount Townsend Summit**
The steepest section of trail is beyond **Silver Lakes junction,** but it doesn't last long. The trees thin and scarlet paintbrush, fireweed, and other plants add color as the next 0.7 mile puts you atop the ridge. From here the incline

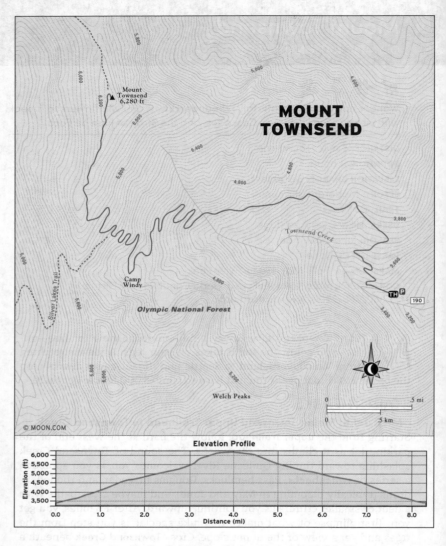

is gradual as you walk the final 0.3 mile (staying right at the **intersection** just below the high point).

The bird's-eye view is the highlight of any trip to the summit. Dungeness Spit reaching out into the Strait of Juan de Fuca, Townsend's Olympic neighbors, Seattle's glistening skyline, Puget Sound, and the Cascades all unfurl below you. Rock outcroppings give hikers plenty of places to sit and enjoy lunch or duck out of the wind. A USGS benchmark is affixed to one of the rocks.

Recharge your legs with a little break before asking them to carry you back down the same trail they just hauled you up.

▲ MOUNT TOWNSEND

DIRECTIONS

Follow U.S. 101 to Penny Creek Road (0.9 mile south of Quilcene Ranger Station and 50.5 miles north of Shelton) and turn west. Drive 1.5 miles and bear left on Big Quilcene River Road/Forest Road 27 and drive 13.5 miles (past the Mount Townsend Trail sign directing traffic to the lower trailhead) to Forest Road 27-190 and turn left. Follow the road 0.8 mile to the small trailhead parking lot. A toilet is located at the trailhead.

GPS COORDINATES: 47.85611, –123.03597 / N47° 51.3666' W123° 2.1582'

BEST NEARBY BITES

At Quilcene's **Gear Head Deli** (294963 U.S. 101, 360/301-3244, 10am-4pm Tues.-Sat.), grab lunch for your hike or relax on the deck with a pulled pork sandwich served on a ciabatta roll. The pork is smoked in-house and topped with homemade barbecue sauce. From the trailhead, the 17-mile drive southeast takes less than 45 minutes via Big Quilcene River Road/Forest Road 27 and U.S. 101.

OLYMPIC NATIONAL PARK

Mount Townsend

Combine two trails to experience the vast variety of this rain forest—giant trees, a cedar bog, waterfalls, and Lake Quinault.

BEST: Waterfall Hikes

DISTANCE: 4 miles round-trip

DURATION: 2 hours

ELEVATION CHANGE: 350 feet

EFFORT: Easy

TRAIL: Dirt; boardwalk, paved road when the lakeshore is flooded

USERS: Hikers, wheelchair users (on a short portion of Rain Forest Nature Loop), leashed dogs

SEASON: Year-round

PASSES/FEES: Northwest Forest Pass

MAPS: Green Trails Map 197 for Lake Quinault, Custom Correct Map for Quinault-Colonel Bob

CONTACT: Olympic National Park, Pacific Ranger District, 360/288-2525, www.fs.usda.gov

A long the way, keep an eye out for squirrels scampering up trees, Chinook salmon spawning in the streams during the fall, and bald eagles soaring above the lake.

START THE HIKE

▶ **MILE 0-0.3: Trailhead Kiosk to Quinault Loop Trail**

Moss and a tiny tree grow atop the **trailhead kiosk.** Take about 10 steps up the trail and come to a choice: right or left on the 0.5-mile **Rain Forest Nature Trail Loop**? Either direction works, but turning left is the most direct route for this hike—and it immediately delivers a colossal 400-year-old Douglas fir. (The Forest Service lists the first portion of the nature loop in either direction as wheelchair accessible.) After 0.1 mile, pass a trail on your left (you'll close your loop hike at this intersection) and walk 0.2 mile along the edge of a narrow gorge holding Willaby Creek. At another mossy kiosk, turn left on the **Quinault Loop Trail** (staying to the right takes you on the remainder of the nature loop and back to the trailhead).

▶ **MILE 0.3-2.2: Quinault Loop Trail to Cascade Falls**

Enjoy a quiet walk dwarfed by 15- to 20-story-tall western hemlocks, Douglas firs, western red cedars, and Sitka spruce. Pass a closed trail on the right shortly before crossing a **bridge over Willaby Creek.** In 1 mile, come to the intersection with the **Willaby Creek Trail** and continue straight. The trail can get muddy before **boardwalks** offer a cleaner (but sometimes slippery)

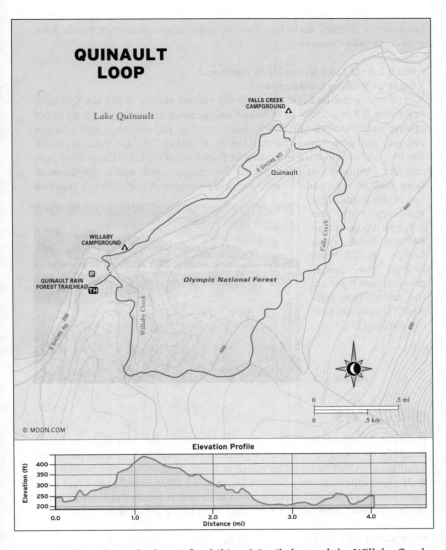

QUINAULT LOOP

Lake Quinault

FALLS CREEK
CAMPGROUND

S SHORE RD

Quinault

Falls Creek

WILLABY
CAMPGROUND

QUINAULT RAIN
FOREST TRAILHEAD

Olympic National Forest

Willaby Creek

S SHORE RD

© MOON.COM

.5 mi

.5 km

Elevation Profile

route through a cedar bog. After hiking 0.6 mile beyond the Willaby Creek Trail intersection, pass a triangle kiosk and a trail on your left heading to historic Lake Quinault Lodge. (This 0.6-mile trail is a good option if you're looking for a shortcut.) Go right and cross a **bridge over Falls Creek.** In another 0.3 mile, cross the bridge at **Cascade Falls** where you're sure to be inspired to pause for a photo.

▶ MILE 2.2–2.8: Cascade Falls to Lake Quinault

An intersection 0.2 mile farther gives you the option to extend your trip. (Turning right on the Gatton Creek Trail delivers more forest, falls, and creeks with an option to visit the "World's Largest Sitka Spruce.") But, to head to the lakeshore, turn left and cross Falls Creek on a **wooden bridge.** In 0.4 mile, cross **South Shore Road** near the ranger station. The trail travels between Falls Creek and a fence before arriving at the shore of nearly four-mile-long **Lake Quinault.**

▶ MILE 2.8–4: Lake Quinault to Trailhead Kiosk or Willaby Campground

A trail traces the **lakeshore** behind the ranger station and Lake Quinault Lodge for 0.9 mile back to **Willaby Campground.** However, the trail is not always passable: The rain forest gets more than 130 inches of precipitation per year and sometimes the trail floods. If this is the case, you can finish the loop by walking Shore Road and then following Lake Loop Road past cabins to Willaby Campground. At the campground, rejoin the **Quinault Loop Trail** as it crosses a concrete **bridge** where Willaby Creek tumbles out of the gorge. The trail climbs into the gorge as it passes under the Shore Road bridge. In 0.2 mile beyond the campground, turn right on the nature loop and walk 0.1 mile back to the parking lot.

LAKE QUINAULT ▶

DIRECTIONS

From northbound U.S. 101, 38 miles north of Hoquiam, turn right on Shore Road. Drive 1.4 miles and turn right into the trailhead parking lot. From southbound U.S. 101, 65 miles south of Forks, turn left on Old State Route 9. Drive 1.1 miles and turn left on Shore Road. Continue 0.4 mile and turn right into the trailhead parking lot. A restroom is located at the trailhead. Willaby Creek Campground is on the left, 0.1 mile down Shore Road.

GPS COORDINATES: 47.459812, –123.862387 / N47° 27.5887' W123° 51.7432'

BEST NEARBY BITES

Nine months before President Franklin D. Roosevelt signed the bill creating Olympic National Park, he had lunch at the **Lake Quinault Lodge** (360/288-2900, www.olympicnationalparks.com, 7:30am-8pm daily). The dining room now bears Roosevelt's name. The lunch menu includes several styles of burgers and sandwiches including a smoked salmon BLT. Reservations are accepted but not required. From the trailhead, the 1-mile drive northeast takes less than 2 minutes via Shore Drive.

Combine two trails into one kid-friendly hike through a mossy forest of towering trees—both upright and fallen—while visiting rumbling rapids and crossing a suspension bridge.

DISTANCE: 4.2 miles round-trip

DURATION: 2 hours

ELEVATION CHANGE: 300 feet

EFFORT: Easy

TRAIL: Wide dirt path, suspension bridge

USERS: Hikers, wheelchair users

SEASON: Year-round, but road may close for snow and add 1 mile each way to hike

PASSES/FEES: 7-day national park pass, Olympic Annual Pass, America the Beautiful Passes

MAPS: Green Trails Map 167 for Mount Steel

CONTACT: Olympic National Park, 360/565-3130, www.nps.gov/olym

START THE HIKE

▶ **MILE 0-1: Ranger Station to Shady Lane**
Start from the ranger station and, over the first 0.1 mile, cross the North Fork Skokomish River on a wide **bridge.** Once on the other side, a sign points left to **Shady Lane Trail.** The next 0.1 mile leading to the wooden bridge over Elk Creek is flat and the dirt tread is wheelchair friendly. Beyond the bridge, the trail continues to follow the North Fork Skokomish River opposite the 49-site Staircase Campground. Even on sunny days you'll find the trail is aptly named as you pass under cedars, hemlocks, and Douglas firs. Keep an eye out for elk, birds, and butterflies as you wander 0.8 mile to the trail's end at a small parking lot on Forest Road 2451 (an alternate starting point).

▶ **MILE 1-1.9: Shady Lane to River Bridge**
By the time you follow the trail back to the river **bridge,** you'll have 1.9 miles under your belt. If you're up for part two of this hike, turn left on the **Staircase Rapids Loop.**

▶ **MILE 1.9-2.3: Staircase Rapids Loop to Big Cedar**
Shortly after starting the **Staircase Rapids Loop,** pass a **spur** on the left leading to the small Elk Creek hydro plant that powers the ranger station. Continue another 0.3 mile to a sign pointing left to the **"Big Cedar."** The short side trip (about 0.1 mile round-trip) visits a fallen 14-foot-wide western red cedar. Immediately after finishing this fascinating aside, pass a

Staircase Rapids and Shady Lane

OLYMPIC NATIONAL PARK

235

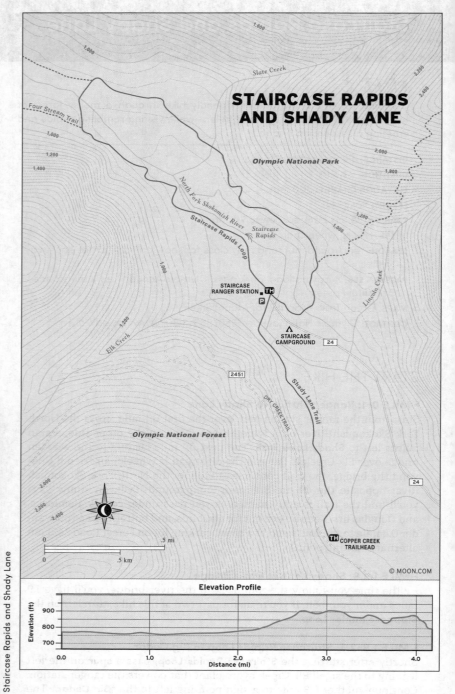

STAIRCASE RAPIDS AND SHADY LANE

Elevation Profile

▲ SUSPENSION BRIDGE ACROSS THE NORTH FORK SKOKOMISH RIVER

viewpoint of the river and its rapids. The park classifies the path up to this point (including the Big Cedar spur) as wheelchair accessible, but I'd concur with the trail brochure's footnote: "May need assistance." Those uncomfortable rolling across this terrain can backtrack to the river.

▶ **MILE 2.3–3: Big Cedar to North Fork Skokomish River Suspension Bridge**
Spend the next 0.6 mile following the river and enjoying the moss-covered trees and boulders until you reach an **intersection** with the Four Stream Trail. Turn right to stay on the loop trail and walk 0.1 mile to a **suspension bridge** crossing the North Fork Skokomish River.

▶ **MILE 3–4.2: North Fork Skokomish River Suspension Bridge to Parking Lot**
After crossing the bridge—and snapping a few photos—stay left and, shortly after, reach the **North Fork Skokomish River Trail.** Turn right where the sign points the way back to the ranger station. This section of the loop is quieter as it travels farther from the river. Cross a couple of creeks and enjoy the lush greenery as the path meanders 1.1 miles back to Staircase's **parking lot.** Follow the parking lot's driveway downhill to return to the ranger station and campground in a short distance.

DIRECTIONS

From U.S. 101 in Hoodsport, head west on Highway 119 for 9.3 miles. At the stop sign turn left on Forest Road 24 and drive 6.6 miles to the Staircase Ranger Station and the trailhead. The driveway to the parking lot is just before the ranger station. Toilets and a campground are located at the trailhead.

GPS COORDINATES: 47.515213, –123.328773 / N47° 30.9128′ W123° 19.7264′

🦌 ❄ 🐾

Let views of Rainier, the Hood Canal, and Lake Cushman inspire you upward to a mountaintop on every Olympic hiker's must-do list.

BEST: Dog-Friendly Hikes
DISTANCE: 3.4 miles round-trip
DURATION: 2.5 hours
ELEVATION CHANGE: 2,400 feet
EFFORT: Moderate
TRAIL: Dirt, log steps, rock, scree
USERS: Hikers, leashed dogs
SEASON: July–October
PASSES/FEES: Northwest Forest Pass
MAPS: Custom Correct Map for Mount Skokomish–Lake Cushman, Green Trails Map 168SX for Olympic Mountains East
CONTACT: Olympic National Forest, Hood Canal Ranger District, 360/765-2200, www.fs.usda.gov

There are three trailhead options for climbing Mount Ellinor, but don't think that starting from the upper parking lot makes this trip easy. You'll just get to the steep stuff (and some of the best views in the Olympics) a little quicker.

START THE HIKE

▶ **MILE 0-0.7: Mount Ellinor Upper Trailhead to Winter Trail Junction**
Find the **upper trailhead** on the west edge of the parking lot and quickly enter the woods. The trail climbs gradually for 0.3 mile until it **intersects** with the trail approaching from the lower lot. Turn right to continue upward. In another 0.4 mile, a sign marks the **junction** with the winter trail. Unless you have mountaineering gear and the requisite skills and the rocky upper slopes are covered with snow, the winter route isn't advised. Continue straight to stay on the **summer trail** as the climbing starts to get serious.

▶ **MILE 0.7-1.7: Winter Trail Junction to Mount Ellinor Summit**
The woods soon give way to **subalpine meadows** where daisies, purple Jeffrey's shooting stars, yarrow, and other wildflowers grow. There is no shade as you scamper up rocky steps and steep pitches. On hot summer days you'll be happy to have packed extra water, sunglasses, and a hat.

The higher you climb the more spectacular the view becomes. Lake Cushman and Hood Canal glisten in the glacier-carved landscape. Mount

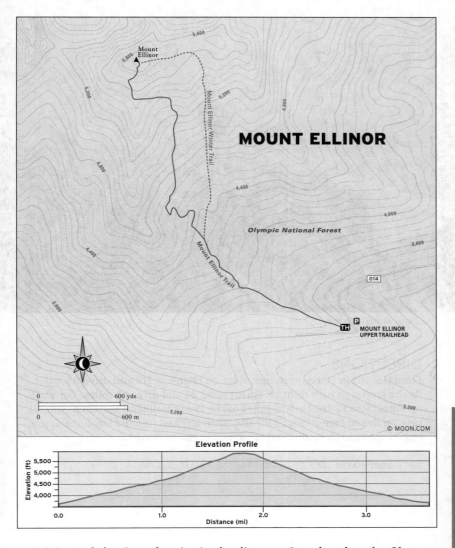

MOUNT ELLINOR

Mount Ellinor

Mount Ellinor Winter Trail

Mount Ellinor Trail

Olympic National Forest

014

MOUNT ELLINOR UPPER TRAILHEAD

© MOON.COM

Elevation Profile

Rainier and the Cascades rise in the distance. Introduced to the Olympics in the 1920s, mountain goats have long frequented Mount Ellinor. Keep your distance if you encounter these creatures, but the likelihood of crossing paths with goats is decreasing: In 2018, federal and state agencies started moving the peninsula's estimated 725 goats to the Cascades. After 1 mile of climbing, the argillite rock of Ellinor's 5,944-foot **summit** offers numerous places to sit, have a snack, and enjoy the scenery from the edge of the Olympics.

If you can pry yourself away from the view, the route back is the same steep trail you used to get here.

▲ ATOP MOUNT ELLINOR

DIRECTIONS

From U.S. 101 in Hoodsport, turn west on Highway 119 and drive 9.3 miles.
At the stop sign turn right on Forest Road 24 and drive 1.6 miles. Turn left
on Forest Road 2419. Drive 5 miles to the lower trailhead and then continue 1.7 miles to Forest Road 2419-014. Turn left and find the trailhead at the
end of the road. A vault toilet is located in the parking lot.

GPS COORDINATES: 47.510271, –123.247888 / N47° 30.6163′ W123° 14.8733′

BEST NEARBY DRINKS

Hoodsport has several options for a post-hike adult beverage. **The
Hardware Distillery Co.** (24210 N. Highway 101, 206/300-0877, www.
thehardwaredistillery.com, hours vary) serves artisan whiskey, gin,
vodka, and other spirits. From the trailhead, the 18-mile drive southeast to Hoodsport takes 45 minutes via Highway119.

Follow a beloved all-ages trail to a picturesque emerald lake surrounded by timber-covered slopes in Olympic National Forest.

DISTANCE: 6.8 miles round-trip
DURATION: 3 hours
ELEVATION CHANGE: 1,300 feet
EFFORT: Moderate
TRAIL: Dirt trail
USERS: Hikers, leashed dogs
SEASON: April-November
PASSES/FEES: Northwest Forest Pass
MAPS: Green Trails Map 168 for The Brothers
CONTACT: Olympic National Forest, Hood Canal Ranger District, 360/765-2200, www.fs.usda.gov

One of the most popular trails on the Olympic Peninsula, Lena Lake fits neatly into a lot of agendas. It's an easy first backpacking trip for the kids, while those looking for a challenge have the option of a butt-kicking extension to a higher lake. Get started early and come on a weekday if you want to avoid the crush of hikers.

START THE HIKE

▶ **MILE 0-1.9: Lena Lake Roadside Trailhead to First Bridge**
Start from the **roadside trailhead** on a wide, mostly smooth path that soon begins its gradual, switchbacking climb through second-growth forest. Listen for the sound of Lena Creek as it rolls downhill to the Hamma Hamma River. After 1.9 miles, reach a **wooden bridge** that inspires many hikers to pause and pose for pictures. The gully beneath the bridge is dry as Lena Creek flows underground in this area.

▶ **MILE 1.9-3: First Bridge to Ledge Viewpoint**
Reach a second photo-worthy **bridge** in another 0.7 mile as you close in on your destination. A **junction** 0.4 mile beyond the bridge allows the option of going left to Upper Lena Lake. Instead, turn right and in a matter of seconds find yourself standing on a **ledge** overlooking the 55-acre lake. Keep an eye out for bear, elk, deer, and a variety of birds.

▶ **MILE 3-3.4: Ledge Viewpoint to Lena Lake**
This space at the edge of the trees is an ideal and scenic destination for day hikers, but you can explore a little more by following the path along the west side of lake for another 0.4 mile (passing campsites and a pit toilet) to another **intersection**. Here you get a second chance to turn left and climb to Upper Lena Lake (note this will quickly take you into

OLYMPIC NATIONAL PARK

Lena Lake

241

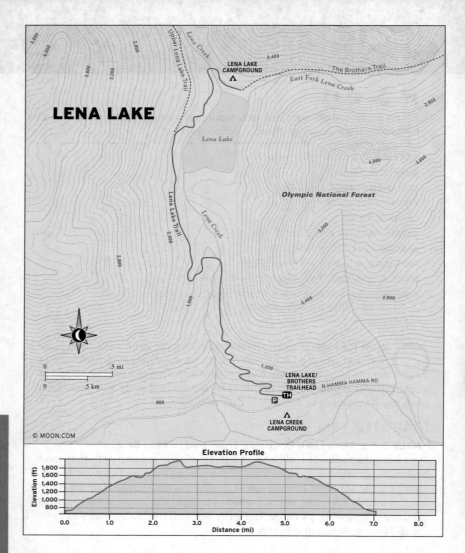

LENA LAKE

Elevation Profile

Olympic National Park, where dogs are not allowed). Go right and in a few steps you'll arrive at an appealing **rest stop** where Lena Creek cascades toward to the lake.

When it's time to leave, return to your car via the Lena Lake Trail.

DIRECTIONS

From U.S. 101 near milepost 318 (14 miles north of Hoodsport and 23 miles south of Quilcene), turn west on Hamma Hamma River Road/Forest Road 25 and drive 7.5 miles to the trailhead. A toilet is located at the trailhead.

GPS COORDINATES: 47.599739, –123.150884 / N47° 35.9843' W123° 9.053'

▲ LENA LAKE

BEST NEARBY BREWS

Located in the small Hood Canal town of Quilcene, **101 Brewery** (294793 U.S. 101, 360/765-6485, www.101brewery.com, 7am-7pm Sun.-Thurs., 7am-8pm Fri.-Sat.) crafts four beers and offers a menu that includes pizza, burgers, pie, and ice cream. Make sure to sample Quilcene's most famous export: oysters. From the trailhead, the 30-mile drive northeast takes less than 45 minutes via Hamma Hamma Road/Forest Road 25 and U.S. 101.

Lena Lake

NEARBY CAMPGROUNDS

NAME	DESCRIPTION	FACILITIES	SEASON	FEE
Sol Duc Campground	situated in thick old-growth forest on the Sol Duc River	82 RV and tent sites, restrooms	year-round	$21

Sol Duc Hot Springs Road, Olympic National Park, 360/565-3130, www.recreation.gov

NAME	DESCRIPTION	FACILITIES	SEASON	FEE
Heart O' the Hills Campground	ideally located for adventures into northern Olympic National Park and Hurricane Ridge	105 RV and tent sites, restrooms	year-round	$20

Hurricane Ridge Road, Port Angeles, Olympic National Park, 360/565-3131, www.nps.gov/olym

NAME	DESCRIPTION	FACILITIES	SEASON	FEE
Staircase Campground	old-growth forest along the Skokomish River	49 RV and tent sites, restrooms	year-round	$20

Staircase Road, Hoodsport, Olympic National Park, 360/565-3131, www.nps.gov/olym

NAME	DESCRIPTION	FACILITIES	SEASON	FEE
Willaby Campground	steps from Lake Quinault and the Quinault Rain Forest Nature Trail Loop	21 RV and tent sites, restrooms	April–November	$25

South Shore Road, Quinault, Olympic National Forest, 360/288-0203, www.recreation.gov

NAME	DESCRIPTION	FACILITIES	SEASON	FEE
Hoh Campground	immersed in the lush greenery of the rain forest	78 RV and tent sites, restrooms	year-round	$20

Hoh Valley Road, Hoh Rain Forest, Olympic National Park, 360/565-3131, www.nps.gov/olym

COLUMBIA RIVER GORGE

Roughly 15,000 years ago, the first of several floods—part of a larger event later dubbed the Missoula Floods—swept through the Columbia River and carved out one of the region's most iconic natural features: the Columbia River Gorge. Some 80 miles long and up to 4,000 feet deep, the river canyon cuts through the Cascades and forms the boundary between Washington and Oregon. Trails on both sides of the Gorge draw nature lovers with their dramatic beauty. The National Scenic Area comprises old-growth forests, spectacular waterfalls, and iconic bluffs and ridges, making it one of the Pacific Northwest's most popular hiking destinations, even after the 2017 Eagle Creek Fire burned nearly 50,000 acres on the Oregon side.

▲ FOOTBRIDGE ON LARCH MOUNTAIN

▲ MOUNT HOOD FROM MCCALL POINT

1 **Latourell Falls Loop**
DISTANCE: 3.1 miles round-trip
DURATION: 1.5 hours
EFFORT: Easy/moderate

2 **Angel's Rest**
DISTANCE: 4.9 miles round-trip
DURATION: 2.5 hours
EFFORT: Moderate

3 **Wahkeena Falls-Multnomah Falls Loop**
DISTANCE: 5.9 miles round-trip
DURATION: 3 hours
EFFORT: Moderate

4 **Larch Mountain Crater Loop**
DISTANCE: 7.1 miles round-trip
DURATION: 3.5 hours
EFFORT: Easy/moderate

5 **Beacon Rock**
DISTANCE: 2 miles round-trip
DURATION: 1 hour
EFFORT: Easy/moderate

6 **Dry Creek Falls**
DISTANCE: 5 miles round-trip
DURATION: 2.5 hours
EFFORT: Moderate

7 **Dog Mountain**
DISTANCE: 6.9 miles round-trip
DURATION: 4 hours
EFFORT: Moderate/strenuous

8 **Coyote Wall (Labyrinth Loop)**
DISTANCE: 6.3 miles round-trip
DURATION: 3.5 hours
EFFORT: Easy/moderate

9 **Mosier Plateau**
DISTANCE: 3.7 miles round-trip
DURATION: 1.5 hours
EFFORT: Easy/moderate

10 **Tom McCall Point Trail**
DISTANCE: 3.8 miles round-trip
DURATION: 2 hours
EFFORT: Easy/moderate

▾ VIEW FROM DOG MOUNTAIN

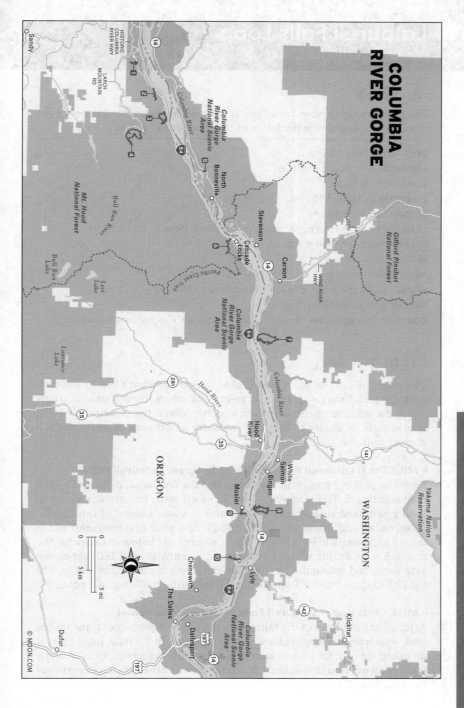

Latourell Falls Loop

GUY W. TALBOT STATE PARK, OR

This breezy loop crescendos at one of the most photographed waterfalls in the Gorge, set against a backdrop of columnar basalt pillars.

BEST: Waterfall Hikes
DISTANCE: 3.1 miles round-trip
DURATION: 1.5 hours
ELEVATION CHANGE: 880 feet
EFFORT: Easy/moderate
TRAIL: Dirt trail, paved path, roots, rocks, stone steps
USERS: Hikers, leashed dogs
SEASON: Year-round
PASSES/FEES: None
MAPS: USGS topographic map for Bridal Veil, OR-WA
PARK HOURS: 6am-10pm daily
CONTACT: Oregon State Parks, 503/695-2261, www.oregonstateparks.org

START THE HIKE

The waterfall is at its most powerful as winter snowpack begins melting, during which time its splash may freeze and create dangerous conditions along the trail; be cautious in cold weather. Given the popularity of this hike and its proximity to Portland, consider an off-season weekday for a dose of solitude.

▶ **MILE 0-1.1: Latourell Falls Trailhead to Upper Latourell Falls**
From the parking area, find the **Latourell Falls Trailhead,** indicated by the map signboard. The clockwise loop kicks off with five stone steps, and then you'll head steeply uphill and south through a forest of Douglas fir, alder, cedar, and maple. At 0.3 mile you'll find your first **viewpoint** of Latourell Falls, marked by a bench. The trail parallels **Latourell Creek** for the next 0.8 mile, during which you'll ascend a gently graded 280 feet alongside ferns and salmonberries (in summer), before arriving at the foot of the 120-foot, two-tiered **Upper Latourell Falls**—the trail's highest point.

▶ **MILE 1.1-2: Upper Latourell Falls to Outcrop Viewpoint**
After taking in views of the falls, cross the footbridge and continue on the trail, which begins looping back north from here. In 0.8 mile, head right at an unsigned fork for a short **spur trail.** This path can get rocky at times; it ends at an **outcrop** that affords dramatic views of the Washington side of the Columbia River Gorge.

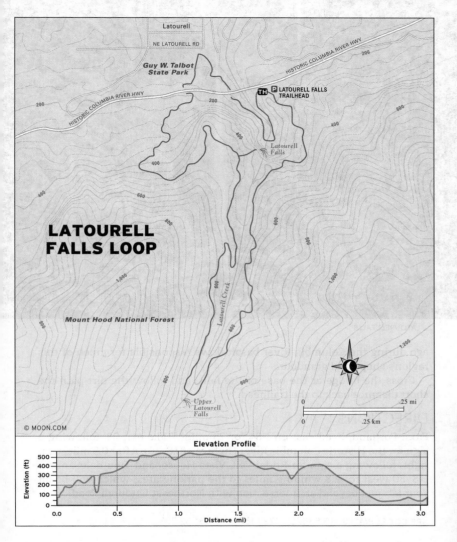

Elevation Profile

▶ **MILE 2-3.1: Outcrop Viewpoint to Latourell Falls and Trailhead**

Back on the main trail, you'll climb gently for the next 0.25 mile before steadily descending back toward the Columbia River. Cross the Historic Columbia River Highway in another 0.6 mile, and pick up the unmarked trail on the north side of the road. Take a sharp left onto the paved path at the first unsigned intersection almost immediately after crossing the highway. The trail descends a small stone staircase and immediately forks; turn right to head east, following a sign for the Loop Trail and Base of Lower Falls and passing some shaded picnic benches to your left. The paved path curves back south and continues under the highway, once again paralleling Latourell Creek. After 0.2 mile, you'll arrive at the misty base of photogenic **Latourell Falls,** which tumbles 200 feet amid lichen-colored columnar basalt pillars—created more than 10 million years

▲ LATOURELL FALLS

ago during the Columbia River basalt flows responsible for much of this region's shape and grandeur.

Cross the bridge at the base of the falls, and follow the dirt path the short distance back to the trailhead.

DIRECTIONS

From Portland, head east on I-84 for 25 miles. Take exit 28, following a sign for the Historic Columbia River Highway (U.S. 30). After 0.5 mile, turn right, following a sign for Bridal Veil, Vista House, and Troutdale. Follow U.S. 30 west for 2.8 winding miles to the parking area, which will be on your left just beyond an intersection with Northeast Latourell Road.

GPS COORDINATES: 45.53873, –122.21804 / N45° 32.3238′ W122° 13.0824′

BEST NEARBY BREWS

Built in 1911 as the Multnomah County poor farm, today **McMenamins Edgefield** (2126 SW Halsey St., Troutdale, 503/669-8610, www.mcmenamins.com, hours vary by individual venue) is a hotel and part of the McMenamins regional chain, which is known for refurbishing historic properties while adding a modern sense of whimsy. This property hosts numerous bars and restaurants serving McMenamins' libations from its on-site brewery, winery, and distillery, not to mention a popular concert venue and two par-3 golf courses. From the trailhead, the 16-mile drive west takes 25 minutes via the Historic Columbia River Highway and I-84.

Angel's Rest
COLUMBIA RIVER GORGE NATIONAL SCENIC AREA, OR

Hike through a wildfire-scarred landscape and past waterfalls to arrive at the summit of an exposed bluff offering spectacular views of the Columbia River Gorge.

DISTANCE: 4.9 miles round-trip
DURATION: 2.5 hours
ELEVATION CHANGE: 1,300 feet
EFFORT: Moderate
TRAIL: Dirt trail, rock scrambles, roots
USERS: Hikers, leashed dogs
SEASON: Year-round
PASSES/FEES: None
MAPS: USGS topographic map for Bridal Veil, OR-WA
PARK HOURS: 6am-10pm daily
CONTACT: Columbia River Gorge National Scenic Area, 541/308-1700, www.fs.usda.gov

START THE HIKE

Damaged by the Eagle Creek Fire, this trail reopened after months of restoration and has quickly regained its popularity; make this a midweek hike in the off-season if you can to avoid crowds.

▶ **MILE 0-0.6: Angel's Rest Trailhead to Upper Coopey Falls**
From the main parking area, head south to cross the Historic Columbia River Highway and find the **Angel's Rest Trailhead.** In a couple of hundred feet, you'll arrive at an unsigned, Y-shaped junction; head left to continue uphill. Here you'll see several burned tree trunks, evidence of the Eagle Creek Fire, though for the most part this early stretch comprises dense forest including ferns, old-growth trees, and white trillium blossoms in early spring. For the first 0.4 mile, you'll steadily ascend a gentle slope to arrive at the top of 150-foot **Coopey Falls.** After another 0.1 mile along the trail, you'll cross a bridge over **Coopey Creek** and, almost immediately, find a short spur trail to your left offering views of the 35-foot **Upper Coopey Falls.**

▶ **MILE 0.6-2.1: Upper Coopey Falls to Rockslide**
Back on the main trail, the hike begins to intensify, gaining 300 feet before arriving, in another 0.6 mile, at Eagle Creek Fire-devastated forest; from here to the summit, the greenery gradually gives way to downed logs, snags, and blackened tree trunks. After another 0.5 mile, you're almost entirely surrounded by toothpick-like snags littering the hillsides (much

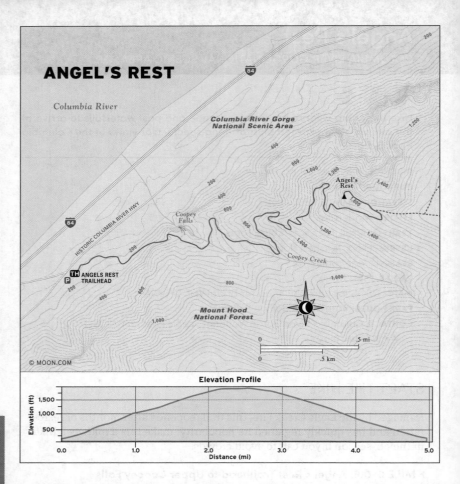

ANGEL'S REST

Columbia River

Columbia River Gorge
National Scenic Area

Angel's Rest

Coopey Falls

HISTORIC COLUMBIA RIVER HWY

Coopey Creek

ANGELS REST TRAILHEAD

Mount Hood National Forest

© MOON.COM

0   .5 mi
0   .5 km

Elevation Profile

of this area burned in a 1991 wildfire as well). As you switchback up the slopes—with the summit of Angel's Rest now visible to the east—you'll see several shortcuts filled in with rocks and spur trails blocked off with logs; stay on the established trail at all times, as there's a high risk of falling trees, uneven ground, and erosion as the area recovers. In roughly 0.4 mile, you'll arrive at a 150-foot-long rockslide that can be slippery after rainfall.

▶ **MILE 2.1-2.45: Rockslide to Angel's Rest Summit**
After another 0.25 mile of steep climbing, you'll arrive at an unsigned Y-junction. Continue straight to head north, and delicately climb a 15-foot rock scramble. As soon as you navigate this tricky stretch, you'll arrive at the **Angel's Rest summit,** featuring epic views: To the east, you'll see Beacon Rock, Hamilton Mountain, and some charred forests; to the west is the Vista House, built in 1916 as a rest stop for travelers on the Historic Columbia River Highway, on the basalt promontory of Crown Point.

Return the way you came.

▲ UPPER COOPEY FALLS

DIRECTIONS
From Portland, head east on I-84 east for 25 miles. Take exit 28, following a sign for the Historic Columbia River Highway (U.S. 30). You'll arrive at the main parking area to your right after 0.5 mile, just beyond a sign for Bridal Veil, Vista House, and Troutdale. Additional parking is also available farther west along the Historic Columbia River Highway.

GPS COORDINATES: 45.56022, –122.17264 / N45° 33.6132' W122° 10.3584'

BEST NEARBY BREWS
Choose among a well-rounded selection of balanced beers at **Migration Brewing** (18188 NE Wilkes Rd., Portland, 971/274-3770, http://migrationbrewing.com, 11am-9pm Sun.-Thurs., 11am-10pm Fri.-Sat.). Its lineup includes a mix of lagers, barrel-aged beers, and hop-forward IPAs and pale ales. From the trailhead, the 16-mile drive west takes 17 minutes via I-84.

Wahkeena Falls-Multnomah Falls Loop

COLUMBIA RIVER GORGE NATIONAL SCENIC AREA, OR

Enjoy dense, old-growth forest and plenty of waterfalls along this loop, including iconic Multnomah Falls—the tallest in Oregon.

BEST: Waterfall Hikes

DISTANCE: 5.9 miles round-trip

DURATION: 3 hours

ELEVATION CHANGE: 1,670 feet

EFFORT: Moderate

TRAIL: Dirt trail, paved path, stream crossings, rocks, gravel

USERS: Hikers, leashed dogs

SEASON: Year-round, but trail may be icy or snowy winter-early spring

PASSES/FEES: None

MAPS: USGS topographic map for Multnomah Falls, OR–WA; free trail maps available at the U.S. Forest Service information center inside Multnomah Falls Lodge

CONTACT: Columbia River Gorge National Scenic Area, 541/308-1700, www.fs.usda.gov

The loop between Wahkeena Falls and Multnomah Falls is one of the most popular hikes in Oregon—no surprise, given that Multnomah Falls is among the state's biggest tourist draws.

START THE HIKE

Plan to share portions of this trail with scores of fellow hikers; consider saving this hike for a weekday if possible, or start before 9am.

▶ MILE 0-0.8: Multnomah Falls Lodge to Wahkeena Falls

From the parking lot, follow the pedestrian crosswalk south under I-84, crossing Multnomah Creek and the Historic Columbia River Highway, to the plaza in front of **Multnomah Falls Lodge,** which has a snack stand and restrooms; you can also grab a free trail map inside. Pause to appreciate views of **Multnomah Falls** from here now or at the end of the hike. From the lodge head west to begin the counterclockwise loop along the shoulder of the **Historic Columbia River Highway.** After 0.1 mile, take a slight left onto the **Return Trail.** This mostly flat dirt and gravel path parallels the highway and connects the parking areas at Multnomah and Wahkeena Falls (so you could start the hike from either end—but there's more parking at this trailhead). After 0.5 mile, you'll descend a short series of stone steps before coming to a junction; turn left to head west on the **unnamed paved path.** You'll shortly see a sign for Wahkeena Falls; proceed up the paved path, ascending through a forest of Douglas fir and hemlock. In 0.2

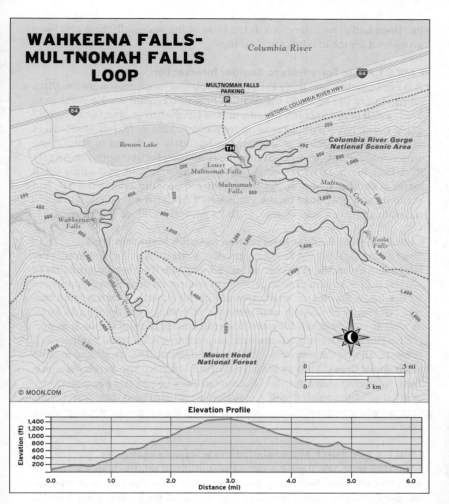

WAHKEENA FALLS-MULTNOMAH FALLS LOOP

Columbia River

MULTNOMAH FALLS
PARKING
P

HISTORIC COLUMBIA RIVER HWY

84

84

Benson Lake

TH

Columbia River Gorge
National Scenic Area

Lower
Multnomah Falls

Multnomah
Falls

Multnomah Creek

Wahkeena
Falls

Ecola
Falls

Wahkeena Creek

Mount Hood
National Forest

0   .5 mi

0   .5 km

© MOON.COM

Elevation Profile

Elevation (ft): 1,400 / 1,200 / 1,000 / 800 / 600 / 400 / 200

Distance (mi): 0.0   1.0   2.0   3.0   4.0   5.0   6.0

mile, you'll emerge at the base of the upper tier of **Wahkeena Falls,** which cascades more 240 feet total and gets its name from the Yakama Nation's word for "most beautiful."

▶ MILE 0.8–1.4: Wahkeena Falls to Lemmons Viewpoint

The paved path switchbacks steeply uphill beyond the falls, arriving in 0.6 mile at a junction; turn right for a short spur trail to **Lemmons Viewpoint,** named for a firefighter who died nearby; it offers unfettered views of the Columbia River Gorge, including Beacon Rock and Hamilton Mountain to the east.

▶ MILE 1.4–1.7: Lemmons Viewpoint to Fairy Falls

Back at the junction, head south on the **Wahkeena Trail,** a dirt path that parallels **Wahkeena Creek** through a lush canyon before arriving, in 0.3 mile, at the base of **Fairy Falls.** Good news: This marks the end of the hardest part of the ascent, and the trail levels out from here. A wooden plank has been laid across the creek at the base of the waterfall; cross and keep an eye out for ice in winter and spring.

▸ MILE 1.7–2.6: Fairy Falls to Boulder Intersection

A 0.1-mile amble past Fairy Falls brings you to a junction; ignore the Vista Point Trail to the left, and instead head right to remain on the Wahkeena Trail. You'll begin to spot burned-out tree trunks—by-products of the 2017 Eagle Creek Fire—with increasing frequency along here, but wildflowers including purple phlox, bear grass, and dandelions bloom in spring and summer along this stretch. In 0.4 mile is an intersection with the Angel's Rest Trail, but head left to remain on the Wahkeena Trail. In 0.4 mile you'll arrive at another junction; again ignore the Vista Point Trail to the left, and continue straight ahead on the Wahkeena Trail. This intersection is also a pleasant spot for a snack break, with its several boulders for sitting.

▸ MILE 2.6–3.5: Boulder Intersection to Larch Mountain Trail

Soon after you'll hit yet another junction, with the Devil's Rest Trail; veer left to remain on the Wahkeena Trail. Shortly you'll come upon the first of several minor stream crossings, and then enter an area heavily damaged by the Eagle Creek Fire; every tree along this stretch is burned and barren, but plenty of undergrowth remains, including vine maple and ferns, as well as variety of wildflowers in spring and early summer, such as purple foxglove, yellow tiger lilies, and purple fireweed. After 0.9 mile, you'll come to another stream crossing as you descend the canyon alongside **Multnomah Creek.** Shortly after you'll turn left onto the **Larch Mountain Trail,** following a sign for the Multnomah Falls Lodge and heading north, parallel to Multnomah Creek. Cross the last stream, and then watch your step as you continue along the trail, which gets especially rocky along here.

▸ MILE 3.5–4: Larch Mountain Trail to Wiesendanger Falls

After 0.25 mile, you'll pass a pair of waterfalls in relatively quick succession: 55-foot **Ecola Falls,** only partially visible from the trail, and **Wiesendanger Falls,** also cascading 55 feet into a small gorge. You'll get a better look at Wiesendanger Falls in another 0.2 mile when the trail switchbacks to its base; where the waterfall enters the creek makes a popular swimming hole in summer.

▸ MILE 4–4.7: Wiesendanger Falls to Multnomah Falls Viewpoint Spur

Another 0.1 mile past Wiesendanger Falls you'll pass **Dutchman Falls,** a series of three short waterfalls. In 0.3 mile, head left at the junction, following a sign for the **Multnomah Falls Viewpoint.** The 0.3-mile round-trip spur ends at a plaza at the top of Multnomah Falls; while you don't see much of the waterfall itself from here, it's worth the short side trip for its views of the Columbia River Gorge.

▸ MILE 4.7–5.9: Multnomah Falls Viewpoint Spur to Multnomah Falls Lodge

Back at the junction, turn left onto the Larch Mountain Trail, following the Multnomah Falls Lodge sign. You'll ascend briefly before descending via

▲ MULTNOMAH FALLS

11 paved switchbacks, crossing **Benson Bridge** near the base of **Multnomah Falls;** the 635-foot waterfall tumbles over basalt cliffs in two major steps and is among the most popular natural attractions in the Pacific Northwest, drawing more than two million visitors each year. After 1.2 miles, the trail levels out back at the Multnomah Falls Lodge.

DIRECTIONS

From Portland, head east on I-84 for 28.3 miles. Take exit 31—off to the left—and follow the signs for Multnomah Falls to arrive in the parking area.

The many parking areas near Multnomah Falls fill to capacity regularly, even on weekdays, so consider taking the **Columbia Gorge Express** (888/246-6420, http://columbiagorgeexpress.com), a shuttle between Portland and several popular destinations in the Gorge, including Multnomah Falls (US$7.50 round-trip). The shuttle departs Portland at the **Gateway Transit Center** (9900 NE Multnomah St., Portland), and the ride takes 35-45 minutes. Buses operate year-round, but check the website for the schedule because it varies seasonally.

GPS COORDINATES: 45.57769, -122.11719 / N45° 34.6614' W122° 7.0314'

> ### BEST NEARBY BITES
>
> Enjoy an upscale meal at **Multnomah Falls Lodge** (53000 E. Historic Columbia River Hwy., Bridal Veil, 503/695-2376, www.multnomah-fallslodge.com, 8am-9pm daily). Located at the base of Multnomah Falls, its on-site restaurant offers fine Northwest-inspired cuisine.

Hike into an eroded crater atop Larch Mountain—and enjoy jaw-dropping views of Mount Hood and other Cascade peaks.

DISTANCE: 7.1 miles round-trip
DURATION: 3.5 hours
ELEVATION CHANGE: 1,200 feet
EFFORT: Easy/moderate
TRAIL: Dirt trail, rocks, roots, stream crossings, paved path, stairs, roadside
USERS: Hikers, leashed dogs
SEASON: June–October
PASSES/FEES: Northwest Forest Pass
MAPS: USGS topographic map for Multnomah Falls, OR-WA
CONTACT: Columbia River Gorge National Scenic Area, 541/308-1700, www.fs.usda.gov

Larch Mountain is an extinct volcano near the western edge of the Columbia River Gorge. On this clockwise loop hike, you'll descend into a crater near the mountain's 4,055-foot peak.

START THE HIKE

▶ **MILE 0–2.1: Larch Mountain Trail to Multnomah Creek Way Trail**
Start hiking on the unsigned paved path—the **Larch Mountain Trail**—framed by two wooden posts at the northwestern edge of the parking lot. The path forks almost immediately; take the trail that heads slightly downhill to the left. It soon becomes a dirt trail and goes past a restroom. Old-growth Douglas fir and hemlock forest surrounds you. After about 0.2 mile you'll arrive at an unsigned T-shaped junction; head left to continue downhill. As you descend, vine maple, rhododendron, and summertime huckleberries flank the trail. You'll lose about 600 feet of elevation over the next 1.4 mile, at which point you'll arrive at an old roadbed and well-signed junction; cross the road to continue downhill on the Larch Mountain Trail. Enjoy the purple, bell-shaped foxglove along this stretch; it blooms in late spring and remains vibrant through midsummer. You'll come to a T-shaped junction in another 0.5 mile; head right to take the **Multnomah Creek Way Trail.**

▶ **MILE 2.1–5.2: Multnomah Creek Way Trail to Oneonta Trail**
The trail flattens out in 0.2 mile, where you'll cross **Multnomah Creek** on a wooden footbridge; this trickling creek feeds Multnomah Falls a few miles downstream. Red cedar and salmonberries grow along the trail here. Immediately after the bridge crossing, turn right to remain on the Multnomah Creek Way Trail and begin looping back south from where you came. You'll head into a marshy area, for a brief moment out from under the forest

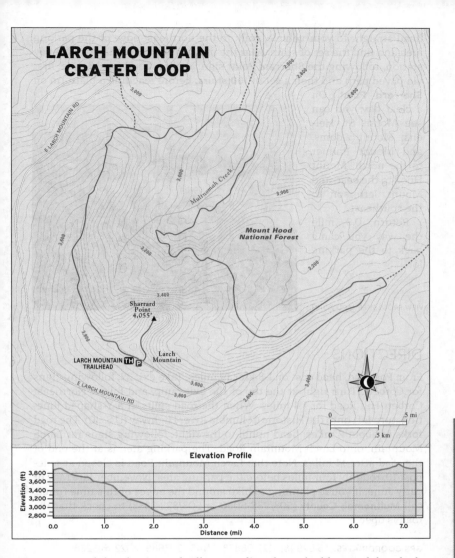

LARCH MOUNTAIN CRATER LOOP

Mount Hood
National Forest

Sharrard
Point
4,055'

LARCH MOUNTAIN
TRAILHEAD

Larch
Mountain

E LARCH MOUNTAIN RD

0   .5 mi
0   .5 km

Elevation Profile

canopy, and then begin gradually ascending through old-growth hemlock. The trail crosses numerous small, trickling streambeds over its next winding stretch, but the flow won't rise much above your boot sole. Along this stretch you'll find vibrant undergrowth and wildflowers in spring-summer, including twinflowers, noted for their Y-shaped stalks, and the three-petaled trillium. Some 2.9 miles beyond the Multnomah Creek crossing, you'll arrive at a T-shaped junction; turn right onto the **Oneonta Trail.**

▶ **MILE 5.2–7.1: Oneonta Trail to Sherrard Point and Parking Lot**
Steadily ascend the ridgeline; to your left is the **Bull Run Watershed,** the primary source of drinking water for the city of Portland. After 0.9 mile, the trail ends at **Larch Mountain Road;** turn right to head uphill, walking along its shoulder. The road ends, after 0.4 mile, at the parking area. Rather than

head straight to your vehicle, walk to the northeast edge of the parking area and find the set of stairs near the information board/day-use fee pay station, following the Sherrard Point sign. You'll ascend for 0.3 mile, first via paved path and then a set of **100 stairs,** before reaching a platform on **Sherrard Point.** On a clear day, you can see Mount St. Helens, Mount Adams, and Mount Rainier to the north, Mount Hood to the east, and Mount Jefferson to the southeast.

Return 0.3 mile the way you came back to the parking lot.

VIEW FROM SHERRARD POINT ▶

DIRECTIONS

From Portland, head east on I-84 for 19 miles. Take exit 22, following signs for Corbett. Turn right at the top of the exit ramp, and follow Northeast Corbett Hill Road for 1.4 miles. When the road splits at a Y-shaped junction, turn left onto the Historic Columbia River Highway (U.S. 30). The road forks in about 2 miles; head uphill to the right, following signs for Larch Mountain, onto Larch Mountain Road. The parking area is at the end of the road after 14 miles. Note that Larch Mountain Road is closed at milepost 10, roughly four miles before the parking area, November-late May or early June. If you're planning to hike around the edges of this time frame, call **Multnomah County** (503/988-5050 or 503/823-3333) to check that the road is open.

GPS COORDINATES: 45.52948, –122.08878 / N45° 31.7688′ W122° 5.3268′

BEST NEARBY BREWS

Located at the edge of Glendoveer Golf Course, **Von Ebert Brewing Glendoveer** (14021 NE Glisan St., Portland, 503/878-8708, http://glendoveer.vonebertbrewing.com, 11am-10pm Sun.-Thurs., 11am-11pm Fri.-Sat.) serves beers brewed on-site, as well as at its other location in Portland's Pearl District, alongside classic pub fare. From the trailhead, the 30-mile drive east takes 50 minutes via Larch Mountain Road and I-84.

Beacon Rock

BEACON ROCK STATE PARK, WA

🦌 ✿ 🚶

Follow a shelf-like path blasted into the side of a towering monolith to a sweeping view of the Columbia River Gorge.

DISTANCE: 2 miles round-trip
DURATION: 1 hour
ELEVATION CHANGE: 650 feet
EFFORT: Easy/moderate
TRAIL: Dirt, wooden bridges, paved path
USERS: Hikers
SEASON: Year-round
PASSES/FEES: Discover Pass
MAPS: Green Trails Map 429 for Bonneville Dam
PARK HOURS: 8am-dusk daily
CONTACT: Washington State Parks, 509/427-8265, http://parks.state.wa.us

R ising above the Columbia River, Beacon Rock is the core of an ancient volcano. Lewis and Clark gave the rock its name when they camped here in 1805. Hiking to its top wouldn't be possible without the considerable efforts of Henry Jonathan Biddle, a wealthy engineer and geologist from Philadelphia who developed a love for the area and purchased Beacon Rock, saving it from demolition. From 1916 to 1918, Biddle and his friend Charles Johnson built a harrowing trail up the side of the rock. They blasted a 4-foot-wide path into the cliff and spanned narrow fissures with 22 wooden bridges and more than 100 concrete slabs.

START THE HIKE

▶ **MILE 0-1: Monolith West Side to Beacon Rock**
The path starts in the woods on the west side of the monolith and after a few bends passes through a **gate.** From there, 52 easy-to-manage **switchbacks** are packed into the 1 mile it takes reach the top. Hand-rails line the route, giving visitors a bit of comfort as they shift their attention between views of the Co-lumbia River, the moss and

SWITCHBACKS ▶

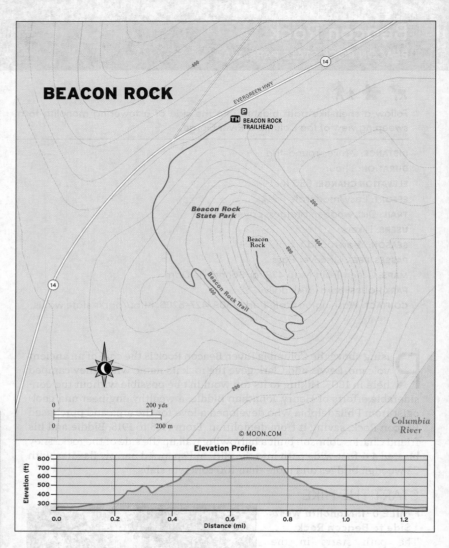

BEACON ROCK

Beacon Rock State Park

Beacon Rock

Beacon Rock Trail

BEACON ROCK TRAILHEAD

EVERGREEN HWY

Columbia River

© MOON.COM

0 — 200 yds
0 — 200 m

Elevation Profile

lichen growing on the rock, and occasional wildflowers blooming in the crevices. Warblers, flycatchers, pigeons, hummingbirds, woodpeckers, and other birds frequent the area.

▶ MILE 1-2: Beacon Rock to Monolith West Side

Stone steps deliver you to the **top** (848 feet above sea level) and a view that stretches miles up and down the Columbia River Gorge. Ships motor up the river, and trains chug along the banks following the route the Lewis and Clark expedition pioneered two centuries ago. There's not much room at the top, so on nice days you might have to wait for an opportunity to stand at the railing and snap pictures of the Gorge.

After your turn, zigzag your way back to your car.

▲ TRAIL ALONG BEACON ROCK

DIRECTIONS

From I-205 in Vancouver, Washington, take exit 27 and merge onto Highway 14. Drive east for 28 miles. Beacon Rock and trailhead parking is on the right side of the road. Toilets are near the parking lot.

GPS COORDINATES: 45.628571, –122.022222 / N45° 37.7143' W122° 1.3333'

BEST NEARBY BITES

The riverside community of Stevenson, 8.5 miles (12 minutes) northeast of the trailhead via Highway 14, offers tasty post-hike options that include a salmon sandwich at the **Big River Grill** (192 2nd St., Stevenson, WA, 509/427-4888, www.thebigrivergrill.com, hours vary) and burgers and brews in the century-old saloon at **Clark & Lewie's Traveler's Rest Saloon & Grill** (130 SW Cascade Ave., Stevenson, WA, 509/219-0097, www.clarkandlewies.com, hours vary).

COLUMBIA RIVER GORGE NATIONAL SCENIC AREA, OR

Located just a couple of miles east of the Eagle Creek Fire's origin point, this trail offers some of the most gripping views of the devastation wrought by the wildfire—but it also shows signs of life, and concludes at a lovely waterfall.

DISTANCE: 5 miles round–trip

DURATION: 2.5 hours

ELEVATION CHANGE: 1,240 feet

EFFORT: Moderate

TRAIL: Dirt trail, roots, rocks, gravel roads

USERS: Hikers, leashed dogs, horseback riders

SEASON: Year-round

PASSES/FEES: Northwest Forest Pass

MAPS: USGS topographic maps for Bonneville Dam, OR-WA, and Carson, WA-OR

CONTACT: Columbia River Gorge National Scenic Area, 541/308-1700, www.fs.usda.gov

START THE HIKE

▸ **MILE 0-0.3: Bridge of the Gods Trailhead Parking to Eagle Creek Fire-Burned Forest**

From the southern edge of the **Bridge of the Gods Trailhead** parking area, walk south across the road leading to the Bridge of the Gods tollbooth, following a sign onto the **Pacific Crest Trail (PCT).** Walk 0.1 mile on the gently sloping trail, then turn right onto **Southwest Moody Avenue,** under I-84, heading uphill. After a few hundred feet, turn right onto the **unsigned gravel road,** following it for a couple of hundred feet before turning left to rejoin the **PCT.** In 0.1 mile you'll come upon Eagle Creek Fire-charred tree trunks, downed trees, and jagged snags lining the trail. But even with all the damage, signs of life are everywhere: You'll hear the occasional bird over nearby highway noise, and find ferns and raspberry bushes along the narrow trail.

▸ **MILE 0.3-1.3: Eagle Creek Fire-Burned Forest to Power Lines and PCT**

You'll gain 495 feet over the next 1 mile, steadily yet gently ascending, before arriving at a T-shaped intersection. Head right onto the **unnamed gravel road,** following a sign for the PCT, as the road curves uphill and ducks under a set of power lines. Just past the power lines, turn left, back onto the **PCT.**

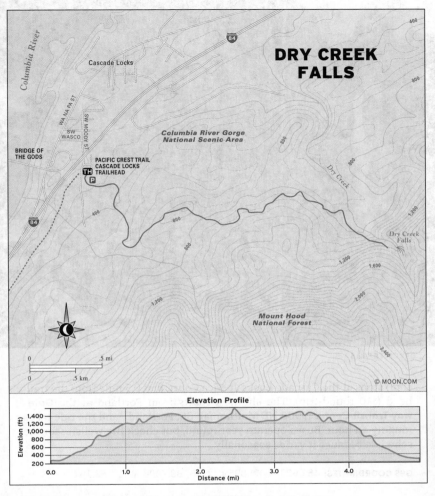

DRY CREEK FALLS

Columbia River

Cascade Locks

I-84

WA NA PA ST

SW MOODY ST

SW WASCO

BRIDGE OF THE GODS

PACIFIC CREST TRAIL CASCADE LOCKS TRAILHEAD

Columbia River Gorge National Scenic Area

Dry Creek

Dry Creek Falls

Mount Hood National Forest

© MOON.COM

Elevation Profile

▶ **MILE 1.3–2.5: Power Lines and PCT to Dry Creek Falls**

Continue your gradual ascent through a forest of Douglas fir, vine maple, and hemlock for another 0.9 mile, at which point you'll arrive at a junction; make a hard right onto the wide **Dry Creek Falls Trail** for 0.3 mile. The trail ends at the base of **Dry Creek Falls,** a 75-foot plume in the heart of a narrow basalt canyon.

Return the way you came.

DIRECTIONS

From downtown Cascade Locks, head south on Wa Na Pa Street toward the Bridge of the Gods. Turn left at a sign for the Bridge of the Gods toll bridge, and follow the road as it loops around to the east. After a few hundred feet, turn right into a parking area at a sign for the Bridge of the Gods Trailhead in Toll House Park.

If you'd rather not drive and fight for parking at this popular trailhead, the **Columbia Gorge Express** (888/246-6420, http://columbiagorgeexpress.

▲ DRY CREEK FALLS

com) stops at the Cascade Locks Justice Court, just 0.5 mile from the trailhead ($10 round-trip). The shuttle departs from Portland at the **Gateway Transit Center** (9900 NE Multnomah St., Portland), and the ride takes roughly an hour. Buses operate year-round, but check the website for the schedule because it varies seasonally.

GPS COORDINATES: 45.66233, –121.8959 / N45° 39.7398' W121° 53.754'

BEST NEARBY BITES

Enjoy hearty pizza and pub fare—and wash it down with a refreshing craft beer—at **Cascade Locks Ale House** (500 Wa Na Pa St., Cascade Locks, 541/374-9310, http://cascadelocksalehouse.com, noon-5pm Wed., noon-9pm Thurs.-Mon.). The pub serves pizza, sandwiches, and burgers alongside a selection of craft beer from Portland and the Columbia River Gorge. From the trailhead, the 0.5-mile drive takes 5 minutes via Wa Na Pa St.

Climb through colorful fields of wildflowers to a sweeping view of Mount Hood and the Columbia River Gorge.

BEST: Spring Hikes, Wildflower Hikes
DISTANCE: 6.9 miles round-trip
DURATION: 4 hours
ELEVATION CHANGE: 2,900 feet
EFFORT: Moderate/strenuous
TRAIL: Dirt, talus fields
USERS: Hikers, leashed dogs
SEASON: March–December
PASSES/FEES: Northwest Forest Pass, permit required March 31–July 1 ($1.50 per person)
MAPS: Green Trails Map 430 for Hood River, OR
CONTACT: Columbia River Gorge National Scenic Area, 541/308-1700, www.fs.usda.gov/crgnsa

Even if its slopes were barren and dusty, Dog Mountain's striking view of the Columbia River Gorge would draw a crowd. But they aren't. The upper mountain comes alive with color each spring as wildflowers bloom and hikers arrive by the busload. Springtime traffic is so heavy that in 2018 the Forest Service started requiring permits during the season, designed to encourage hikers to take public transportation and alleviate congestion at the trailhead. Permits are free for those riding the shuttle bus from Stevenson. Otherwise, buy a permit (www.recreation.gov) and arrive before sunrise for the best chance of staying ahead of the crowds.

START THE HIKE

▶ **MILE 0-0.6: Parking Lot to First Old Trail Junction**
From the 100-car parking lot, there are three options for making the 2,900-foot climb: Long but gradual (Augspurger Trail), shorter but steeper (the new Dog Mountain Trail), or even shorter and steeper (the old Dog Mountain Trail). Ascending on the new trail and returning via the Augspurger Trail makes an enjoyable loop with loads of inspiring scenery.

From the east end of the parking lot, follow the **new trail,** which tilts upward as heads east and arrives at a toilet in a matter of steps. Here, the real climbing commences, through a forest of Douglas fir. Trailside flora includes Oregon grape, snowberry, and poison oak. After 0.6 mile, pass the **old trail** on your left.

Dog Mountain

COLUMBIA RIVER GORGE

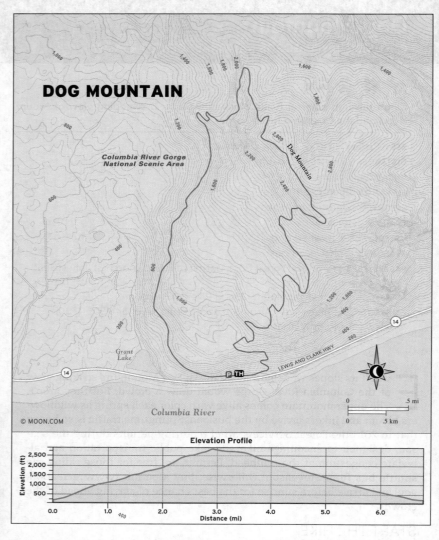

Elevation Profile

© MOON.COM

▶ **MILE 0.6-2.1: First Old Trail Junction to Second Old Trail Junction**
After another 1.5 steep miles of hard work, pass the **upper junction with the old trail.** Views of the Gorge and the knowledge that the old trail is even steeper help distract you from the grind.

▶ **MILE 2.1-3: Second Old Trail Junction to**
  Columbia River Gorge Viewpoint
Push on for another steep 0.4 mile before finding yourself in vibrant **Puppy Dog Meadow.** Yellow balsamroot, scarlet paintbrush, purple lupine, red columbine: The kaleidoscope of colors coupled with views of Mount Hood and the Columbia River is so stunning some hikers choose to make this their destination. Look for a USGS survey disc on the trail before

continuing upward 0.3 mile, then turning right on a 0.2-mile **spur** that takes you to the high point and another breathtaking view of the Gorge.

▶ MILE 3–4.1: Columbia River Gorge Viewpoint to Augspurger Trail Junction

Wherever you choose to stop climbing, you can return the way you came or take the Old Trail shortcut. But to finish the loop retrace your steps on the spur and turn right to follow the **Dog-Augspurger Tie Trail** north along the ridge for 0.9 mile. At the junction with **Augspurger Trail,** turn left (right makes a 4-mile-each-way side trip to Augspurger Mountain)

▶ MILE 4.1–6.9: Augspurger Trail Junction to Parking Lot

Descend through the forest for about 0.8 mile before reaching the first of several **talus fields.** These rocky sections are easy to navigate if you watch your step, although I have seen hikers slowed enough by these stretches during evening hikes that they found themselves not finishing until after dark.

Expect more of the same for the final 2 miles to the car, with occasional views through the evergreens to Grant Lake. After all that work to get up Dog Mountain, this comparatively gradual descent is a knee's best friend.

DIRECTIONS

From I-205 in Vancouver, Washington, take exit 27 and merge on to Highway 14. Drive east for 47 miles. The well-marked Dog Mountain parking lot is on the left side of the road. A vault toilet is located near the trailhead.

Gorge TransLink (www.gorgetranslink.com) offers shuttle service to the busy trailhead 7:30am-4:30pm on weekends March 31-July 1. The $1-each-way service from the Skamania County Fairgrounds (710 SW Rock Creek Dr., Stevenson, WA) includes a Dog Mountain hiking permit and discounts at Stevenson businesses. Leashed dogs are permitted.

GPS COORDINATES: 45.699265, –121.708174 / N45° 41.9559' W121° 42.4904'

BEST NEARBY BREWS

Brewers stir every batch of beer by hand at **Walking Man Brewing** (240 SW 1st St., Stevenson, WA, 509/427-5520, www.walkingman-beer.com, 11:30am-9pm Wed.-Sun.) in Stevenson. The old-fashioned approach has served the two-decade-old, award-winning brewery well. Pizza, burgers, and salads supplement the beer selection. From the trailhead, the 9.5-mile drive west takes about 15 minutes via Highway 14.

Dog Mountain

Link trails to visit fields of wildflowers, views of the Columbia River, and the edge of a basalt cliff.

BEST: Brew Hikes, Dog-Friendly Hikes

DISTANCE: 6.3 miles round-trip

DURATION: 3.5 hours

ELEVATION CHANGE: 1,200 feet

EFFORT: Easy/moderate

TRAIL: Dirt, rocks, paved and dirt road

USERS: Hikers, leashed dogs, off-leash dogs (July-Nov.), mountain bikers, horseback riders (May-Sept.)

SEASON: Year-round

PASSES/FEES: Northwest Forest Pass

MAPS: Green Trails Map 432S for Columbia River Gorge East; free maps at www.fs.usda.gov/crgnsa

CONTACT: Columbia River Gorge National Scenic Area, 541/308-1700, www.fs.usda.gov/crgnsa

When your hiking route is called "the Labyrinth," it's a good idea to double-check that you packed a good map. At Coyote Wall, for good measure, you might even snap a photo of the large map on the back of the trailhead kiosk or download a map from the Forest Service website (www.fs.usda.gov/crgnsa). With the Columbia River visible most of the way it's hard to stay lost, but a multitude of paths and sparse signage make it easy to wander off course.

START THE HIKE

▶ **MILE 0-0.4: Parking Lot East End to Trail Junction**

Starting at the east end of the parking lot beneath **Coyote Wall,** it's quickly evident why **Old Highway 8** was retired. The paved road is littered with huge rocks that fell from the basalt cliff. Look for jumping fish in Locke Lake, watch trains chug along the Columbia River, and gaze into Oregon as you walk the flat road. At 0.4 mile, pass a trail you'll use to finish the loop.

▶ **MILE 0.4-1.1: Trail Junction to Labyrinth Creek**

In another 0.3 mile, turn left on **Co7** (the Labyrinth Trail) and begin heading upward. Stay right at a junction a few steps up the hill, passing through a short rocky section. Pass a **small cave** in 0.3 mile and stay left at the intersection that follows. Check out a waterfall and cross **Labyrinth Creek** over the next 0.1 mile.

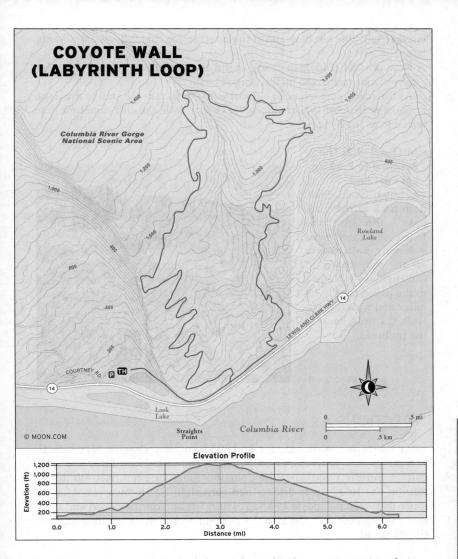

COYOTE WALL
(LABYRINTH LOOP)

Columbia River Gorge
National Scenic Area

Rowland
Lake

LEWIS AND CLARK HWY 14

COURTNEY RD P TH

14

Look
Lake

Straights
Point

Columbia River

© MOON.COM

0 .... .5 mi
0 .... .5 km

Elevation Profile

Elevation (ft): 1,200 / 1,000 / 800 / 600 / 400 / 200

Distance (mi): 0.0 / 1.0 / 2.0 / 3.0 / 4.0 / 5.0 / 6.0

Watch boats motor up and down the Columbia as Mount Hood rises above the panorama. In the spring, wildflowers add color to the slopes. Stay alert for rattlesnakes and poison oak.

▶ **MILE 1.1–2.5: Labyrinth Creek to Atwood Road**
Meander 0.7 mile beyond the **creek crossing** before turning left on **Co8** (Upper Labyrinth Trail) and walking another 0.7 mile (with some of the best views) to abandoned **Atwood Road.**

▶ **MILE 2.5–4.3: Atwood Road to the Syncline**
Turn left and follow the road 0.5 mile as it passes through a stand of trees, dips in and out of the Labyrinth Creek drainage, and arrives at a **three-way**

intersection. Stay left here and at the intersection that follows a few steps later.

Now on **Co4** (Old Jeep Trail), spend the next 1 mile descending the grassy slopes transfixed by the Gorge's beauty.

As the road approaches an old barbwire fence, take the trail to the right for a 0.3-mile uphill walk to look over Coyote Wall, the cliff sometimes referred to as the Syncline.

▶ **MILE 4.3–6.3: The Syncline to Parking Lot East End**

To finish your hike, drop back to the road, pass through the fence, and then make sweeping **switchbacks** all the way down to Old Highway 8. Return to the paved road in 1.3 miles and turn right to walk 0.4 mile back to the trailhead.

COYOTE WALL ▶

DIRECTIONS

From Vancouver, Washington, take I-205 south into Oregon. Take exit 22 and merge onto eastbound I-84. Drive 54.7 miles to Hood River and take exit 64. Turn left and cross the Columbia River (and return to Washington) on the Hood River Bridge then turn right on Highway 14. After 11 miles (between mileposts 69 and 70) turn left on Courtney Road and then make an immediate right into the parking area. Toilets are located near the trailhead.

GPS COORDINATES: 45.700604, –121.401706 / N45° 42.0362' W121° 24.1024'

BEST NEARBY BREWS

Burritos and brews await in White Salmon, less than 5 miles (less than 10 minutes) west of the trailhead via Highway 14. The food and beer are locally sourced at **Everybody's Brewing** (177 E. Jewett Blvd., 509/637-2774, www.everybodysbrewing.com, 11:30am-9:30pm Sun.-Thurs., 11:30am-10pm Fri.-Sat.), where the outdoor seating area includes views of Mount Hood.

Mosier Plateau

COLUMBIA RIVER GORGE NATIONAL SCENIC AREA, OR

One of the newest trails in the Columbia River Gorge boasts waterfalls, wildflowers, and some of the region's best sunset views.

BEST: Winter Hikes
DISTANCE: 3.7 miles round-trip
DURATION: 1.5 hours
ELEVATION CHANGE: 560 feet
EFFORT: Easy/moderate
TRAIL: Dirt trail, gravel, roots, rocks, wooden steps
USERS: Hikers, leashed dogs
SEASON: Year-round
PASSES/FEES: None
MAPS: USGS topographic map for White Salmon, WA-OR
CONTACT: Friends of the Columbia Gorge, 541/386-5268, http://gorgefriends.org

This hike is a year-round gem, with bald eagles abundant in winter, more than 30 species of wildflower blooming each spring, Gorge breezes to keep you cool in summer, and fewer crowds than most Gorge hikes in the fall. Sunset views from the viewpoint on Mosier Plateau are stunning—just be sure to bring a flashlight for your return descent.

START THE HIKE

Note that ticks, rattlesnakes, and poison oak can be found along the trail, so long pants are strongly recommended, especially at the height of summer. Sensitive plants also line it, as does some private property; keep to the trail at all times.

▶ **MILE 0-0.3: Parking Area to Mosier Pioneer Cemetery**
From the parking area, head east for 0.2 mile along the **Historic Columbia River Highway** and cross **Mosier Bridge.** Just past the bridge you'll spot a bench on the south side of the highway, which is where the **Mosier Plateau Trail** begins. Some confusing unofficial trails converge near this early stretch, but head uphill on the well-maintained dirt trail and you'll be on the right track. In 0.1 mile, you'll arrive at **Mosier Pioneer Cemetery,** home to some of Mosier's earliest settlers.

▶ **MILE 0.3-1.3: Mosier Pioneer Cemetery to Mosier Viewpoint**
Continue up the gently graded trail through grassy fields, oak trees, and stands of ponderosa pine. After 0.25 mile, you'll find a **viewpoint** off to your right. Here you can see **Mosier Creek Falls** and, farther south, **Mosier Creek.** In another 0.25 mile, climb a set of wooden steps, the first of several while ascending Mosier Plateau. This stretch of trail is especially

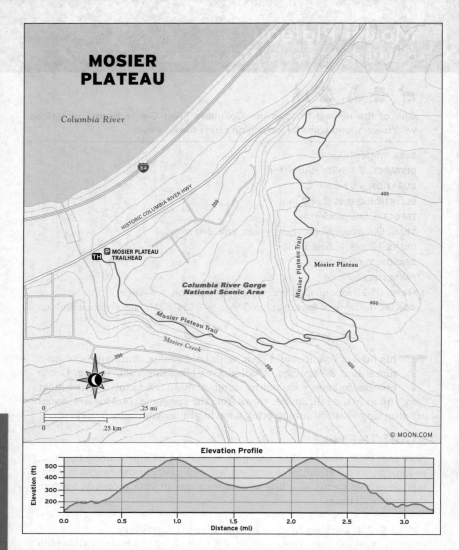

MOSIER PLATEAU

Columbia River

Columbia River Gorge National Scenic Area

Mosier Plateau Trail

Mosier Plateau

Mosier Creek

Mosier Plateau Trail

HISTORIC COLUMBIA RIVER HWY

MOSIER PLATEAU TRAILHEAD

84

200

400

600

0   .25 mi
0   .25 km

© MOON.COM

Elevation Profile

Elevation (ft)

500
400
300
200

0.0   0.5   1.0   1.5   2.0   2.5   3.0

Distance (mi)

rich with wildflowers, including bighead clover, yellow arrowleaf balsamroot, and Columbia desert parsley, noted for its reddish-purple petals. In 0.5 mile, after steadily ascending an open hillside, you'll arrive at **Mosier viewpoint,** just below the summit of Mosier Plateau, from which you'll have views of Mosier, Hood River, and the Columbia River Gorge that are particularly spectacular during sunset.

▶ MILE 1.3-2: Mosier Viewpoint to Trail Loop

Continue on the trail, heading downhill for 0.4 mile. Yellow balsamroot and purple lupine bloom along this stretch each spring. Just beyond a concrete pad, once the site of a mobile home, you'll see a sign to your left indicating the **Trail Loop.** Follow the 0.25-mile loop for river views and a quiet respite just above the highway.

▲ MOSIER VIEWPOINT

▶ **MILE 2–3.7: Trail Loop to Parking Area**
After completing the loop to rejoin the main trail, return 1.7 miles the way you came.

DIRECTIONS

From Hood River, follow I-84 east for 5.5 miles. Take exit 69, following signs for Historic Columbia River Highway (U.S. 30) and Mosier. Follow the off-ramp for about 0.2 mile; at the first intersection, turn right to head south onto U.S. 30. Follow the road as it passes through the town of Mosier. After 0.3 mile, turn left onto a gravel driveway, following a sign for public parking. The road ends in a gravel parking area between the highway and railroad tracks.

GPS COORDINATES: 45.68478, –121.39391 / N45° 41.0868′ W121° 23.6346′

BEST NEARBY BREWS

Near the banks of the Columbia River, **pFriem Family Brewers** (707 Portway Ave., Suite 101, Hood River, 541/321-0490, www.pfriembeer. com, 11am–10pm daily) delivers a lineup of outstanding beers, including a heavy-hitting Belgian dark strong ale, a piney IPA, and a crisp pilsner. From the trailhead, the 7-mile drive west takes 10 minutes via I-84.

This trail traverses celebrated wildflower-strewn meadows and an oak savanna to a hillside boasting grand views of Mount Hood and the Columbia River Gorge.

BEST: Spring Hikes, Wildflower Hikes
DISTANCE: 3.8 miles round-trip
DURATION: 2 hours
ELEVATION CHANGE: 1,080 feet
EFFORT: Easy/moderate
TRAIL: Dirt trail, rocks, roots, stone staircase
USERS: Hikers
SEASON: March–October
PASSES/FEES: None
MAPS: USGS topographic map for Lyle, WA–OR
CONTACT: The Nature Conservancy, 503/802-8100, www.nature.org

McCall Point's location between the forested western part of the Gorge and the drier prairies and highlands of eastern Oregon make this fertile ground for wildflowers. The trail is maintained by The Nature Conservancy. Arrive at the height of wildflower season, and you'll likely encounter a docent along the path; these friendly volunteers are happy to help identify plant species and offer best practices for preventing further erosion.

START THE HIKE
Keep an eye out for poison oak, ticks, and rattlesnakes on this trail.

▸ **MILE 0–0.3: Tom McCall Point Trailhead to Viewpoint**
Start hiking from the **Tom McCall Point Trailhead** at the base of the turn-around at Rowena Crest, heading south through a meadow. If you're here May-June, this meadow offers your first glimpse of why McCall Point is among the most popular wildflower hikes in the Columbia River Gorge: purple lupine, shooting stars, and yellow balsamroot mingle in the grasses, splaying out in seemingly every direction. After 0.3 mile, stop at a **viewpoint** to your right for your first vistas of the eastern edge of the Columbia River Gorge; good as these views are, they only improve from here.

▸ **MILE 0.3–1.9: Viewpoint to McCall Point Summit**
Gently ascending, you'll briefly enter an oak grove in 0.7 mile. You might catch a glimpse here of a western meadowlark, Oregon's state bird. In another 0.2 mile, you'll climb a short stone staircase through another oak

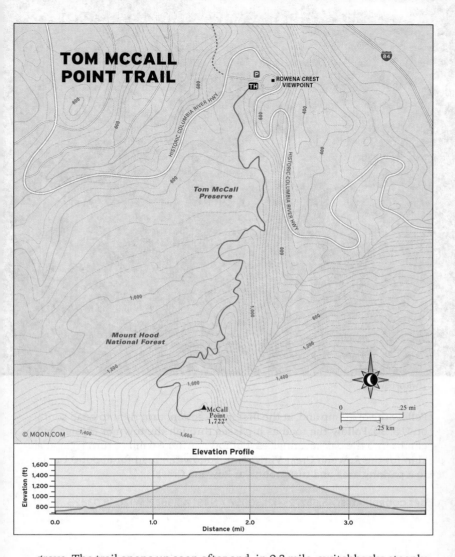

TOM MCCALL POINT TRAIL

Elevation Profile

grove. The trail opens up soon after and, in 0.3 mile, switchbacks steeply through exposed hillsides. Mount Adams to the north, and wildflowers in every direction, soon come into view. Look for fields of prairie stars, foxglove, and more. You'll reach the **McCall Point summit** in 0.4 mile. The hillside meadow is awash in yellow balsamroot, clumps of purple grass widow, and red paintbrush, and affords gorgeous Gorge views including Mount Hood to the west and Mount Adams, Rowena Plateau, and the town of Lyle to the north.

Return the way you came.

DIRECTIONS

From Hood River, follow I-84 east for 5.5 miles. Take exit 69, following signs for the Historic Columbia River Highway (U.S. 30) and Mosier.

▲ WILDFLOWERS

Follow the off-ramp and, at the first intersection, turn right to head south on U.S. 30. Follow the road as it passes through the town of Mosier and climbs into the oak savannas east of town. After 6.6 miles, turn right at a sign for the Rowena Crest Viewpoint. Follow the road for about 0.1 mile to a parking area and turnaround at Rowena Crest.

GPS COORDINATES: 45.68272, –121.30057 / N45° 40.9632' W121° 18.0342'

BEST NEARBY BREWS

Full Sail Brewery (506 Columbia St., Hood River, 541/386-2247, http://fullsailbrewing.com, 11am-9pm daily) has been churning out quality craft beer in the heart of Hood River for more than 30 years. Full Sail prides itself on sustainable practices, and its pub patio delivers sweeping views of the Columbia River. From the trailhead, the 13-mile drive west takes 20 minutes via I-84.

NEARBY CAMPGROUNDS

NAME	DESCRIPTION	FACILITIES	SEASON	FEE
Ainsworth State Park	popular campground in the Columbia River Gorge	40 full-hookup sites, 6 walk-in tent sites, restrooms	March–October	$7-26

I-84, Cascade Locks, OR, 503/793-9885, www.oregonstateparks.org

NAME	DESCRIPTION	FACILITIES	SEASON	FEE
Beacon Rock State Park	4,464-acre park on the Columbia River with scenic trails	28 RV and tent sites, restrooms	year-round	$12-50

34841 Hwy. 14, Skamania, WA, 888/226-7688, www.washington.goingtocamp.com

NAME	DESCRIPTION	FACILITIES	SEASON	FEE
Skamania County Fairgrounds	fairgrounds that sometimes hosts events (call ahead)	60 RV and tent sites, restrooms	year-round	$20-25

710 SW Rock Creek Dr., Stevenson, WA, 509/427-3980, www.skamaniacounty.org

NAME	DESCRIPTION	FACILITIES	SEASON	FEE
Wyeth Campground	former Civilian Conservation Corps campsite	13 tent and RV sites, 3 group sites, restrooms	May–September	$20-30

Wyeth Rd., Cascade Locks, OR, 541/308-1700, www.fs.usda.gov

NAME	DESCRIPTION	FACILITIES	SEASON	FEE
Memaloose State Park	campground overlooks the Columbia River	43 full-hookup sites, 66 tent sites, restrooms	March–October	$19-31

I-84, Mosier, OR, 541/478-3008, www.oregonstateparks.org

NAME	DESCRIPTION	FACILITIES	SEASON	FEE
Maryhill State Park	park has more than 4,500 feet of waterfront on the Columbia River	70 RV and tent sites, restrooms	year-round	$12-50

50 U.S. 97, Goldendale, WA, 888/226-7688, www.washington.goingtocamp.com

CENTRAL WASHINGTON

In stark contrast to the Cascades, Puget Sound, and the Pacific Ocean beaches, Central Washington adds to the breadth of the state's diversity. With topography shaped by lava flows and massive ice age floods, it is a wonderland for geology lovers. Hiking here challenges your imagination more than your legs. What was the view like from atop Badger Mountain when ancient Lake Lewis covered the Tri-Cities area? What was it like 15 million years ago when the lava flows that helped form Yakima's Cowiche Canyon covered most of the state east of the Cascades? What would Steamboat Rock look like before dams created the Banks Lake reservoir in Grand Coulee? Whether you want to cap a day of hiking with a dip in a lake or indulge your inner scientist, this region has you covered.

▲ VIEWS ON THE YAKIMA SKYLINE TRAIL   ▲ STEAMBOAT ROCK

1 **Steamboat Rock**
DISTANCE: 3.2 miles round-trip
DURATION: 1.5 hours
EFFORT: Easy/moderate

2 **Ancient Lakes**
DISTANCE: 4.4 miles round-trip
DURATION: 2.5 hours
EFFORT: Easy

3 **Yakima Skyline Trail**
DISTANCE: 6 miles round-trip
DURATION: 3 hours
EFFORT: Moderate

4 **Cowiche Canyon**
DISTANCE: 5.6 miles round-trip
DURATION: 3 hours
EFFORT: Easy/moderate

5 **Badger Mountain: Trailhead Park Loop**
DISTANCE: 3 miles round-trip
DURATION: 1.5 hours
EFFORT: Easy/moderate

▾ WATERFALL AT ANCIENT LAKES

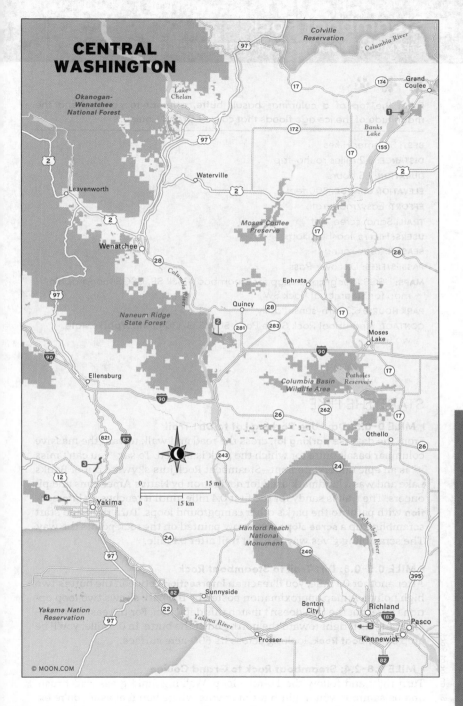

1 Steamboat Rock
STEAMBOAT ROCK STATE PARK, ELECTRIC CITY

From the top of a columnar basalt butte, attempt to comprehend the magnitude of the ice age floods that carved Grand Coulee.

BEST: Summer Hikes
DISTANCE: 3.2 miles round-trip
DURATION: 1.5 hours
ELEVATION CHANGE: 800 feet
EFFORT: Easy/moderate
TRAIL: Sand, scree, dirt
USERS: Hikers, leashed dogs
SEASON: Year-round
PASSES/FEES: Discover Pass
MAPS: USGS topographic map for Steamboat Rock SE, USGS topographic map for Steamboat Rock SW
PARK HOURS: 6:30am–sunset daily
CONTACT: Steamboat Rock State Park, 509/633-1304, http://parks.state. wa.us

START THE HIKE

▶ **MILE 0-0.5: Day-Use Parking Lot to Dirt Trail**
From the day-use **parking lot,** cross the road and walk toward the massive columnar basalt butte for which the park is named. To say "you can't miss it" is an epic understatement—Steamboat Rock juts skyward out of Banks Lake and was a landmark used for navigation by Native Americans and pioneers. The trail is sandy for the first 0.4 mile, until it reaches an **intersection** with paths to the park's other campground loops. Turn right and start scrambling up a **scree slope**. An arrow painted on the rock points the way. The scrambling gives way to a dirt trail after 0.1 mile.

▶ **MILE 0.5-0.8: Dirt Trail to Steamboat Rock**
After another 0.1 mile, you'll reach an **intersection** between the butte's two high points. A map approximation posted by the park shows two loop options here, but the trail doesn't match this depiction. For the easiest-to-follow path, turn right toward the north end of the butte. In 0.2 mile, you'll be atop **Steamboat Rock,** looking across its 600-acre surface.

▶ **MILE 0.8-2.4: Steamboat Rock to Grand Coulee**
Turn right and follow the 1.6-mile loop. Walking amid grass, sagebrush, and balsamroot, you might have moments where you feel as if you're exploring a typical patch of arid Central Washington wilderness. Then the trail runs along the rim of the butte, and you're reminded that you're in the

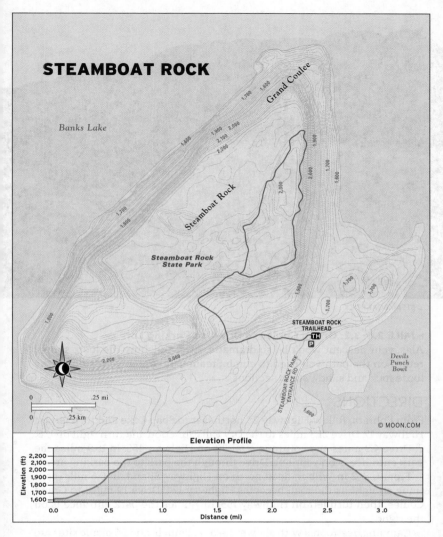

STEAMBOAT ROCK

Banks Lake

Grand Coulee

Steamboat Rock

Steamboat Rock State Park

STEAMBOAT ROCK TRAILHEAD

Devils Punch Bowl

STEAMBOAT ROCK PARK ENTRANCE RD

0   .25 mi
0   .25 km

© MOON.COM

Elevation Profile

middle of a geological marvel. As the name implies, **Grand Coulee** is the most famous of the deep channels that ice age floods carved in eastern Washington. Steamboat Rock was an island in that ancient, diverted Columbia River bed. When the waters subsided and the Columbia returned to its usual route, the island became a massive butte. From atop the butte you can hear chatter from boats and the nearby campground as you look out over the lake toward **Northrup Canyon.** Keep an eye out for bald and golden eagles and peregrine falcons.

You may be thinking that the steep slopes of the coulee may look familiar. They made a six-second cameo in the 1984 adventure classic *Indiana Jones and the Temple of Doom*, part of a scene in which Indy and friends jumped out of a plane with nothing but an inflatable raft.

▲ STEAMBOAT ROCK

▶ MILE 2.4–3.2: Grand Coulee to Day-Use Parking Lot

Alas, your descent won't be so dramatic. After finishing the loop, simply return on the path you used to climb Steamboat. Watch your step on the loose rock and sandy, steep sections.

DIRECTIONS

From Ephrata, follow Highway 28 northeast to Soap Lake and turn left on Highway 17. Drive 21.3 miles to the Dry Falls Junction and turn right on U.S. 2. Drive 4.3 miles and continue straight on Highway 155. In 18.9 miles the park entrance is on your left. Drive through the park to the parking area.

From U.S. 2 in Wilbur, head north on Highway 21 and, in 0.6 mile, continue straight as the road becomes Highway 174. Drive 19 miles to Grand Coulee, then turn left on Highway 155. In 7 miles the park entrance is on the right.

Camping, restrooms with showers, a boat launch, and 56 picnic sites are located in the park.

GPS COORDINATES: 47.863779, –119.121098 / N47° 51.8267' W119° 7.2659'

2 Ancient Lakes

COLUMBIA BASIN WILDLIFE AREA, QUINCY

🦌 ❁ 🎇 🐾 🚶

Enjoy pothole lakes and a waterfall deep inside Potholes Coulee, carved out by the ice age floods.

DISTANCE: 4.4 miles round-trip
DURATION: 2.5 hours
ELEVATION CHANGE: 250 feet
EFFORT: Easy
TRAIL: Sand, dirt, road, single track
USERS: Hikers, leashed dogs, mountain bikers, horseback riders
SEASON: March-November
PASSES/FEES: Discover Pass
MAPS: USGS topographic map for Babcock Ridge
CONTACT: Columbia Basin Wildlife Area, 509/765-6641, www.wdfw.wa.gov

W hile many people explore this area in the summer, bring plenty of water and be prepared for intense, triple-digit heat. Consider doing this hike early in the morning, in the evening, or in the spring or fall when temperatures are a little lower.

If you hike here on a summer afternoon when triple-digit temperatures bake the shrub-steppe desert, you might be shocked to find lakes at the end of this sandy trail. Such is the wonder of Washington's channeled scablands. The setting stands in stark contrast to the forested and mountainous hikes just over an hour away in the Cascades—a reminder of the diversity that makes Washington such a fascinating place

START THE HIKE

▶ **MILE 0-0.3: Jeep Trailhead to First Trail Junction**
The hike starts on a sandy **Jeep trail** beyond the gate at the south end of the parking lot. Fat bulrushes rise from trailside wetlands as you walk along **Babcock Bench** above the Columbia River. Be sure to look up for American kestrels, hawks, and other birds. But also look down for rattlesnakes sunning along the path. After 0.3 mile, reach the first of several paths heading east along the floor of the ravine. Any of the trails will take you to Ancient Lakes, but turning left on the first keeps you closest to the wall with the added bonus of taking you past a waterfall.

▶ **MILE 0.3-1.2: First Trail Junction to Waterfall and Boulder**
In another 0.9 mile, the **waterfall** splashes over the edge of the coulee. Pass a **boulder** so large it blocks the sound of the falling water. Continue following the path east through sagebrush and perennial wildflowers such as lupine and balsamroot.

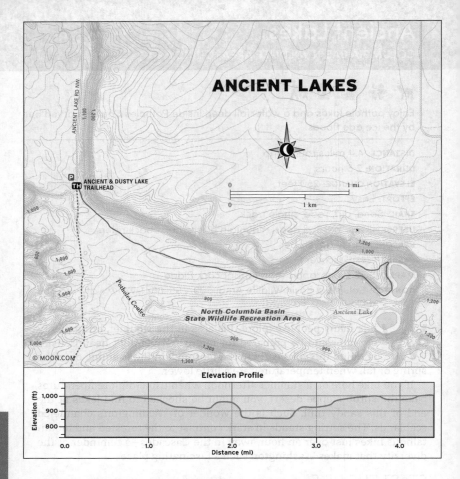

ANCIENT LAKES

ANCIENT LAKE RD NW

ANCIENT & DUSTY LAKE
TRAILHEAD

Potholes Coulee

North Columbia Basin
State Wildlife Recreation Area

Ancient Lake

© MOON.COM

Elevation Profile

▶ MILE 1.2-2.7: Waterfall and Boulder to Lakeshore

The **lakes** come into view after another 0.3 mile. Use the faint, dusty trails to find your way to the **lakeshore** at the northeast corner of the coulee. In another 0.6 mile you'll reach the north end of the lake. Spend some time here admiring the striking view: a multilevel **waterfall** cascading down a basalt slope. Walk the vegetated horseshoe-shaped shoreline for 0.6 mile and keep a lookout for ducks and other waterfowl as the trail turns back to the west.

▶ MILE 2.7-4.4: Lakeshore to Jeep Trailhead

At the west end of the lake, turn right on a dirt path and climb uphill for 0.1 mile to rejoin the trail you used to get to the lake. You can return the way you came 1.6 miles back to the car or find another path to walk along the open canyon floor.

DIRECTIONS

From I-90 near George, take exit 149 (eastbound) or exit 151 (westbound) and follow Highway 281 north (5.5 miles from exit 249 or 4.5 miles from

▲ THE ANCIENT LAKES ARE IN A CANYON CARVED BY ICE AGE FLOODS.

exit 251). Turn left on White Trail Road at the north end of Colockum Ridge Golf Course (on the left). Drive 7.8 miles and turn left on Road 9 NW. After 2 miles the road becomes Ancient Lake Road and continues for 3.8 miles to the trailhead. A toilet is available.

GPS COORDINATES: 47.15995, -119.98061 / N47° 9.597' W119° 58.8366'

BEST NEARBY BITES

Quell your post-hike hunger in Ephrata, where you won't have any trouble finding tasty Mexican food at restaurants like **El Agave** (906 Basin St. SW, 509/717-2062, 11am-9pm Sun.-Thurs., 11am-10pm Fri.-Sat.) and **Tequila's** (222 Basin St. NW, 509/754-1306, hours vary). From the trailhead, the 11-mile drive northeast takes about 20 minutes via Ancient Lake Road and Highway 28.

3 Yakima Skyline Trail

WENAS WILDLIFE AREA, SELAH

Walk the rim of the Yakima River canyon while enjoying views of Roza Dam, two towering volcanoes, and spring wildflowers.

BEST: Brew Hikes
DISTANCE: 6 miles round-trip
DURATION: 3 hours
ELEVATION CHANGE: 1,600 feet
EFFORT: Moderate
TRAIL: Dirt road, dirt and rock trail
USERS: Hikers, leashed dogs, horseback riders, off-road vehicles
SEASON: March–November
PASSES/FEES: Discover Pass
MAPS: WDFW maps available at www.wdfw.wa.gov
CONTACT: Wenas Wildlife Area, 509/697–4503, www.wdfw.wa.gov

Yakima—"The Palm Springs of Washington" as its famous I-82 sign proclaims—gets about 200 days of sunshine annually, making it an ideal escape for vitamin D-deprived hikers from the Seattle area. The Yakima Skyline Trail is a scenic place to enjoy that sunshine in full: There is no shade, so pack plenty of water and sunscreen.

START THE HIKE

▶ MILE 0–0.7: Buffalo Road Gate to Yakima Skyline Trail

From the gate, where the state Department of Natural Resources hopes to soon build a small parking lot, walk **Buffalo Road** northeast for 0.7 mile. This section of the road above the Roza Canal and Yakima River is often closed to motorized vehicles to protect soils and vegetation. Enjoy the view to the southeast of the imposing Fred G. Redmon Memorial Bridges over Selah Creek Canyon. Find the **Yakima Skyline Trail** next to a battered post at a hairpin bend on Buffalo Road. The dirt and rock path climbs gradually from the north side of the road. The path can be muddy and slippery after a rain. In the spring, lupine, bitterroot, larkspur, and other wildflowers add splashes of purples and pinks to the landscape.

Wenas Wildlife Area is home to such a diverse collection of wildlife that my hiking partner and I found ourselves playing "Name that Scat." Elk, deer, bears, bighorn sheep, grouse, turkey, quail, raptors, and reptiles (stay alert for rattlesnakes) frequent the area. Check hunting regulations and plan accordingly. Wearing hunter orange is a wise move. Ornithologists frequent the area, too, in hopes of catching glimpses of Bullock's orioles, warblers, sparrows, and other birds.

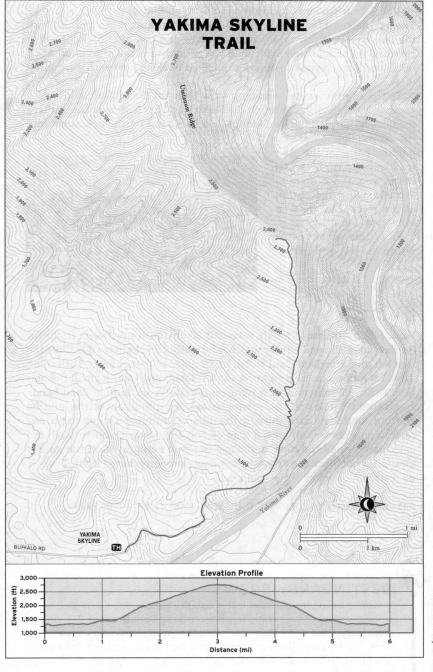

YAKIMA SKYLINE TRAIL

Elevation Profile

▶ MILE 0.7–3: Yakima Skyline Trail to Canyon Rim

The trail makes its way east for 0.5 mile before turning north and climbing the **canyon rim**. A few false summits might lure you into thinking you're closer to the scenic high point than you actually are, but after another 1.8 miles you'll reach your destination: a **hilltop hitching post** with a stunning view.

To the southwest the sweeping view includes Selah, farmland, and a sliver of Yakima visible through the Selah Gap. On clear days, the scenery includes Mount Rainier and Mount Adams. To the north, look down into the canyon holding the serpentine paths of the Yakima River and Highway 821. Below you, the 67-foot-tall Roza Dam diverts a portion of the river into the 94.8-mile Roza Canal.

From this scenic perch, return the way you came.

SUNSET ON YAKIMA
SKYLINE TRAIL ▶

DIRECTIONS

From I-82 northeast of Selah, take exit 26 and turn northwest (right for eastbound traffic and left for westbound traffic) on Highway 821. Take the first left onto Harrison Road and drive 1.9 miles to Wenas Road. Turn right, drive 2.9 miles, and turn right on Gibson Road, just after a small fire station. Drive 0.2 mile and turn right on Buffalo Road. Buffalo Road bends south after 0.5 mile and immediately passes a parking area on the left (the starting point for another hike up the ridge). Continue 1.5 miles on the dirt road to an intersection with a gate on the left. Let yourself through the gate, park beside the road, and close the gate behind you. If the gate is locked, do not block the driveway to private property on the right. There is no restroom or water at the trailhead.

GPS COORDINATES: 46.708167, –120.486566 / N46° 42.49′ W120° 29.194′

BEST NEARBY BREWS

It would be a shame to visit the country's most prolific hop-producing valley without sampling the product. **Bale Breaker Brewing Company** (1801 Birchfield Rd., 509/424-4000, www.balebreaker.com, hours vary) is on a commercial hop farm. Wander through the fields, grab a pint in the taproom, and play games on the lawn. Food is not prepared on-site; visitors often have pizza delivered or bring their own food. From the trailhead, the 15-mile drive northeast takes less than 30 minutes via I-82 and Highway 24.

Listen to singing birds while following a creek through a canyon formed by ancient lava flows.

BEST: Wildflower Hikes

DISTANCE: 5.6 miles round-trip

DURATION: 3 hours

ELEVATION CHANGE: 200 feet

EFFORT: Easy/moderate

TRAIL: Wide dirt path

USERS: Hikers, leashed dogs, mountain bikers, horseback riders (no bikes and horses when the trail is muddy)

SEASON: Year-round

PASSES/FEES: None

MAPS: Trail maps available at www.cowichecanyon.org

CONTACT: Cowiche Canyon Conservancy, 509/248-5065, www.cowichecanyon.org

START THE HIKE

▶ **MILE 0-0.6: Parking Lot East End to First Cowiche Creek Bridge**
From the small **parking lot** at the east end of the **Cowiche Canyon Trail,** follow the wide gravel path westward past an organic hop farm as it enters the canyon. In 0.6 mile, you'll reach the first of nine bridges crossing **Cowiche Creek.** The creek gives life to a lush green riparian swath cutting through the otherwise brown, arid environment. You'll walk past golden balsamroot and pink bitterroot growing amid the sagebrush. This trail is especially popular for bird-watching. Hummingbirds, turkey vultures, red-tailed hawks, wrens, Bullock's orioles, and robins are canyon regulars. Keep an eye out for rattlesnakes and other wildlife as well. Marmots are sometimes spotted playing among the rocks.

▶ **MILE 0.6-1: First Cowiche Creek Bridge to Vineyard Trail Detour (1.6 miles)**
At 0.4 mile beyond the **first bridge,** you'll reach an intersection with the **East Upland Trails.** A few steps farther (just over a bridge) is the **Vineyard Trail,** a 1.6-mile one-way digression especially alluring to wine lovers. The spur leads out of the canyon to views of Mount Rainier and Mount Adams—and the tasting room at Wilridge Estate Vineyard, Winery & Distillery (250 Ehler Rd., Yakima, 509/966-0686, www.wildridgewinery.com).

CENTRAL WASHINGTON

Cowiche Canyon

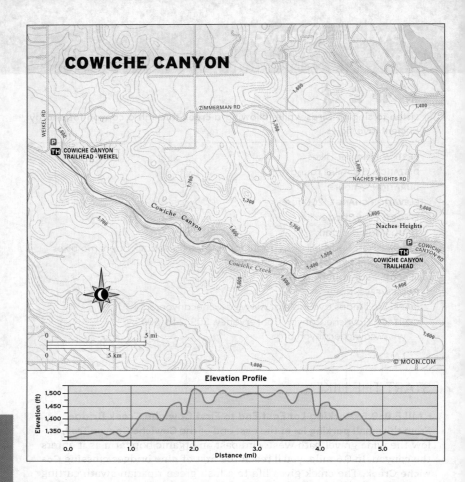

COWICHE CANYON

ZIMMERMAN RD

WEIKEL RD

P TH COWICHE CANYON
TRAILHEAD - WEIKEL

NACHES HEIGHTS RD

Cowiche   Canyon

Naches Heights

Cowiche Creek

P
TH   COWICHE
CANYON RD

COWICHE CANYON
TRAILHEAD

© MOON.COM

0   .5 mi

0   .5 km

Elevation Profile

Elevation (ft)

1,500
1,450
1,400
1,350

0.0   1.0   2.0   3.0   4.0   5.0

Distance (mi)

▶ **MILE 1-1.7: First Cowiche Creek Bridge to Cowiche Canyon Floor**
If you're not detouring, continue 0.7 mile along the creek to the narrowest section of the **canyon**. About 15 million years ago, lava flowed from fissures near Pullman and covered much of eastern Washington and Oregon. The rocky canyon floor and south wall are just the tip of the basalt-berg that reaches about a mile beneath the earth's surface.

▶ **MILE 1.7-2.4: Cowiche Canyon Floor to Lone Pine Trail**
Walk another 0.7 mile past the narrow stretch to another **intersection,** this time with the **Lone Pine Trail,** which leads south (left) to a collection of short trail loops you can explore. If you don't want to investigate these trails, continue straight.

▶ **MILE 2.4-2.8: Lone Pine Trail to Weikel Road**
At 0.4 mile beyond the intersection, the trail passes a few homes as it arrives at its **west trailhead** on Weikel Road, the stopping point. Return the way you came through the canyon.

▲ COWICHE CANYON TRAIL

DIRECTIONS

From U.S. 12 in Yakima, turn southwest on Ackley Road and then make a quick left on Powerhouse Road. Drive 0.2 mile and turn right on Cowiche Canyon Road. Continue 2.2 miles to the east trailhead. A portable toilet is at the small trailhead parking lot.

GPS COORDINATES: 46.622220, –120.614727 / N46° 37.3332' W120° 36.8836'

BEST NEARBY BITES

Miner's Drive-In (2415 S. 1st St., Yakima, 509/457-8194, 8am-2am Sun.-Thurs., 8am-3:30am Fri.-Sat.) has been a fixture in the Yakima Valley since 1948. The vast menu is highlighted by the famous Big Miner Burger, which is roughly the size of a human head. From the trailhead, the 12-mile drive southeast takes less than 20 minutes via U.S. 12 and I-82.

Cowiche Canyon

Badger Mountain: Trailhead Park Loop

BADGER MOUNTAIN CENTENNIAL PRESERVE, RICHLAND

Hike to a view of the Columbia River, Eastern Oregon, and the Tri-Cities without ever leaving Richland's city limits.

BEST: Dog-Friendly Hikes
DISTANCE: 3 miles round-trip
DURATION: 1.5 hours
ELEVATION CHANGE: 800 feet
EFFORT: Easy/moderate
TRAIL: Dirt, pavement, crushed rock
USERS: Hikers, leashed dogs, mountain bikers, horseback riders
SEASON: Year-round
PASSES/FEES: None
MAPS: USGS topographic map for Badger Mountain, Friends of Badger Mountain map available at www.friendsofbadger.org
CONTACT: Benton County Parks, 509/736-3053, www.co.benton.wa.us; Friends of Badger Mountain, 509/783-6558, www.friendsofbadger.org

Badger Mountain Centennial Preserve comprises more than one square mile, with eight miles of trails that attract more than 200,000 visitors per year. The Trailhead Park Loop links three trails for a direct and scenic visit to the top of Badger Mountain. On toasty summer days, early morning and evening are ideal times to hike this trail.

START THE HIKE

▶ **MILE 0-1.1: Trailhead Park Parking Lot to Skyline Trail**

Starting from the parking lot, skirt the perimeter of **Trailhead Park**'s play area before arriving at a **kiosk** with a map, a bird-viewing display, and a history of the area's geology. Leashes are available to borrow at the trailhead. A restroom is located nearby. Continue 0.1 mile, the climbing already underway, to an intersection; continue straight to follow the popular **Canyon Trail.** On warm summer evenings and mornings, you might catch some shade in the canyon before following the trail upward through the dryland grass on the opposite slope.

Keep ascending as you start to get a sense of the view that awaits. Pasco, Richland, and Kennewick are visible below. At 1,250 feet, notice the **Lake Lewis marker** and ponder the fact that thousands of years ago everything beneath you was underwater.

After 1 mile on **Canyon Trail** (and passing wildflowers like balsamroot and phlox in the spring), arrive at the **Skyline Trail** and the fence surrounding the radio towers. Turn left here, but first take time to appreciate the view. Walk past the fence and let your gaze trace the path of the Columbia

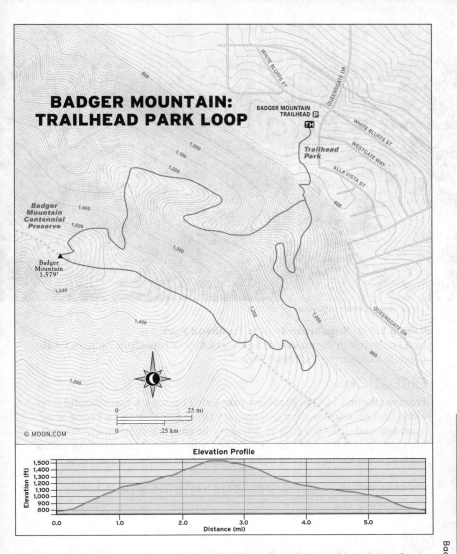

BADGER MOUNTAIN: TRAILHEAD PARK LOOP

Elevation Profile

River. Look across miles of fertile farmland and, on clear days, see as far as Mounts Hood, Adams, and Rainier.

▶ MILE 1.1-2.5: Skyline Trail to Sagebrush Trail

The Skyline Trail is wide and rocky in places but easily navigated as it descends over the next 0.5 mile under power lines. Turn left on the **Sagebrush Trail**. Named for the predominant trailside shrubbery, the path descends more gradually than the Canyon Trail and offers a view of the Columbia. After 0.9 mile, turn left following the direction of a "Hikers Only" sign.

▲ VIEW FROM BADGER MOUNTAIN

▶ **MILE 2.5-3: Sagebrush Trail to Trailhead Park**
In 0.1 mile, rejoin the stairs on the lower Canyon Trail. Turn right and walk 0.4 mile to return to Trailhead Park.

DIRECTIONS

From eastbound I-182 in Richland, take exit 3 (exit 3A for westbound travelers) and go southeast on Queensgate Drive for 0.5 mile to Keene Road. Turn left and drive 0.6 mile to Shockley Road. Turn right and in 0.5 mile Shockley bends left and becomes Queensgate Drive. In another 0.4 mile a parking lot is located on the right. A restroom is located at Trailhead Park.

GPS COORDINATES: 46.237583, –119.307161 / N46° 14.255' W119° 18.4297'

BEST NEARBY BREWS

The world's first industrial-size nuclear reactor was built north of Richland during World War II. Today, **Atomic Ale Brewpub & Eatery** (1015 Lee Blvd., 509/946-5465, www.atomicalebrewpub.com, 11am-9pm Sun.-Thurs., 11am-10pm Fri.-Sat.) pays tribute to this history while practicing its own science: brewing. Cap your hike with a thin-crust pizza like the spicy Reactor Core (salami, sausage, red onions, red pepper, jalapeños, and "nuclear butter") and hand-crafted beers like the Proton Pale Ale, Atomic Amber, and Plutonium Porter. From the trailhead, the 5-mile drive northeast takes about 10 minutes via I-182 and George Washington Way.

Badger Mountain: Trailhead Park Loop

NEARBY CAMPGROUNDS

NAME	DESCRIPTION	FACILITIES	SEASON	FEE
Steamboat Rock State Park	situated on Banks Lake at the foot of Steamboat Rock and one of the most popular campgrounds east of the Cascades	174 tent and RV campsites, restrooms	year-round	$12–50
51052 Highway 155, Electric City, 888/226-7688, www.washington.goingtocamp.com				
Yakima Sportsman State Park	situated on nearly 270 acres of green in the desert and popular among anglers and bird-watchers	67 RV and tent sites, restrooms	March–October	$20–50
904 University Parkway, Yakima, 888/226-7688, www.washington.goingtocamp.com				
Big Pines Campground	the largest of the four BLM campgrounds in the Yakima Canyon	40 camper and tent sites, restrooms	year-round	$15
Canyon Road, Roza, Big Pines Recreation Site, 509/665-2100, www.recreation.gov				
Hood Park Campground	on the shore of Lake Wallula, formed by the McNary Dam on the Columbia River	67 RV and tent sites, restrooms	mid-May–early September	$24–26
123 Ice Harbor Road, Burbank, 509/547-2048, www.recreation.gov				
Quincy Lakes Unit	a wilderness area with dispersed camping for those with tents and small campers	dispersed camping, restrooms	March–October	Discover Pass
Road 3 NW, Quincy, 509/754-4624, www.wdfw.wa.gov				

EASTERN WASHINGTON

From amber waves of grain to Blue Mountains majesties, Eastern Washington offers a variety of lightly visited settings. Explore nature trails and rock formations in a protected natural area minutes from Spokane, one of Washington's largest cities. Hike up Kamiak Butte in the rolling hills of the Palouse. Or head to the state's most secluded corners: To the northeast, look for bighorn sheep on the slopes above Sullivan Lake and ascend Abercrombie Mountain for a panorama that includes Idaho, British Columbia, and the Pend Oreille River. In the southeast, wander the Blue Mountains to a staffed fire lookout with views of peaks in three states.

▲ MARKER ON ABERCROMBIE MOUNTAIN

▲ ROCK FORMATION NEAR ILLER CREEK

◄ ABERCROMBIE MOUNTAIN

1 **Abercrombie Mountain**
DISTANCE: 7.8 miles round-trip
DURATION: 4 hours
EFFORT: Moderate

2 **Sullivan Lakeshore Trail**
DISTANCE: 8.4 miles round-trip
DURATION: 4 hours
EFFORT: Moderate

3 **Iller Creek Conservation Area**
DISTANCE: 5 miles round-trip
DURATION: 2.5 hours
EFFORT: Easy/moderate

4 **Kamiak Butte**
DISTANCE: 2.5 miles round-trip
DURATION: 1.5 hours
EFFORT: Easy/moderate

5 **Oregon Butte**
DISTANCE: 5.8 miles round-trip
DURATION: 3 hours
EFFORT: Easy/moderate

▾ SULLIVAN LAKE

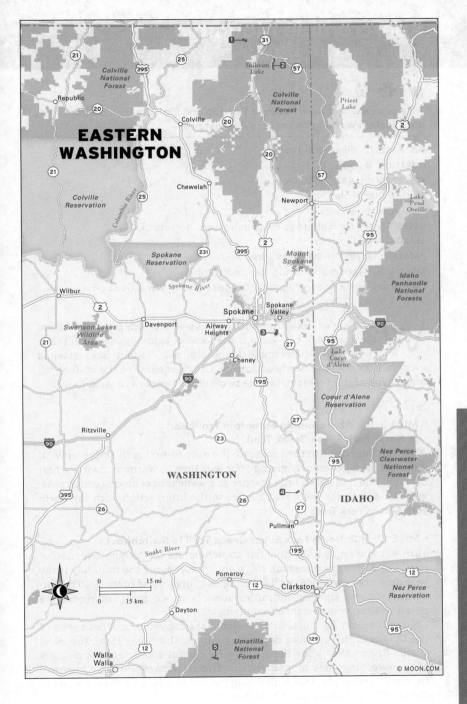

EASTERN WASHINGTON

© MOON.COM

Take in a view that stretches from Canada and Idaho to the Cascades from atop Eastern Washington's second-highest peak.

DISTANCE: 7.8 miles round-trip

DURATION: 4 hours

ELEVATION CHANGE: 2,400 feet

EFFORT: Moderate

TRAIL: Dirt, loose rock

USERS: Hikers, leashed dogs, mountain bikers, horseback riders

SEASON: June–October

PASSES/FEES: Northwest Forest Pass

MAPS: USGS topographic map for Abercrombie

CONTACT: Colville National Forest, 509/684-7000, www.fs.usda.gov

When you're hankering for a great view, hikes to fire lookouts are always a safe bet—even if the lookout is long gone. Such is the case with Abercrombie Mountain, a 7,308-foot peak stashed away in Washington's northeast corner. Only remnants of the 20-foot-tall tower's foundation remain, but the two-nation view is as a good as ever.

START THE HIKE

▶ **MILE 0-1.5: Abercrombie Mountain Trailhead to North Fork Silver Creek Trail**

After the long drive to the trailhead, the easy-to-find path slopes upward gently at first, generously giving your legs time to warm up over the first 0.4 mile. The trail gets a little steeper as it **switchbacks** among cedar, pine, and Douglas fir for the next 1.1 miles to the intersection with the **North Fork Silver Creek Trail.**

▶ **MILE 1.5-3.2: North Fork Silver Creek Trail to Switchbacks**

Turn left and enjoy a 0.3-mile flat stretch before the toughest section of climbing. There are more than 100 plant species along the trail. July is the best time to see wildflowers like bear grass, lupine, and fireweed. The Forest Service says sightings of rattlesnakes, bears, cougars, and moose are possible. Keep your distance from them all.

Over the next 1.4 miles, more **switchbacks** deliver occasional views of the Columbia River before depositing you on the ridge. Here, the Pend Oreille River valley joins the scenery. Be careful about sending pictures of the sweeping view to your envious friends, however: I got a message from my service provider welcoming me to Canada (less than 5 miles to the north) and to substantially higher rates.

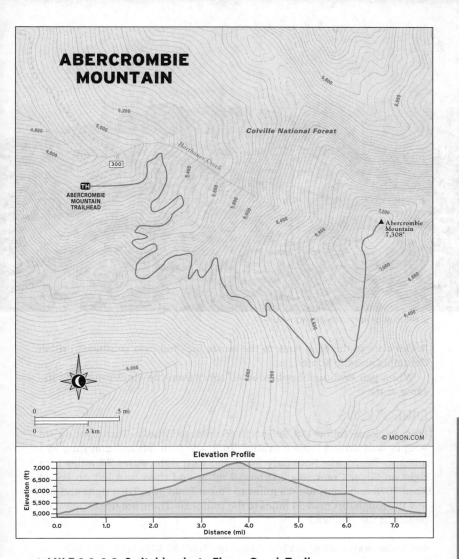

ABERCROMBIE MOUNTAIN

Colville National Forest

ABERCROMBIE
MOUNTAIN
TRAILHEAD

Hartbauer Creek

▲ Abercrombie
Mountain
7,308'

© MOON.COM

Elevation Profile

▶ **MILE 3.2-3.6: Switchbacks to Flume Creek Trail**

Put your phone on airplane mode and follow the trail up Abercrombie's south side for 0.4 mile to the intersection with the **Flume Creek Trail.** Turn left but snap a mental image of the intersection for the return trip. It can be easy to miss.

▶ **MILE 3.6-3.9: Flume Creek Trail to Abercrombie Mountain Summit**

It's just another 0.3 mile to the **summit.** Pass gnarly snags and spend the final 100 yards walking over the **loose rock** that covers the broad Selkirk peak. Note the remains of a tower, look for a battered USGS benchmark, and soak in the view. Sherlock and Hooknose Peaks are nearby. The Kettle Range is visible to the west and, on clear days, so are the Cascades. The

▲ THE PEAK OF ABERCROMBIE MOUNTAIN

Rockies are to the east. And, to the north, look out over southeast British Columbia and the Kootenays.

When you eventually pull yourself away from the view, return via the same route.

DIRECTIONS

From Spokane, follow U.S. 395 north 65 miles to Colville. Turn right on 3rd Avenue and drive 1.1 miles to Aladdin Road. Turn left and continue 25.5 miles to Deep Lake Boundary Road and turn right. After 7.3 miles turn right on Silver Creek Road. Drive 1.9 miles and then turn left on Forest Road 7078 and continue 4.3 miles to Forest Road 300. Turn right and follow the rough dirt road 3.1 miles to the trailhead. There are no restroom facilities at the trailhead.

GPS COORDINATES: 48.932052, –117.482448 / N48° 55.9231' W117° 28.9469'

BEST NEARBY BREWS

In Colville, **Fired Up Brewing** (1235 S. Main St., 509/684-3328, hours vary) bakes pizza in an earthenware oven and brews beer using locally grown hops. The beer names are a tip of the hat to local landmarks, such as Little Pend Oreille Pale Ale and Red Dome Red; hard ciders are also on tap. From the trailhead, the 43-mile drive southwest takes 1 hour, 20 minutes via Deep Lake Boundary and Aladdin Roads.

Sullivan Lakeshore Trail

COLVILLE NATIONAL FOREST, METALINE FALLS

Trace the eastern shore of Sullivan Lake on an easy trail and maybe catch a glimpse of a bighorn sheep on Hall Mountain.

DISTANCE: 8.4 miles round-trip
DURATION: 4 hours
ELEVATION CHANGE: 1,000 feet
EFFORT: Moderate
TRAIL: Dirt single track, rocky slopes
USERS: Hikers, leashed dogs
SEASON: April–November
PASSES/FEES: Northwest Forest Pass
MAPS: USGS topographic map for Metaline Falls
CONTACT: Colville National Forest, 509/446-7500, www.fs.usda.gov

From spring wildflowers to summer swims to golden fall larches to opportunities to see bears and bighorn sheep, Sullivan Lake has plenty to offer. Tucked away in the lightly traveled northeast corner of the state, this National Scenic Trail in the Colville National Forest starts at East Sullivan Campground at the north end of the lake. However, it's just as easy to start from the Noisy Creek Campground at the lake's southern end.

START THE HIKE

▸ **MILE 0-0.3: Trailhead Kiosk to Nature Loop Trail**

Starting from the **kiosk** at the small roadside parking area, the trail climbs gently and briefly. In about 100 yards, pass the 0.6-mile **Nature Loop Trail.** To take the self-guided tour and learn about a 200-year-old larch and a resilient Douglas fir, borrow the worn paper pamphlet at the trailhead kiosk (but remember to return it when you're done). About 0.25 mile beyond the nature loop, the trail crests above the campground and the **lake** comes into view. A trailside bench offers a spot to enjoy the sight of swimmers and water-skiers playing in one of Colville National Forest's largest lakes. The waters are clear and, in the summer, surprisingly warm (but still chilly).

▸ **MILE 0.3-1.6: Nature Loop Trail to Trailside Picnic Spot**

The lake will be in view for most of the rest of this hike. The trail passes under trees and undulates a bit. After 1.3 miles pass a small **clearing** between the trail and the lake. It's just big enough to pitch a tent or to have a picnic. Spots like these are scarce on the trail, which runs along the base of Hall Mountain. It's not uncommon to come across resting hikers on the narrow stretches, sitting on the trail with their legs hanging over the slope. The steep slopes of Hall Mountain above are home to a herd of bighorn sheep. Biologists are studying the herd, and signs posted at the

EASTERN WASHINGTON

Sullivan Lakeshore Trail

307

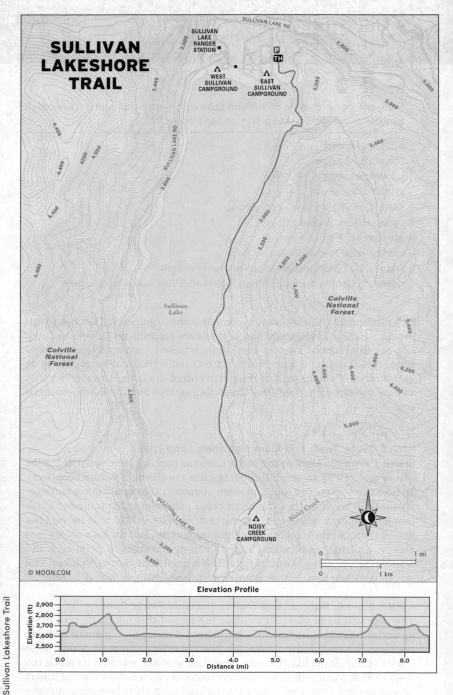

SULLIVAN LAKESHORE TRAIL

SULLIVAN LAKE RD

SULLIVAN
LAKE
RANGER
STATION

WEST
SULLIVAN
CAMPGROUND

EAST
SULLIVAN
CAMPGROUND

P
TH

Sullivan
Lake

Colville
National
Forest

Colville
National
Forest

SULLIVAN LAKE RD

SULLIVAN LAKE RD

NOISY
CREEK
CAMPGROUND

Noisy Creek

© MOON.COM

0   1 mi

0   1 km

Elevation Profile

| | 0.0 | 1.0 | 2.0 | 3.0 | 4.0 | 5.0 | 6.0 | 7.0 | 8.0 |

Elevation (ft): 2,900 / 2,800 / 2,700 / 2,600 / 2,500

Distance (mi)

trailheads ask hikers to report sightings to the national forest or the state Department of Fish and Wildlife.

▶ **MILE 1.6-4.2: Trailside Picnic Spot to Noisy Creek Campground**
For 2.2 miles beyond the **trailside picnic spot**, cross rockslides, pass trees charred by wildfires, and listen to the sounds of small planes taking off and landing at the north end of the lake. Near a bench overlooking a bay at the south end of the lake you might find an old spur trail and option for a side trip to a closed mine. To continue to the Noisy Creek Campground, enjoy a flat 0.4 mile beyond the bluff. This section passes through the trees and offers several places to access the lake. The trail ends in a parking lot near a restroom and a popular swimming hole at **Noisy Creek Campground.**

For the return trip, simply follow the path back to your car.

DIRECTIONS

From Spokane, follow U.S. 2 north for 36 miles and turn left on Highway 211. Drive 15.2 miles to Highway 20 and turn left. Drive 31 miles along the Pend Oreille River; when the road becomes Highway 31, continue straight for 3.1 miles. Turn right on Sullivan Lake Road; just after crossing the Ione bridge, stay left to keep on Sullivan Lake Road. Drive 12.4 miles to Forest Road 22 and turn right. After 0.4 mile, turn right at the sign for the East Sullivan Lake Campground. A small trailhead parking area is on the left before the campground. There are toilets at the campground, but not at the trailhead.

GPS COORDINATES: 48.840494, -117.278366 / N48° 50.4296' W117° 16.702'

SULLIVAN LAKE ▶

BEST NEARBY BITES
The Farmhouse Café (221 E. 5th Ave., Metaline Falls, 509/446-2447, 6am-6:30pm Mon.-Fri., 7am-2pm Sat.-Sun.) in the old mining town of Metaline Falls dishes up biscuits and gravy, burgers, pie, and more. The train footage in the opening credits of the 1993 Johnny Depp film *Benny & Joon* was filmed nearby. From the trailhead, the 7.5-mile drive west takes 15 minutes via Sullivan Lake Road and Highway 31.

Stroll through a riparian setting before ascending to views of the Spokane Valley and the Palouse from a ridge crowned with granite monoliths.

DISTANCE: 5 miles round-trip

DURATION: 2.5 hours

ELEVATION CHANGE: 1,200 feet

EFFORT: Easy/moderate

TRAIL: Single track

USERS: Hikers, leashed dogs, mountain bikers, horseback riders

SEASON: Year-round

PASSES/FEES: None

MAPS: USGS topographic map for Spokane SE, www.spokanecounty.org/1406/Trail-Maps

CONTACT: Spokane County Parks, 509/447-4730, www.spokanecounty.org

The 966-acre Iller Creek/Stevens Creek Unit of the Dishman Hills Conservation Area allows visitors easy access to a forest of ponderosa pine, hemlock, and larch and wildflowers such as Oregon grape and balsamroot. It's also home to moose, elk, coyotes, and numerous bird species. One of 51 stops on the National Audubon Society's Palouse to Pines Loop, Iller Creek is a place to see red crossbills, hummingbirds, cedar waxwings, wrens, and more.

START THE HIKE

▶ **MILE 0-0.9: Parking Lot South End to Iller Creek Marker**
At the south end of the small parking area, slip past the fence and follow the trail right for a counterclockwise loop through one of the Spokane Valley's most beloved conservation projects. Start with a shaded, gradually climbing stretch along **Iller Creek** (typically dry by midsummer). As squirrels, snakes, and birds rustle the bushes, it's easy to forget you're about 5 miles from downtown Spokane. The first 0.9-mile stretch brings you to a **marker** directing you to head right. Here, the climbing gets a little steeper.

▶ **MILE 0.9-2.2: Iller Creek Marker to Rock Monolith**
In another 0.7 mile, pass the **intersection** with the Upper Valley Trail; this trail is a good option if you're looking to abbreviate your trip by about 0.7 mile, but you'll also bypass the best views. The steepest sections of the trail come during the next 0.4 mile, but you'll get a little inspiration as you step out into an **opening** and the Rocks of Sharon come into view to your left. Descend gradually over the next 0.2 mile and arrive at the first house-size **rock monolith**. (Here, a spur trail ascends to the right and visits more rock outcrops but leaves the conservation area in about 0.2 mile.)

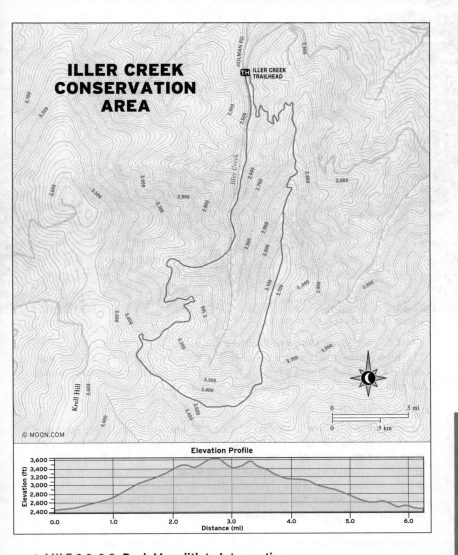

ILLER CREEK
CONSERVATION
AREA

Elevation Profile

▶ MILE 2.2–2.6: Rock Monolith to Intersection

Continue past the **spur trail,** following the sign toward the Stevens Creek
Trail, and, 0.2 mile farther, keep straight at the **intersection** and climb a little higher to a sweeping view that includes Steptoe Butte rising above the
Palouse. Keep going and, 0.2 mile after the Stevens Creek Trail intersection, reach another **intersection**. Continue straight as the ridge descends.

▶ MILE 2.6–4.3: Intersection to Trail Ridge

In 0.5 mile, pass the eastern **intersection** with the Upper Valley Trail. Keep
following the **Iller Creek Trail** along the ridge and in a short distance reach
a stretch where the forest was thinned by fire. Enjoy views of the Spokane
Valley and Mount Spokane at times over the next 1.2 miles.

▲ ROCK FORMATIONS NEAR ILLER CREEK

▶ **MILE 4.3–5: Trail Ridge to Trailhead**
The hike winds down with a 0.4-mile descent on switchbacks built by volunteers. The switchbacks deposit you back in the riparian setting along Iller Creek for a flat 0.3-mile jaunt to the trailhead.

DIRECTIONS

From Spokane, follow I-90 east to exit 287 and turn south on Argonne Road. Continue for 3.5 miles as the road becomes Dishman-Mica Road then turn right on Schafer Road. In 0.9 mile the road ends at East 44th Avenue. Turn right and drive 0.2 mile to Farr Road. Turn left and continue 0.3 mile to Holman Road. Turn right and drive 0.75 mile to the trailhead located at the turn where the road becomes Rockcrest Lane. The trailhead is well marked. There is limited parking and one portable toilet.

GPS COORDINATES: 47.601881, –117.281793 / N47° 36.1129' W117° 16.9076'

BEST NEARBY BREWS

Spokane's **Iron Goat Brewing Company** (1302 W. 2nd Ave., 509/474-0722, www.irongoatbrewing.com, 11am-close daily) is known for crafting creative beers and a vegan-friendly menu. They'll even add tofu to your thin-crust pizza. The brewery has created 150 different beers, but consider a classic like the fruity Impaler Imperial IPA. Iron Goat gets its name from Spokane's most famous trash can: Built for the 1974 world's fair, an iron goat sculpture in Riverfront Park has a built-in vacuum allowing it to eat trash. From the trailhead, the 12-mile drive northwest takes 20 minutes via I-90.

Kamiak Butte
KAMIAK BUTTE COUNTY PARK, PALOUSE

Take in sweeping views of the Palouse's fertile farmland from atop an isolated, tree-covered hill standing in contrast to its surroundings.

BEST: Spring Hikes
DISTANCE: 2.5 miles round-trip
DURATION: 1.5 hours
ELEVATION CHANGE: 750 feet
EFFORT: Easy/moderate
TRAIL: Dirt, gravel, steps
USERS: Hikers, leashed dogs
SEASON: March-November
MAPS: USGS topographic map for Albion
PARK HOURS: 7am-dusk daily
CONTACT: Whitman County Parks and Recreation, 509/397-6238, www.whitmancounty.org

START THE HIKE

▶ **MILE 0-0.5: Picnic Area Kiosk to Pine Ridge Trail**

To explore this steptoe (an isolated hill surrounded by lava flows), start from the **picnic area kiosk** by ascending a short section of **steps** to a wide path. In a few steps, pass the **Larch Shelter** on the left and, to the right, the trail you'll use to finish the loop. For the next 0.5 mile, the **Pine Ridge Trail** climbs through a forest of ponderosa pine, Douglas fir, and western larch. Keep an eye out for wildlife such as deer, porcupines, chipmunks, owls, and squirrels. The park is home to about 30 types of mammals and more than 130 bird species. Once you've switchbacked your way up the ridge, Washington State University and the University of Idaho, across the border in Moscow, are both part of the panorama.

▶ **MILE 0.5-1.5: Pine Ridge Trail to Kamiak Butte Summit**

Atop the ridge, turn right to continue on the **Pine Ridge Trail** as it climbs gradually for the next 0.9 mile. Along the way, take note of the contradicting microclimates of the butte's north- and south-facing slopes. Shade and cooler temperatures on the north side allow for dense forest and wildflowers like trillium and yellowbells. Meanwhile, more direct sunlight on the south side creates difficult growing conditions. Pass areas scarred by fire and reach an **intersection** in the woods. Continue straight for 0.1 mile to the 3,641-foot **summit.** This section is on private property and signs ask hikers to stick to the trail.

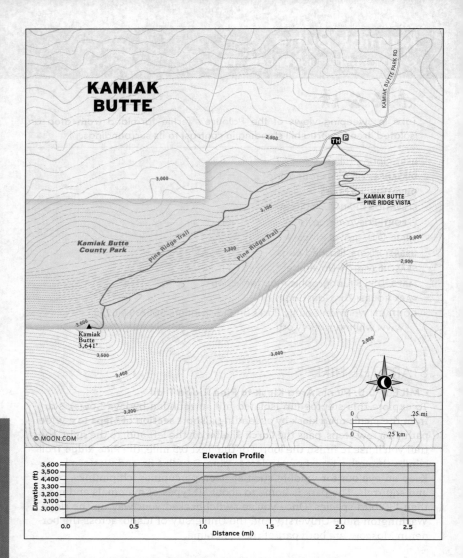

KAMIAK BUTTE

KAMIAK BUTTE PARK RD

2,900

TH P

KAMIAK BUTTE
PINE RIDGE VISTA

3,000

Kamiak Butte
County Park

Pine Ridge Trail

3,100

3,300

Pine Ridge Trail

3,000

2,900

3,600

Kamiak
Butte
3,641'

2,800

3,500

3,000

3,400

3,200

© MOON.COM

0   .25 mi

0   .25 km

Elevation Profile

Elevation (ft)

3,600
3,500
3,400
3,300
3,200
3,100
3,000

0.0   0.5   1.0   1.5   2.0   2.5

Distance (mi)

▶ **MILE 1.5–1.6: Kamiak Butte Summit to Backside Trail**

From the **summit**, you can create a longer loop by following the West End Primitive Trail (this adds 1.4 miles to your trip and dogs are prohibited on this section), but for the most direct descent return 0.1 mile and turn left on the **Backside Trail.** The trail passes through a narrow band of young trees reclaiming a slope cleared in the 1950s for a ski run.

▶ **MILE 1.6–2.5: Backside Trail to Larch Shelter and Trailhead**

After a 0.4-mile descent, turn right to stay on the trail. Keep right at **two intersections** over the next 0.2 mile (trails to the left lead to the campground). Continue through a spring-fed **thicket** teeming with trees and shrubs that attract birds and other animals. After 0.25 mile arrive back at the **Larch Shelter**. Turn left to return to the trailhead.

▲ WINTER ON KAMIAK BUTTE

DIRECTIONS

From Colfax follow Highway 272/Canyon Street east for 5.4 miles and turn right on Clear Creek Road. Drive 8.1 miles to Fugate Road/Road 5100 and turn right. In 0.7 mile, turn left on Kamiak Butte Park Road. Drive 0.8 mile to the trailhead near the picnic area and restrooms. Camping is available in the park.

GPS COORDINATES: 46.870298, –117.152982 / N46° 52.2179' W117° 9.1789'

BEST NEARBY BITES

Get a taste of college life in Pullman—14 miles (20 minutes) south of the trailhead via Highway 27—by dining at a classic WSU hangout. Grab a huge burger and fries at **Cougar Cottage,** better known as **The Coug** (900 NE Colorado St., 509/332-1265, 11am–2am daily).

🦌 ❀ 🐾 🚶

Wander across the top of the Blue Mountains to a nearly 90-year-old fire lookout with a 360-degree view spanning three states.

DISTANCE: 5.8 miles round-trip
DURATION: 3 hours
ELEVATION CHANGE: 1,200 feet
EFFORT: Easy/moderate
TRAIL: Dirt
USERS: Hikers, leashed dogs, hunters, horseback riders
SEASON: June–November
PASSES/FEES: Northwest Forest Pass
MAPS: USGS topographic map for Oregon Butte, USFS map for Wenaha-Tucannon Wilderness
CONTACT: Umatilla National Forest, Pomeroy Ranger District, 509/843-1891, www.fs.usda.gov

O regon Butte isn't in the state it's named for, but you can see it from here. The views of Idaho and Washington are pretty spectacular too. In fact, the views of the Blue Mountains start the moment you step out of your car, more than a mile above sea level. This sample panorama is a reward for a drive you might find more taxing than the hike.

START THE HIKE

▶ **MILE 0-1: Mount Misery Trailhead to West Butte**

Find the **Mount Misery Trail** at the east end of the parking lot and step immediately into 176,557-acre Wenaha-Tucannon Wilderness. Take note of the sandy trail surface. It is composed of wind-deposited silt (loess) and ash from an ancient eruption. The trail offers several day-hiking and backpacking options as it travels across hilltops and through a forest of Douglas fir, spruce, larch, and lodgepole pine. After 1 mile of gradual climbing, reach an **unmarked intersection**. Veer right to visit the top of West Butte.

▶ **MILE 1-1.8: West Butte to Mount Misery Trail**

In another 0.5 mile, pass just below the summit of **West Butte** (6,292 feet). Catch your first glimpse of your destination, the fire lookout on the neighboring peak. Enjoy the south-facing slopes that are often adorned with spring and summer wildflowers. From West Butte, descend **switchbacks** and rejoin the **Mount Misery Trail** in 0.3 mile.

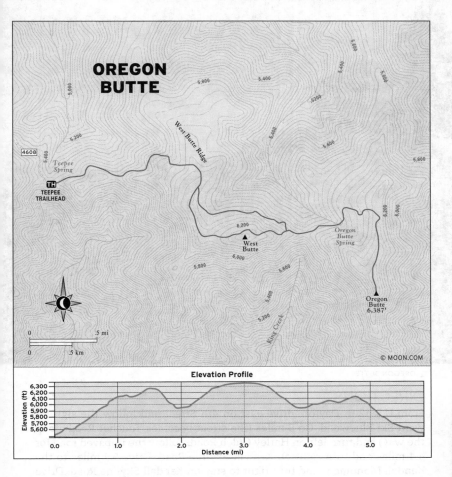

OREGON BUTTE

Elevation Profile

▶ MILE 1.8-2.9: Mount Misery Trail to Sawtooth Ridge Trail and Lookout

Descend another 0.3 mile to **Oregon Butte Spring.** The spring pumps water into a trough carved into a tamarack log. The lookout stationed atop Oregon Butte all summer relies on the spring as her water source. From here, the trail ascends 0.3 mile to an intersection with the **Sawtooth Ridge Trail.** Turn right and continue upward for 0.1 mile to the ridge. Turn south and enjoy the view as you ramble another 0.4 mile to the **lookout**.

Built in 1931, the lookout stands on the highest point (6,387 feet) in the wilderness and is staffed in the summer. Rows of peaks and valleys seem to stretch forever in every direction. Idaho's Seven Devils Range is visible to the southeast, while to the south the view includes Oregon's Wallowa and Elkhorn Mountains. The Oregon border is about 7.5 miles away. It can be chilly in late summer and fall, and mid-September snowfall isn't uncommon. Snow can also linger on the north-facing slopes into summer.

When you're ready to return, retrace your steps.

▲ OREGON BUTTE

DIRECTIONS

From U.S. 12 in Dayton, drive east on 4th Street and follow the sign toward Ski Bluewood. Go 5 miles (the street becomes Touchet Road along the way) and turn left on Hatley Gulch Road. Follow the unpaved road for 4.4 miles and turn right on Kendall Skyline Road. Drive 5.9 miles to the Kendall Monument and turn right to stay on Kendall Skyline Road. Drive 11.5 miles and then turn left on Forest Road 4608 at the Godman Guard Station. Drive 6 miles to the trailhead. A vault toilet is located at the parking area.

GPS COORDINATES: 46.11808, –117.71393 / N46° 7.0848' W117° 42.8358'

BEST NEARBY BREWS

Chief Spring's Brew Pub (148 E. Main St., Dayton, 509/382-4677, www.fireandironsbrewpub.com, hours vary) is named for co-owner and brew master Mike Spring, a local fire chief. Spring and his wife, Ann, own the pub and the neighboring pizzeria. Enjoy slices, pints, tacos, burgers, chili, and more while admiring the firehouse décor. From the trailhead, the 36-mile drive northwest takes about 1 hour, 20 minutes via Kendall Skyline Road and U.S. 12.

NEARBY CAMPGROUNDS

NAME	DESCRIPTION	FACILITIES	SEASON	FEE
Noisy Creek Campground	on the southern end of Sullivan Lake	19 RV and tent sites, restrooms	mid-May-early September	$18
Sullivan Lake Road, Ione, Colville National Forest, 877/444-6777, www.recreation.gov				
Tucannon Campground	on the Tucannon River bordering the W. T. Wooten State Wildlife Area	18 RV and tent sites, restrooms	year-round	$8
Forest Road 47, Mountain Top, Umatilla National Forest, 509/843-1891, www.fs.usda.gov				
Bowl and Pitcher Campground	one of four campgrounds in Riverside State Park; access to giant basalt formations via a suspension bridge across the Spokane River	32 tent and RV sites, restrooms	May 15-September 15	$12-50
9711 W. Charles Road, Nine Mile Falls, 888/226-7688, www.washington. goingtocamp.com				
Kamiak Butte	situated in the woods at the base of Kamiak Butte, just minutes from Pullman	8 tent sites, restrooms	year-round	$15
Road 6710, Palouse, 509/397-4622, www.whitmancounty.org				
Liberty Lake Campground	in a county park east of Spokane, just a short walk from Liberty Lake	27 RV and tent sites, restrooms	May-September	$22-40
3719 S. Zephyr Road, Liberty Lake Regional Park, 509/954-0808, www.spokanecounty.org				

Safety

BEFORE YOU GO

All too often, when hikers find themselves in distress, the trouble didn't start on the trail. It started in their living room. It's the seemingly tiny mistakes made at home that can compound into significant problems in the wilderness. Forgetting to let somebody know where you're going. Not checking the weather or time of nightfall. Forgetting to pack rain gear, food, water, or extra batteries. Maybe even (and, yes, at least one of us has done this) forgetting your entire day pack. You have a map and compass, but do you know how to use them? Were you honest about your limitations and fitness level (your current fitness level) when you selected the hike?

Safe and fun hikes start during the preparation process. Here's what you need to get ready for your day hike:

The 10 Essentials

Since 1974, when it was formalized by the Seattle-based outdoor group The Mountaineers, the 10 Essentials has been widely regarded as the standard list of gear hikers and climbers need to stay safe and respond to an emergency when traveling in the backcountry.

1. Extra food: Pack more than you think you'll need.

2. Extra water: Carry more than you think you'll need or, if there are water sources along your route, carry a water purification system.

3. First aid: In a waterproof bag, carry a first-aid kit with items to care for yourself and those depending on you (including pets). Don't forget insect repellent, foot care, and medications.

4. Emergency shelter: Take a lightweight bivy, waterproof tarp, or an oversized and durable plastic bag.

5. Insulation: Pack extra clothes for warmth and protection from the elements.

6. Illumination: A headlamp and/or flashlight and extra batteries.

7. Fire: A stove, waterproof matches, or lighter and tinder.

8. Sun protection: Bring a hat and sunglasses and always use sunscreen (even on overcast days).

9. Navigation: Start with a map and compass. Consider carrying a GPS device (more resistant to weather than phones), an altimeter, and a personal locator beacon (capable of sending an emergency signal from outside cell coverage). Bring battery backup for electronic devices. While your phone is a wonderful tool, don't treat it as a lifeline: Phones are fragile, and cell coverage in the backcountry is not a given.

10. Repair kit and tools: A multipurpose tool, knife, duct tape, zip ties, safety pins, and a sewing kit are great for solving problems on the trail.

HIKING APPS

Whether you want to identify a bird or a mountain, need help finding your way, or just need directions and the weather forecast, your phone can help. There are numerous apps that can enhance your outdoor excursion. Here are some of our favorites:

- **CAIRN** (www.cairnme.com, Android, IOS, free with in-app purchases) shares your location with friends and family of your choosing and alerts them if you're overdue. The app also helps find cell coverage, records your route, and offers topographical maps to download for offline use.
- **DARK SKY WEATHER** (www.darksky.net, Android, free with in-app purchases; IOS, $3.99) and **WEATHER UNDERGROUND** (www.wunderground.com, Andriod, IOS, free with in-app purchases) are good choices for staying abreast of weather forecasts in the area you're hiking.
- **FIRST AID - AMERICAN RED CROSS** (www.redcross.org, Android, IOS, free) helps diagnose and treat common injuries and ailments you might face on the trail. Videos and written directions offer expert advice on dealing with sprains, heat stroke, hypothermia, and more.
- **GAIAGPS** (www.gaiagps.com, Android, IOS, free with in-app purchases) lets you navigate the wilderness, record your hike, download maps, check weather forecasts, and search for trails.
- **MERLIN BIRD ID** (www.merlin.allaboutbirds.org, Android, IOS, free) helps you identify more than 3,000 bird species by snapping a photo or answering questions. The app then gives you in-depth info on the bird and even lets you listen to birdsongs.
- **PEAKFINDER AR** (www.peakfinder.org, Android, IOS, $4.99) and **PEAKVISOR** (www.peakvisor.com, Andriod, $4.49, IOS, free with in-app purchases) are excellent apps for identifying peaks. Just point your phone's camera at the mountain in question: The apps use augmented reality to overlay a rendering of the peak so you can determine its name.
- **ALLTRAILS** (www.alltrails.com, Andriod, IOS, free with in-app purchases) and **WTA TRAILBLAZER** (www.wta.org, Andriod, IOS, free) are valuable tools for hikers, complete with hiking suggestions and trip reports with details about current trail and road conditions.

Hiking Prep

With the right gear and preparation, you're ready to hit the trail.

Tell a friend: If you get lost or need help, will rescuers know to look for you? It's vital to make sure a friend or family member knows where you are going and understands your itinerary.

Check the forecast: Be prepared for what the weather is supposed to be like, but remember the weather is unpredictable. So, also be ready for sudden and dramatic changes. Check with a ranger station or land manager before your trip to confirm the trail is open, whether you can reach the trailhead (or get close enough to walk). And don't forget to check the avalanche forecast.

Go old school with directions: Siri is wealth of information, but she doesn't seem to hike much. Ask for "directions to Mailbox Peak," and she'll confidently guide you to the wrong place. Same goes for other trailheads around the Northwest. Avoid this problem by researching directions before you go.

Check yourself before you wreck yourself: A mountaintop, five miles from your car, is a bad place to come to the realization that your athletic glory days are behind you. Be honest about your fitness level and how much stress your joints can handle before they turn on you. If it's been a while since you hiked, start slow. And don't worry—the Northwest (and this book) is loaded with dazzling day hikes for every level.

Double-check: Make sure your gear is in working order and double-check that you have everything you need before pulling out of the driveway.

Get trailhead-ready: Opportunistic burglars love trailheads. Lock your car and never leave valuables inside. If you routinely keep stuff in your car, consider leaving those items at home. And if you do leave items in your car, make sure they're out of sight. And don't forget to hang your parking pass.

On the Trail

WEATHER

For hikers, meteorologists are also stylists. They're talking about rain, snow, and high-pressure systems, but what we hear are guidelines for how to dress. After all, almost every day is perfect for hiking if you have the right gear. The Northwest might be famous for rain, but don't let gloomy forecasts get you down. Heading out in the rain can be a good way to avoid crowds. Plus, most rainy days have windows free of precipitation. To really dial in your forecast, head to www.weather.gov, where you can click on a location on a map and NOAA will serve up a personalized prediction.

Be sure to know what time the sun will set, especially in late summer and early fall when it's not uncommon for hikers to be surprised when darkness arrives earlier than they expected. In winter and early spring, check avalanche conditions on the Northwest Avalanche Center website (www.nwac.us).

Check for road closures and mountain pass conditions at www.wsdot. com. It links to numerous webcams that help you better understand what you'll face during your drive.

WILDLIFE

Whether it's a squirrel scurrying up a tree or a black bear foraging in a trailside huckleberry bush, wildlife encounters are an exciting and inevitable part of hiking in the Pacific Northwest. These encounters are usually peaceful if hikers keep their distance, but there's a reason these animals are called wildlife. They are wild and unpredictable. You don't know what they will do if they are startled or feel cornered, and you don't want to find out.

Give the animals plenty of space and never feed them. Feeding animals conditions them to associate humans with food. This can be unsafe for people and the animals. Rangers at Mount Rainier National Park have reported warning people to stop feeding animals out of their car windows only to see animals killed while jumping in front of cars, presumably in the pursuit of food.

Bears

If you stumble across a bear while hiking in the Northwest, it's likely a black bear. However, grizzly bears can be found in the North Cascades and northeastern Washington. Look for fresh scat, tracks, and clawed trees as you hike. Making noise by clapping your hands or talking loudly is often enough to keep bears away. Bears are attracted to scents like perfume, deodorant, and even toothpaste. If you're camping, hang everything that smells (except your hiking partner) at least 10 feet off the ground and at least 100 yards outside of camp.

If you stumble across a black bear, stop and try to stay calm as you assess the situation. If the bear doesn't notice you, slowly back away. If the bear approaches you, don't throw anything and avoid direct eye contact, which the bear could interpret as a threat. Instead, stand up, wave your hands, and talk to it in a low voice. If you are in a group, stand shoulder-to-shoulder and wave your arms to appear intimidating. If the bear charges you, fight the urge to run (bears can run 35 mph, about 7 mph faster than Usain Bolt). Stand your ground. It's likely bluff-charging. If the bear attacks, fight back.

If your encounter is with a grizzly, WDFW suggests a different approach. First, you'll need to know the difference between the bears; a dish face and shoulder hump are the most obvious sign you're dealing with a grizzly. Grizzlies have smaller ears than black bears and claws that can be twice as long. Don't try to tell them apart by their color. Black bears can be brown or cinnamon colored, and grizzly coats can be so brown they appear black. If you can't avoid the grizzly, try to distract it by dropping a coat or another nonfood item and look for a tree you can climb at least 12 feet off the ground. If you can't find a tree and the bear attacks, curl up on the ground and protect your head and neck with your arms. Don't get up until you're certain the bear is gone.

Cougars

Cougars are solitary creatures who usually want nothing to do with humans. If you happen across one of these massive cats, they're likely to scram quicker than you can process what you saw. Attacks are rare. The best way to avoid cougars is to hike in a group, make noise to avoid surprising these beasts, and stay away from animal carcasses. Cougars might be saving these dead animals for their next meal.

If you encounter a cougar, do not run. Instead, keep eye contact and make yourself look as big as possible. Open your jacket, wave your arms, shout, and throw rocks to convince the animal you are a predator, not prey. Pick up small children. Assess the situation and back away slowly if it is safe to do so. If it attacks, fight back.

Mountain Goats

Mountain goats meandering across rocky slopes are a sight to behold, but get too close and they can be dangerous. Try to stay at least 50 yards away from these peaceful-looking creatures. Mountain goats have an insatiable appetite for salt and might follow you in hope of tasting your sweat and urine or scoring a snack. Never feed them. If a goat won't leave you alone, try to scare it off by hollering, waving your arms, and throwing small rocks. They might look harmless, but if a mountain goat charges you it can be deadly.

Rattlesnakes

They slither, they're venomous, and they'll get your adrenaline pumping, but rattlesnakes aren't likely to bite if you give them plenty of space. Found east of the Cascades, rattlesnakes are most active in late spring and summer and usually shake their rattles to warn you of their presence. Don't let them scare you off the trail. Be mindful of where you step—especially when crossing scree fields, logs, and rocks—and where you put your hands (don't reach under rocks). Keep pets and kids close. And wear hiking boots to protect your feet. Rattlesnake bites are rare, but if you end up on the unlucky side of the odds, here's what the Red Cross recommends: Call 9-1-1, gently wash the wound, and keep it lower than your heart. Stay calm and, unless necessary, avoid walking.

Ticks

Ticks hang out on grass and leaves and will latch on to a human or animal if given the chance. Don't be a good host. Wearing a long-sleeve shirt, pants, and lightweight gaiters (or tucking your pants into your socks) makes it hard for these bugs to attach to you. Avoiding overgrown trails and wearing insect repellent with DEET also helps avoid these pests.

Ticks burrow into your skin and, like tiny eight-legged vampires, they want to drink your blood. If a tick attaches to you, use tweezers and grasp the bug as close to your skin as possible and slowly pull it out. Wash the bite area and apply an antibiotic ointment. You can save the tick so your doctor can test it for Lyme disease. Remember to also inspect your pet for ticks. The Red Cross warns against myths regarding removing ticks. Do not try to remove ticks by burning them or applying petroleum jelly or nail polish.

Hazardous Plants

Learning to identify and avoid poison ivy and poison oak is a good way to avoid an itchy situation. Both grow as shrubs or vines with green leaves that turn red in the fall. Poison ivy leaves have three leaflets while poison oak leaves vary in shape. Both can cause an itchy rash that will spoil your hike.

Wearing pants and a long-sleeve shirt will protect your skin. Avoid overgrown trails. If you come in contact with these plants, wash your skin. The oil emitted by the plants can linger on your gear, clothes and pets, so they'll need to be washed too. Anti-itch cream, an ice pack, and a cool shower can give you some relief.

HIKING WITH DOGS

Your dog probably loves playing in the outdoors as much as you, but just like you and your human hiking companions, things can go wrong if you aren't prepared. Here are some recommendations for making sure everything goes smoothly for you and your best friend:

- **KNOW THE RULES:** Don't leave the house before finding a destination where dogs are allowed. They are permitted in many areas, but some places (like national parks and wildlife refuges) don't allow pets.

- **FIRST-AID UPGRADE:** Make sure your first-aid kit has items than can help tend to an injured dog. Duct tape, vet wrap, wound closure strips, and antibiotic ointment are a good idea. Ask your vet about carrying an antihistamine in case of bee sting. Apply canine sunscreen to exposed skin (and don't forget the nose).

- **PAY ATTENTION TO YOUR DOG:** If your dog is panting excessively, drooling, or unsteady on its feet, it's probably overheated. Blue, purple, or bright red gums are also a sign the dog needs to cool off. Get the dog in the shade, off hot surfaces such as rocks and asphalt, and get it water to drink. Put wet towels behind its neck and on its paws, groin, and armpits.

- **FLEA AND TICK PROTECTION:** A flea and tick collar or medication helps keep these pests away. But a tick puller (or tweezers) is a good addition to your first-aid kit.

- **REIGN IT IN:** Always keep your dog on a leash, no matter how well trained it is. A leash can keep your dog from unwanted encounters with wildlife and hikers who might not love dogs as much as you. Ask before letting your dog interact with another hiker's pet.

- **GEAR UP:** Doggy jackets, booties, and sunglasses can keep your pet safe and comfortable. Plus, they're super adorable. A body harness is likely to be most comfortable for your dog. Buy one with pockets so they can carry their own food, water, and doggy doo.

▾ A LUCKY DOG GETS A RIDE

Wildfire

The biggest summer bummer for Northwest hikers in recent years has been wildfires. Local forest fires coupled with smoke blowing in from fires in California and British Columbia have led to a lousy air quality and poor visibility on many popular trails. Visit www.airnow.com to view the air-quality index. Be sure to check the forecast and call or visit a ranger station in the area where you plan to hike to determine if your plans are safe. Don't be shy about changing plans. You can always return at another time. Wildfires are unpredictable.

PROTECT THE ENVIRONMENT

Whether you're looking for inspiring views, a challenging workout, a few hours of solitude, or memories that last a lifetime, the trails of the Pacific Northwest will take care of you. All they need in return is for you to take care of them. Here are some tips for minimizing your impact:

Dirt won't hurt: Too often, hikers walk around the perimeter of trail-blocking puddles, but this often tramples vegetation and creates wide spots in the trails. Hiking through the puddle is usually the best move.

Don't cut switchbacks: It's horrible for the trail and vegetation. Even if you aren't traipsing through vegetation, these shortcuts can change the way water flows in the area and erode the slope and the trail.

Leave nothing, take nothing: Be prepared to pack out all your trash. Bonus points for collecting garbage you find along the way. Don't collect rocks, pick flowers, or take anything else. If you need a souvenir, take a picture. Don't carve initials or anniversary dates in trees or benches. It's not romantic. It's vandalism.

Be a super pooper: If you can't make it back to a trailhead or to a pit toilet, dig a hole at least six inches deep and at least 200 feet from the trail and the nearest water source. Cover the hole when you are done, but don't bury toilet paper. Pack it out. Or use natural TP like grass, leaves, or pinecones. And never bury your business in the snow. Snow melts. Pack it out.

Don't feed the animals: Feeding animals trains them to associate people with food. You don't want bears seeing you as walking beef jerky, so give other hikers the same courtesy.

Be considerate: In a 2017 interview, Ben Lawhon, educational director at Leave No Trace, told me speakers blasting music don't keep bears away (a common excuse). They are just giving users a false sense of security and spoiling the serenity for others. And it might unnecessarily scare other wildlife, he said.

Yield like a boss: Always yield to horses and uphill hikers. Don't step off the trail, if possible.

Volunteer: Several organizations give hikers the chance to give back to the trails that give them so much. Washington Trails Association (www.wta.org) is one of the largest trail volunteer organizations in the country. Call your favorite park or check www.volunteer.gov for more opportunities.

PASSES, PERMITS, AND FEES

At popular Northwest trailheads, it's somewhat common to see cars with a collection of parking passes spread out on their dashboards. For some

BEERS MADE BY WALKING

Beer enthusiast Eric Steen believes in the connection between the great outdoors and good beer. So in 2011, he founded **Beers Made By Walking** (www.beersmadebywalking.com) to bring together those seemingly disparate worlds. Every spring and summer, Steen plans a series of interpretive hikes throughout the United States, where hikers and local brewers learn about the medicinal and edible characteristics of plants they encounter.

Following the hike, the brewers turn those ideas into new beers and hold tasting events to show off the finished products. Since the first Beers Made By Walking event, these brewers have developed ales and lagers with, for example, stinging nettles, huckleberries, pine needles, sagebrush, prickly pear cactus fruit, and dozens of other ingredients. Each beer release generally raises money for conservation efforts and local nonprofits.

Beers Made By Walking is present throughout the Pacific Northwest, with events in Seattle, Carnation, and Bellingham. Hikes are usually free and open to the public, and end-of-season celebrations vary by city; Seattle breweries generally cap each season with a ticketed event where patrons can try hike-inspired beers, while Portland-area brewers have, in recent years, held tapping events at participating breweries. Check the website in spring to see the upcoming list of cities, sign up for a hike, and stay up-to-date on tasting events.

hikers, it's confusing determining who manages the land they're parking on and which pass to use. It's easier just to lay out everything in the glovebox. Generally, you'll be covered if you have passes for state, national forest, and national park land. Here's what you need to legally park at the trailheads for every hike in this book.

A **Northwest Forest Pass** (discovernw.org, $5 per day, $30 annual pass) is required at developed Forest Service recreation sites in Washington and Oregon. Passes are available at Forest Service offices, through hundreds of vendors, and online at www.store.usgs.gov/forest-pass.

A **Discover Pass** (866/320-9933, www.discoverpass.wa.gov, $10 per day, $30 annual pass) is required on Washington state land managed by Washington State Parks, the Washington Department of Natural Resources, and the Washington Department of Fish and Wildlife. Twenty-eight state parks have automated pay stations. Passes are available at state park headquarters, regional offices, and more than 600 vendors and retail stores (find a complete list on the website). Passes are available online, by phone, and as an add-on option when renewing your Washington vehicle license. If you purchase a one-day pass on your phone and can't print it, you can write the transaction number on a piece of paper and display it on your dash. A processing fee of $1.50-5 applies to some pass purchases.

A **Makah Recreational Use Pass** (www.makah.com, $10 annual pass) is required on the Makah Reservation. Those heading to classic coastal

HIKING WITH CHILDREN

It's you and nature vs. Netflix and the Xbox in a battle to capture your kids' imagination, and the odds aren't in your favor. Not only does it take significantly more energy to ready the little ones for an excursion, but it can also be intimidating. But if you want to pass along your love of the outdoors, the sooner you start hiking the better. Here are some tips for keeping it fun (and safe):

- **PLAN:** Your hands are going to be full on hike day, so ready maps, driving directions, gear, food, water, and pass information the night before.

- **START EASY AND INTERESTING:** The joy of testing your toughness on hard trails is usually lost on kids. Choose something you know will be easy on their little legs. And pick something with ponds, big trees, beaches, or other things that will hold their attention.

- **GO AT THEIR PACE:** Give yourself plenty of time to finish the hike. Those puddles, flowers, and ladybugs you didn't even notice are mesmerizing to kids.

- **GEAR UP:** On short, easy trails, tennis shoes are usually fine hiking footwear for kids. But making sure the youngsters are dressed appropriately for the conditions can be the difference between misery and an outing that launches a lifelong love for the outdoors. A comfortable child-carrier backpack is ideal for babies and toddlers who might need to split time between riding and walking.

hikes such as Shi Shi Beach and Cape Flattery should stop in Neah Bay for a pass. Permits are good for the calendar year in which they are purchased. Buy passes at Hobuck Beach Resort, the Makah Cultural and Research Center, Makah Marina, Makah Mini Mart, Makah Tribal Center, and Washburn's General Store.

National Parks

There's no entrance fee at North Cascades National Park, but have your credit card ready if you're visiting the Northwest's other national parks. At Mount Rainier and Olympic, entry is $30 per private vehicle (with a seating capacity of 15 or less) and good for seven consecutive days. Motorcycles are $25 and walkers and cyclists are $15 each. Both parks offer an annual pass for $55. Purchase passes in advance at www.yourpassnow.com.

- **PLAY GAMES:** Don't give kids a chance for their attention to wane. Play games like I Spy, or count squirrels, birds, or mushrooms for an added layer of entertainment.
- **PACK PLENTY OF SNACKS AND WATER:** Take snack breaks along the way and maybe even save a special snack for the halfway point.
- **GO WITH FRIENDS:** No matter how old, hiking with friends enhances the adventure. Plus, having another parent around means extra help in dealing with emotional meltdowns and diaper blowouts. Looking for a kid-friendly hiking group? Hike it Baby (www.hikeitbaby.com), founded in Portland in 2013, is an excellent resource for finding family hiking meetups.
- **TEACH:** Use the outing to start teaching your kids about nature and trail and environmental etiquette.

BEST HIKES WITH KIDS:

- **HOLE-IN-THE-WALL:** Skip rocks and explore tide pools on a 1.5-mile-each-way walk along the Pacific to a sea arch (page 203).
- **BIG FOUR ICE CAVES:** On a mostly flat 2.4-mile forest walk, pass nurse logs and salmonberry plants, cross a bridge spanning the Stillaguamish River, and view caves formed in the snow at the base of Big Four Mountain. It's not safe to go near or inside the caves (page 125).
- **GROVE OF THE PATRIARCHS AND SILVER FALLS:** From the trailhead, it's 1.2 miles round-trip to the giant trees at the Grove of the Patriarchs, and kids will love crossing the Ohanapecosh River on a suspension bridge. You can easily extend this trip to thundering Silver Falls by walking 1.4 miles south (page 82).

America the Beautiful Passes

A must for outdoor lovers, America the Beautiful Passes (888/275-8747, www.nps.gov) cover entry and amenity fees on lands managed by six federal agencies: the National Park Service (national parks), U.S. Forest Service (national forests and grasslands), U.S. Fish and Wildlife Service (national wildlife refuges), Bureau of Land Management, Bureau of Reclamation, and U.S. Army Corps of Engineers. You have several options:

Annual Pass: Buy this $80 pass at a federal recreation site, by phone at 888/275-8747, or online at store.usgs.gov/pass.

Military Pass: Free for current U.S. military members and dependents; obtain a pass by showing a Common Access Card or military ID at a federal recreation site.

4th Grade Pass: Kids and their families get free access to federal recreation lands during the student's fourth-grade year. Fourth-grade teachers and those at organizations serving fourth-graders (youth group leaders, camp directors, etc.) are also eligible. Visit www.everykidinapark.gov for details.

HIKING TIPS

Senior Pass: U.S. citizens and permanent residents 62 and older may buy a lifetime interagency pass for $80 or an annual pass for $20. Passes may be purchased online at www.store.usgs.gov/pass, through the mail, or, to avoid a $10 processing fee, in person at a federal recreation site. Note that Golden Age Passports are no longer sold but are still honored.

Access Pass: Free to U.S. citizens and permanent residents with permanent disabilities. Documentation of permanent disability is required. Passes are available at federal recreation sites and by mail; ordering by mail requires a $10 processing fee.

Volunteer Pass: Once you volunteer 250 hours with federal agencies participating in the Interagency Pass Program, you're eligible for a free pass. Contact your local federal recreation site for specifics. Find volunteer opportunities at www.volunteer.gov.

RESOURCES

CITY AND COUNTY PARKS

SEATTLE PARKS AND RECREATION
100 Dexter Ave. E
Seattle, WA 98109
206/684-4075
www.seattle.gov

DISCOVERY PARK
3801 Discovery Park Blvd.
Seattle, WA 98199
206/386-4236
www.seattle.gov

WHITMAN COUNTY PARKS & RECREATION
400 N. Main St.
Colfax, WA 99111
509/397-4622
www.whitmancounty.org

STATE PARKS AND FORESTS

WASHINGTON STATE PARKS
PO Box 42650
Olympia, WA 98504
360/902-8844
www.parks.wa.gov

DECEPTION PASS STATE PARK
41020 State Route 20
Oak Harbor, WA 98277
360/675-3767
www.parks.wa.gov

OLALLIE STATE PARK
51350 SE Homestead Valley Rd.
North Bend, WA 98045
425/455-7010
www.parks.wa.gov

WALLACE FALLS STATE PARK
14503 Wallace Lake Rd.
Gold Bar, WA 98251
360/793-0420
www.parks.wa.gov

CAPE DISAPPOINTMENT STATE PARK
244 Robert Gray Dr.
Ilwaco, WA 98624
360/642-3078
www.parks.wa.gov

BEACON ROCK STATE PARK
34841 SR 14
Skamania, WA 98648
509/427-8265
www.parks.wa.gov

MOUNT PILCHUCK STATE PARK
Granite Falls, WA 98252
360/793-0420
www.parks.wa.gov

PALOUSE FALLS STATE PARK
Starbuck, WA 99143
509/646-9218
www.parks.wa.gov

PALOUSE TO CASCADES STATE PARK TRAIL
150 Lake Easton State Park Rd.
Easton, WA 98925
509/656-2230
www.parks.wa.gov

STEAMBOAT ROCK STATE PARK
51052 Highway 155
Electric City, WA 99123
509/633-1304
www.parks.wa.gov

WASHINGTON STATE DEPARTMENT OF NATURAL RESOURCES
1111 Washington St. SE
Olympia WA 98504
360/902-1000
www.dnr.wa.gov

NATIONAL PARKS AND MONUMENTS

NORTH CASCADES NATIONAL PARK
810 State Route 20
Sedro-Woolley, WA 98284
360/854-7200
www.nps.gov/noca

MOUNT RAINIER NATIONAL PARK
55210 238th Ave. E
Ashford, WA 98304
360/569-2211
www.nps.gov/mora

OLYMPIC NATIONAL PARK
600 E. Park Ave.
Port Angeles, WA 98362
360/565-3130
www.nps.gov/olym

MOUNT ST. HELENS NATIONAL VOLCANIC MONUMENT
42218 NE Yale Bridge Rd.
Amboy, WA 98601
360/449-7800
www.fs.usda.gov

EBEY'S LANDING NATIONAL HISTORIC RESERVE
162 Cemetery Rd.
PO Box 774
Coupeville, WA 98239
360/678-6084
www.nps.gov/ebla

NATIONAL FORESTS

U.S. FOREST SERVICE—PACIFIC NORTHWEST REGION
1220 SW 3rd Ave.
Portland, OR 97204
503/808-2468
www.fs.usda.gov/r6

COLVILLE NATIONAL FOREST
765 S. Main St.
Colville, WA 99114
509/684-7000
www.fs.usda.gov/colville

GIFFORD PINCHOT NATIONAL FOREST
1501 E. Evergreen Blvd.
Vancouver, WA 98661
360/891-5000
www.fs.usda.gov/giffordpinchot

MOUNT BAKER-SNOQUALMIE NATIONAL FOREST
2930 Wetmore Ave., Suite 3A
Everett, WA 98201
425/783-6000
www.fs.usda.gov/mbs

OKANOGAN-WENATCHEE NATIONAL FOREST
215 Melody Lane
Wenatchee, WA 98801
509/664-9200
www.fs.usda.gov/okawen

OLYMPIC NATIONAL FOREST
1835 Black Lake Blvd. SW
Olympia, WA 98512
360/956-2402
www.fs.usda.gov/olympic

OTHER RESOURCES

BUREAU OF LAND MANAGEMENT OREGON-WASHINGTON
1220 SW 3rd Ave.
Portland, OR 97204
503/808-6001
www.blm.gov

WASHINGTON STATE DEPARTMENT OF FISH AND WILDLIFE
1111 Washington St. SE
Olympia WA 98501
360/902-2200
www.wdfw.wa.gov

WASHINGTON TRAILS ASSOCIATION
www.wta.org

WASHINGTON STATE FERRIES
310 Maple Park Ave. SE
PO Box 47300
Olympia, WA 98504
888/808-7977
206/464-6400
www.wsdot.wa.gov/ferries

WASHINGTON PASS CONDITIONS
www.wsdot.com

THE MOUNTAINEERS
www.mountaineers.org

FRIENDS OF THE COLUMBIA GORGE
www.gorgefriends.org

NATIONAL WEATHER SERVICE
www.weather.gov

NORTHWEST AVALANCHE CENTER
www.nwac.us

AIRNOW AIR QUALITY INDEX
www.airnow.gov

TIDES AND CURRENTS
www.tidesandcurrents.noaa.gov

INDEX

INDEX

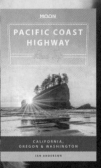

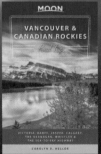

MOON NATIONAL PARKS

In these books:

- Full coverage of gateway cities and towns
- Itineraries from one day to multiple weeks
- Advice on where to stay (or camp) in and around the parks

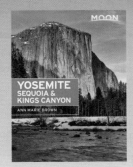

TRAILS AT A GLANCE

PAGE	HIKE NAME	DISTANCE	DURATION
SEATTLE AND VICINITY			
26	Oyster Dome	3.9 mi rt	2 hr
29	Deception Pass: Rosario Head and Lighthouse Point	3.3 mi rt	1.5 hr
32	Ebey's Landing	5.5 mi rt	2.5 hr
35	Discovery Park Loop	2.9 mi rt	1.5 hr
38	Poo Poo Point via Chirico Trail	3.8 mi rt	2 hr
41	Rattlesnake Ledges	4.9 mi rt	2.5 hr
44	Mount Si	7.6 mi rt	4 hr
47	Twin Falls	2.6 mi rt	1.5 hr
50	Mailbox Peak: Old-New Loop	8.2 mi rt	6 hr
54	Nisqually Estuary Boardwalk Trail	4.1 mi rt	2 hr
MOUNT RAINIER			
62	Tolmie Peak	6.2 mi rt	3 hr
65	Spray Park	5.8 mi rt	3.5 hr
68	Second Burroughs Loop	6.4 mi rt	3.5 hr
72	Naches Peak Loop	3.5 mi rt	2 hr
75	Camp Muir	8.2 mi rt	5 hr
78	Skyline Trail Loop	5.8 mi rt	3 hr
82	Grove of the Patriarchs and Silver Falls	2.6 mi rt	2 hr
85	High Rock Lookout	3.2 mi rt	2 hr
NORTH CASCADES			
92	Winchester Mountain	3.6 mi rt	2 hr
95	Skyline Divide	6.8 mi rt	3.5 hr
98	Table Mountain	3 mi rt	1.5 hr
101	Chain Lakes Loop	7.5 mi rt	4 hr
104	Thunder Knob	3.6 mi rt	2 hr

DIFFICULTY	SEASONAL ACCESS	WILDLIFE	WATER-FALLS	DOG-FRIENDLY
Easy/moderate	Year-round	X		X
Easy	Year-round	X		X
Easy/moderate	Year-round	X		X
Easy	Year-round	X		X
Moderate	Year-round	X		X
Moderate	Year-round	X		X
Moderate/strenuous	Apr.-Nov.	X		X
Easy/moderate	Year-round	X	X	X
Strenuous	Apr.-Nov.			X
Easy	Year-round	X		
Easy/moderate	July-Oct.	X		
Moderate	June-Oct.	X	X	
Moderate	July to mid-Oct.	X		
Easy/moderate	June-Oct.	X		
Strenuous	July-Sept.	X	X	
Moderate	Mid-June to mid-Oct.	X	X	
Easy	May-Oct.		X	
Moderate	Mid-June to Oct.	X		X
Moderate	Mid-July to mid-Oct.	X		X
Moderate	July-Oct.	X		X
Easy/moderate	July to mid-Oct.	X		
Moderate	Late July to mid-Oct.	X		X
Easy/moderate	Year-round	X		X

PAGE	HIKE NAME	DISTANCE	DURATION
107	Cascade Pass	7.4 mi rt	4 hr
110	Maple Pass Loop	6.8 mi rt	4 hr
113	Cedar Falls	3.5 mi rt	1.5 hr
116	Green Mountain	8.4 mi rt	5 hr
119	Mount Pilchuck	5.4 mi rt	3 hr
122	Lake Twenty-Two	6.2 mi rt	3.5 hr
125	Big Four Ice Caves	2.4 mi rt	1.5 hr
CENTRAL CASCADES			
132	Wallace Falls	5.2 mi rt	2.5 hr
135	Lake Serene and Bridal Veil Falls	8.2 mi rt	5 hr
138	Barclay Lake	4.4 mi rt	2.5 hr
141	Iron Goat Trail	5.9 mi rt	3.5 hr
144	Colchuck Lake	8.2 mi rt	4.5 hr
147	Talapus and Olallie Lakes	5.6 mi rt	3 hr
150	Granite Mountain	8.6 mi rt	5 hr
153	Snow Lake	6.8 mi rt	3.5 hr
156	Palouse to Cascades State Park Trail: Snoqualmie Tunnel	5.2 mi rt	3 hr
159	Lake Ingalls	9.6 mi rt	4.5 hr
SOUTH CASCADES			
168	Packwood Lake	8 mi rt	4 hr
171	Tongue Mountain	3 mi rt	2 hr
174	Harry's Ridge	8 mi rt	4 hr
177	Killen Creek	6.2 mi rt	3 hr
180	Ape Cave	2.9 mi rt	2 hr

DIFFICULTY	SEASONAL ACCESS	WILDLIFE	WATER-FALLS	DOG-FRIENDLY
Moderate	July to mid-Oct.	X		
Moderate	July-Oct.	X	X	X
Easy	May-early Nov.	X	X	X
Moderate/strenuous	July-Oct.	X		X
Moderate	July-early Nov.	X		X
Moderate	May-Oct.	X	X	X
Easy	June-Sept.	X	X	X
Easy/moderate	Year-round	X	X	X
Moderate	May-Nov.	X	X	X
Easy/moderate	Apr.-Nov.	X		X
Easy/moderate	May-Nov.	X	X	X
Moderate	July-Oct.	X		
Moderate	Mid-May to early Nov.	X		X
Strenuous	Late June-early Nov.	X		X
Moderate	Late June-early Nov.	X		X
Easy/moderate	May-Oct.			X
Moderate/strenuous	July-Oct.	X	X	
Moderate	May-Oct.	X		X
Easy/moderate	May-early Nov.	X		X
Moderate	Late June to mid-Nov.	X		
Moderate	Mid-July to Oct.	X		X
Easy	May-Nov.	X		

TRAILS AT A GLANCE (continued)

PAGE	HIKE NAME	DISTANCE	DURATION
183	Monitor Ridge to Mount St. Helens Summit	10 mi rt	8 hr
187	Lava Canyon	5.8 mi rt	3 hr
WASHINGTON COAST			
194	Cape Flattery	1.5 mi rt	1 hr
197	Point of Arches via Shi Shi Beach	9 mi rt	4.5 hr
200	Ozette Triangle	9.3 mi rt	4.5 hr
203	Hole-in-the-Wall	3 mi rt	1.5 hr
206	North Head Trail	3.8 mi rt	2 hr
OLYMPIC NATIONAL PARK			
214	Dungeness Spit	10.2 mi rt	5 hr
217	Hurricane Hill	3.4 mi rt	2 hr
220	Klahhane Ridge	5.4 mi rt	3 hr
223	Hall of Mosses and Hoh River Trail	6.7 mi rt	3.5 hr
226	Grand Valley	9.3 mi rt	5 hr
229	Mount Townsend	8 mi rt	4 hr
232	Quinault Loop	4 mi rt	2 hr
235	Staircase Rapids and Shady Lane	4.2 mi rt	2 hr
238	Mount Ellinor	3.4 mi rt	2.5 hr
241	Lena Lake	6.8 mi rt	3 hr
COLUMBIA RIVER GORGE			
248	Latourell Falls Loop	3.1 mi rt	1.5 hr
251	Angel's Rest	4.9 mi rt	2.5 hr
254	Wahkeena Falls-Multnomah Falls Loop	5.9 mi rt	3 hr
258	Larch Mountain Crater Loop	7.1 mi rt	3.5 hr
261	Beacon Rock	2 mi rt	1 hr
264	Dry Creek Falls	5 mi rt	2.5 hr
267	Dog Mountain	6.9 mi rt	4 hr

DIFFICULTY	SEASONAL ACCESS	WILDLIFE	WATER-FALLS	DOG-FRIENDLY
Strenuous	Mid-May to Oct.	X		
Moderate	Late May-Nov.	X	X	
Easy	Year-round	X		X
Moderate	Year-round	X		
Moderate/strenuous	Year-round	X		
Easy	Year-round	X		X
Easy	Year-round	X		X
Moderate/strenuous	Year-round	X		
Easy/moderate	June-Oct.	X		
Moderate	Mid-June to Oct.	X	X	
Easy/moderate	Year-round	X	X	
Moderate/strenuous	Mid-July to mid-Oct.	X		
Moderate/strenuous	June-Nov.	X	X	X
Easy	Year-round	X	X	X
Easy	Year-round	X		
Moderate	July-Oct.	X		X
Moderate	Apr.-Nov.	X	X	X
Easy/moderate	Year-round		X	X
Moderate	Year-round		X	X
Moderate	Year-round		X	X
Easy/moderate	June-Oct.			X
Easy/moderate	Year-round	X		
Moderate	Year-round		X	X
Moderate/strenuous	Mar.-Dec.	X		X

PAGE	HIKE NAME	DISTANCE	DURATION
270	Coyote Wall (Labyrinth Loop)	6.3 mi rt	3.5 hr
273	Mosier Plateau	3.7 mi rt	1.5 hr
276	Tom McCall Point Trail	3.8 mi rt	2 hr
CENTRAL WASHINGTON			
284	Steamboat Rock	3.2 mi rt	1.5 hr
287	Ancient Lakes	4.4 mi rt	2.5 hr
290	Yakima Skyline Trail	6 mi rt	3 hr
293	Cowiche Canyon	5.6 mi rt	3 hr
296	Badger Mountain: Trailhead Park Loop	3 mi rt	1.5 hr
EASTERN WASHINGTON			
304	Abercrombie Mountain	7.8 mi rt	4 hr
307	Sullivan Lakeshore Trail	8.4 mi rt	4 hr
310	Iller Creek Conservation Area	5 mi rt	2.5 hr
313	Kamiak Butte	2.5 mi rt	1.5 hr
316	Oregon Butte	5.8 mi rt	3 hr

DIFFICULTY	SEASONAL ACCESS	WILDLIFE	WATER-FALLS	DOG-FRIENDLY
Easy/moderate	Year-round	X	X	X
Easy/moderate	Year-round	X	X	X
Easy/moderate	Mar.-Oct.	X		
Easy/moderate	Year-round	X		X
Easy	Mar.-Nov.	X	X	X
Moderate	Mar.-Nov.	X		X
Easy/moderate	Year-round	X		X
Easy/moderate	Year-round	X		X
Moderate	June-Oct.	X		X
Moderate	Apr.-Nov.	X		X
Easy/moderate	Year-round	X		X
Easy/moderate	Mar.-Nov.	X		X
Easy/moderate	June-Nov.	X		X

MOON WASHINGTON HIKING
Avalon Travel
Hachette Book Group
1700 Fourth Street
Berkeley, CA 94710, USA
www.moon.com

Editor: Rachael Sablik
Acquiring Editor: Nikki Ioakimedes
Series Manager: Sabrina Young
Copy Editors: Brett Keener, Kelly Lydick
Graphics Coordinator: Ravina Schneider
Production Coordinator: Ravina Schneider
Cover Design: Kimberly Glyder Design
Interior Design: Megan Jones Design
Moon Logo: Tim McGrath
Map Editor: Mike Morgenfeld
Cartographers: Lohnes+Wright, Brian
    Shotwell, Karin Dahl
Proofreader: Ann Seifert
Editorial Assistance: Samia Abbasi
Indexer: Greg Jewett

ISBN-13: 9781640495074
Printing History
1st Edition — March 2021
5 4 3 2 1

Front cover photo: North Cascades. © Inge
Johnsson | Alamy Stock Photo
Back cover photo: Olympic National Park.
Sgoodwin481 | Dreamstime.com

Printed in China by RR Donnelley

ICON AND MAP SYMBOLS KEY

- PCT — PCT
- Wildlife
- Wildflowers
- Waterfalls
- Dog-friendly
- Kid-friendly
- Wheelchair accessible
- Public transportation

Expressway	Feature Trail	▲ Park	○ City/Town
Primary Road	Other Trail	✦ Unique Feature	★ Point of Interest
Secondary Road	Contour Line	Waterfall	■ Other Location
Unpaved Road	P Parking Area	Λ Camping	✕ Airport
Rail Line	TH Trailhead	▲ Mountain	Ski Area

QUICK-REFERENCE CHART: TRAILS AT A GLANCE